MW01406002

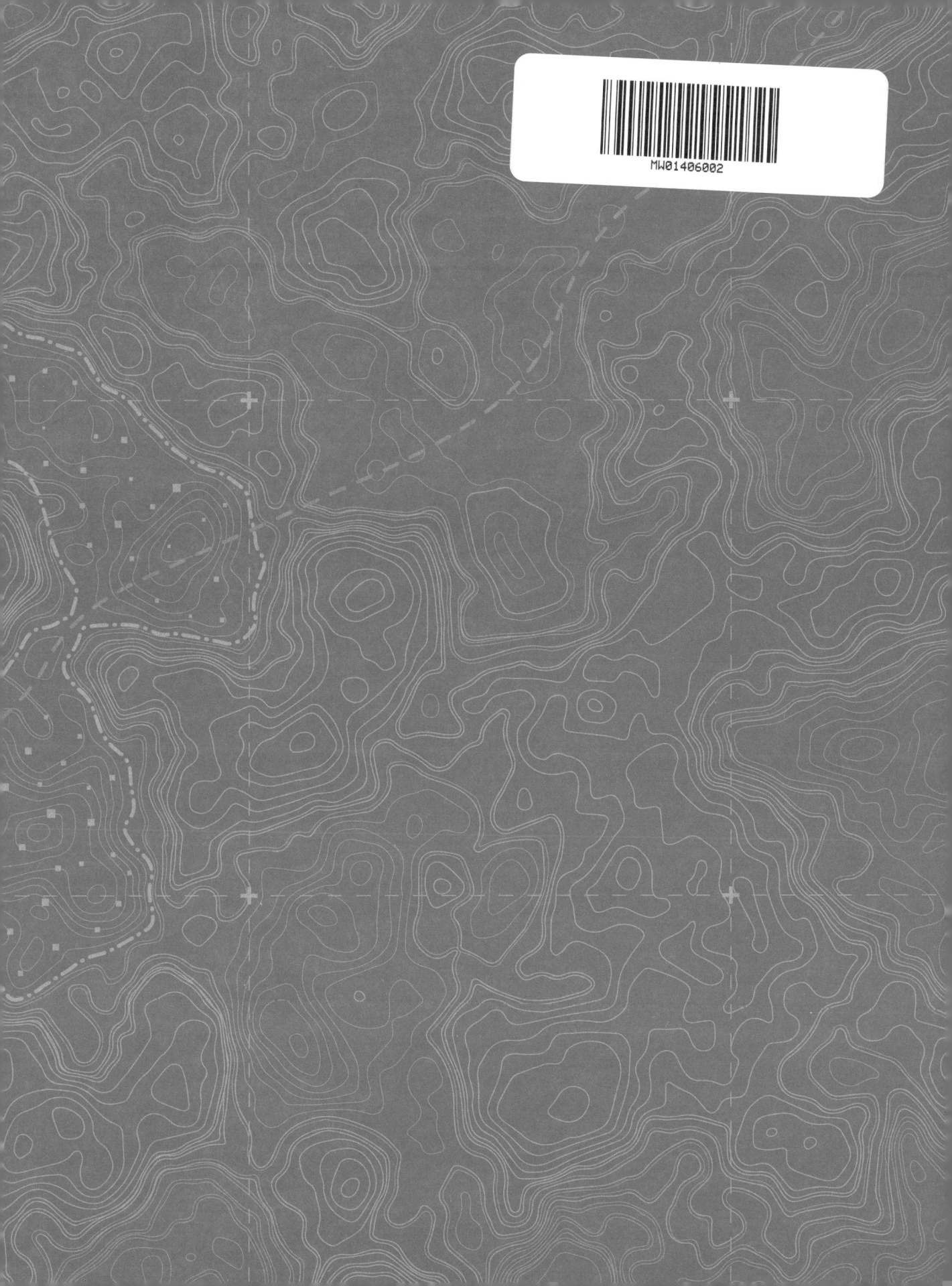

YELLOWSTONE

THE OFFICIAL DUTTON RANCH FAMILY COOKBOOK

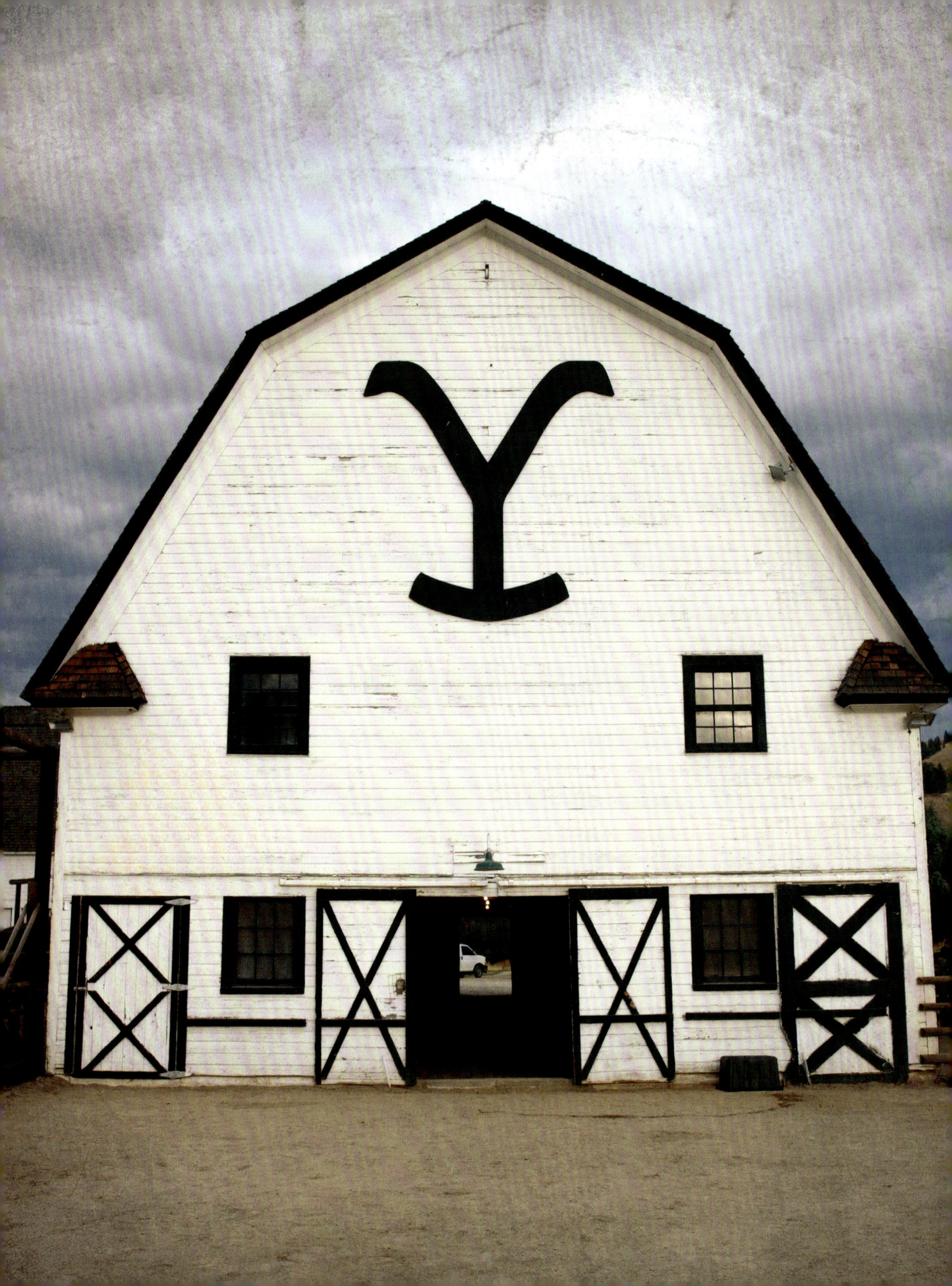

YELLOWSTONE

THE OFFICIAL DUTTON RANCH FAMILY COOKBOOK

DELICIOUS HOMESTYLE RECIPES
FROM CHARACTER AND REAL-LIFE CHEF

GABRIEL "GATOR" GUILBEAU

WITH KIM LAIDLAW

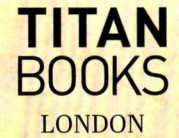

Titan Books
LONDON

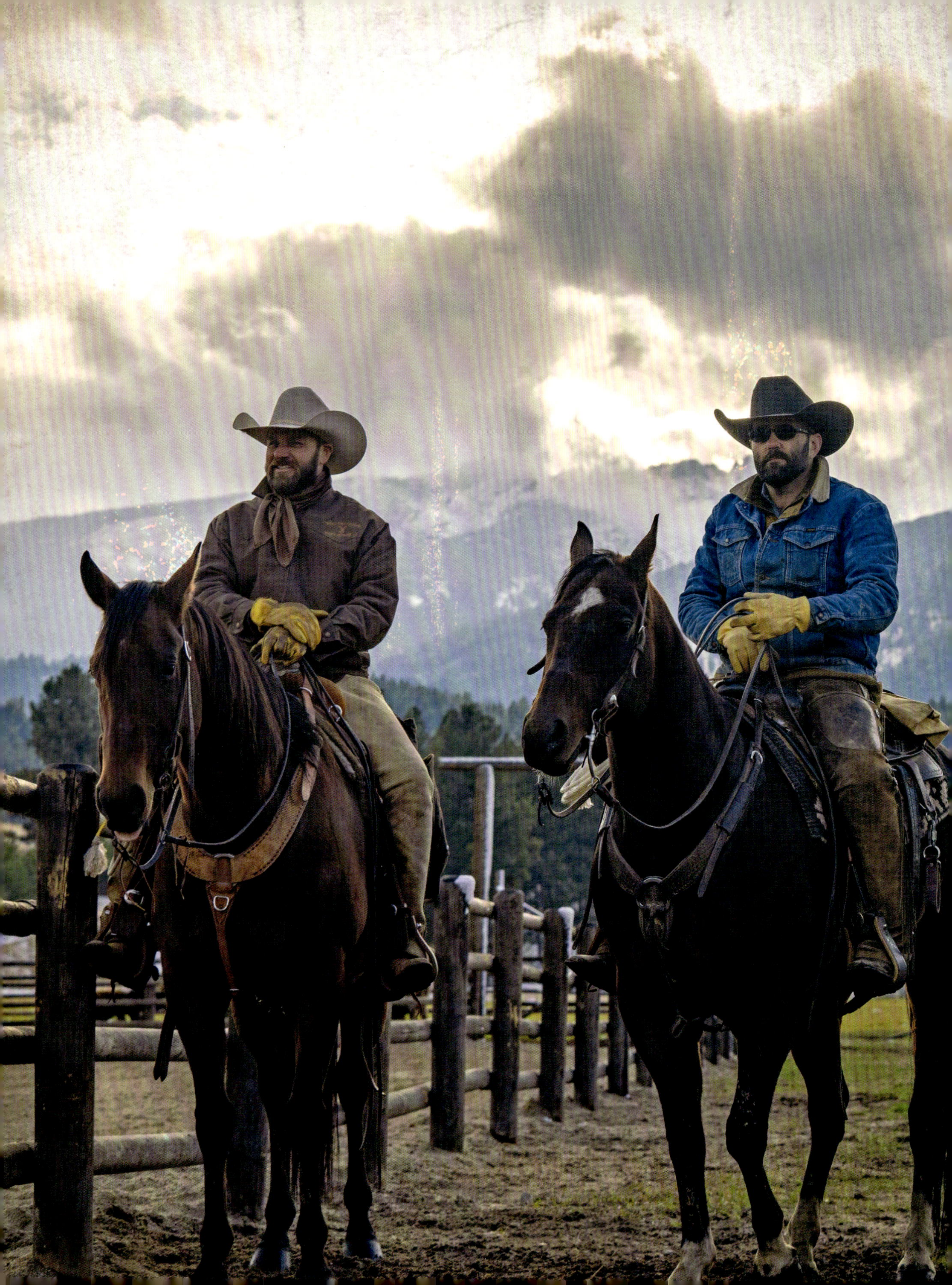

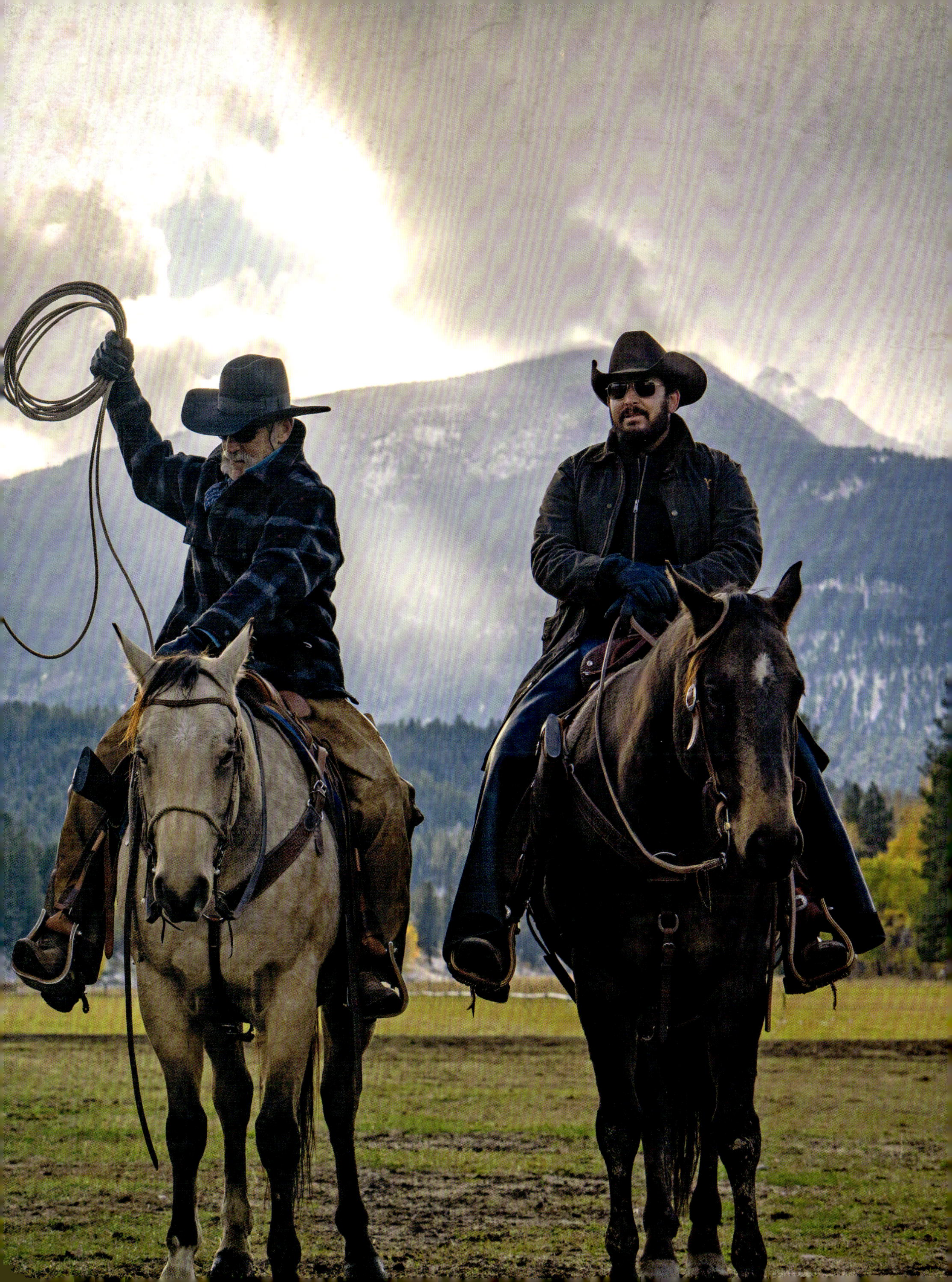

CONTENTS

Introduction 11

STARTERS 16

Chopped Salad with "Dutton Ranch" Dressing 19
Potato Corn Chowder 20
Gator's Louisiana Fried Shrimp 23
Crawfish Cakes with Lime Cream 24
Gator's Butter-Roasted Shrimp 27
John, Kayce, and Tate's Glazed Venison Meatballs 28
Fried Okra 31
Taylor's Beef Jerky 33
Lee's Garlic Butter Steak Bites 34

MAIN DISHES 38

Big Ranch Breakfast 41
Rip's Fry Bread with Scrambled Eggs and Bacon 42
Jimmy's Cowboy Beef Chili 45
John's Perfect Rib Eye Steak 46
Bunkhouse Beer-Braised Beef Stew with Root Vegetables 49
BBQ Bison Burgers with Maple-Bourbon Bacon 52
Helluva Grilled Flank Steak with Mustard-Mushroom Sauce 55
Mama's Beef Pot Roast 56
Gator's Cajun Dirty Rice 59
Grilled Portobello Mushroom Burgers 60
Beth's Cheesy Hamburger Mac Casserole 63
Maw Maw's Honey Bourbon Barbecued Ribs 64
Smoked Pulled Pork 67
Kickin' Chicken Tenders with Pickled Jalapeño Sauce 68
Jamie's Smothered Chicken in Brown Mushroom Gravy 73
Gator's Cajun Chicken and Sausage Gumbo 76
Western Butter Chicken with Rice 79
Rancher's Chicken and Biscuit Dumplings 82
Smoked Turkey Legs with Red Beans and Rice 87
John and Tate's Pan-Roasted Walleye 90
Grilled Octopus with Lemon and Roasted Potatoes 93
Lee, Jamie, and Kayce's Fire-Grilled Wild Trout with Chimichurri 94

SIDE DISHES 100

This Is How You Make a F*$%ing Biscuit 103
Monica's Jalapeño-Cheddar Cornbread 104
Golden Squash Casserole 106
Cornbread Dressing 107
Yeasted Bunkhouse Beer Rolls 108
Hush Puppies 111
Ranch Hand Baked Beans 112
Corn Maque Choux 115
Rodeo Cowboy Caviar 116
Pickled Onions 118
Crunchy Coleslaw 119
Gator's Mustard Potato Salad 120
Wild Rice Pilaf 123
Beth and Jamie's Twice-Baked Potatoes with Bacon and Cheese 124

DESSERTS 128

Beth and Rip's Sweet Blueberry Cobbler 131
Classic Southern Pecan Pie 132
Carter's Cast-Iron Coffee-Chocolate Cake 135
Sweet Potato Bourbon Pie 136
Evadelle's Lace Cookies 141
Bourbon Pineapple Bread Pudding 142
Maw Maw's Chocolate-Pecan Fudge 145
Big-Ass Chocolate Chip Cookies 146

DRINKS 150

Beth's "Two Scoops of Ice Cream, Three Shots of Vodka" Smoothie 153
Summer's Wheatgrass Smoothie 154
Bunkhouse Bitter Beer–Bourbon Cocktail 157
Beth and Rip's Bourbon Apple Cider Old-Fashioned 158
John and Jamie's Huckleberry Whiskey Sour 161
Beth's Coffee Vodka Martini 162
Great Aunt Cara's Iced Irish Whiskey Coffee 165

Index 168
Acknowledgments 173
About the Author 173

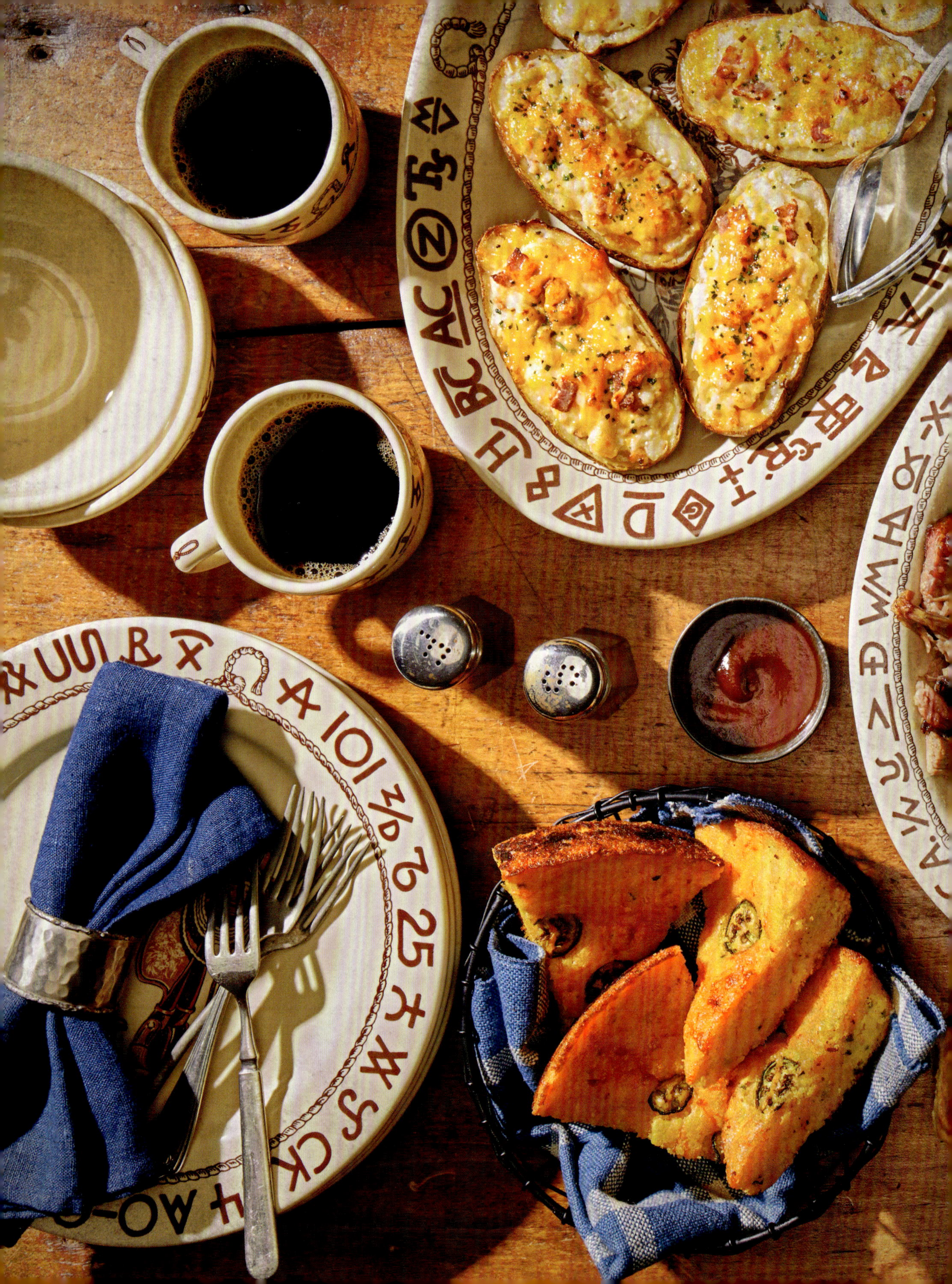

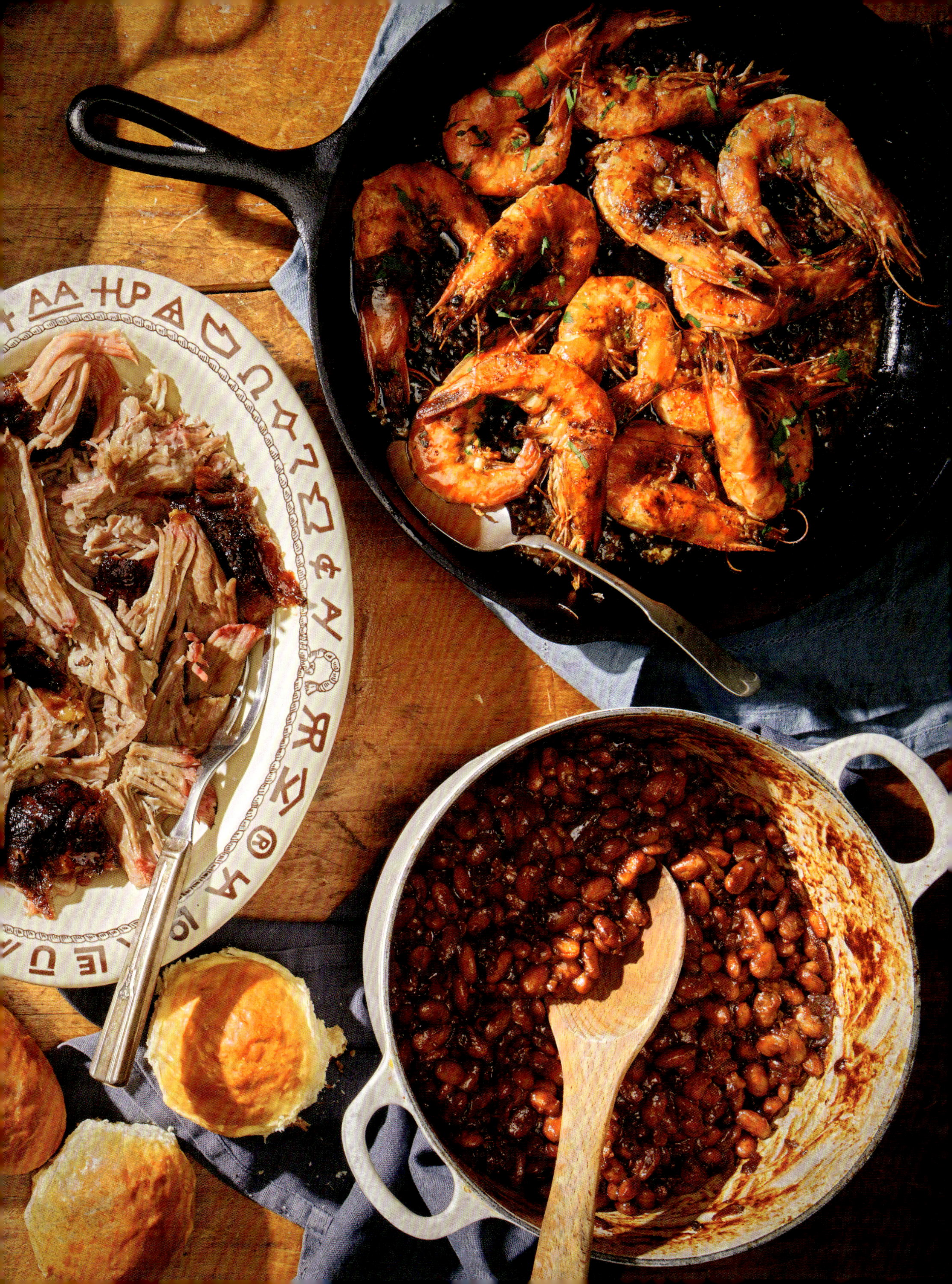

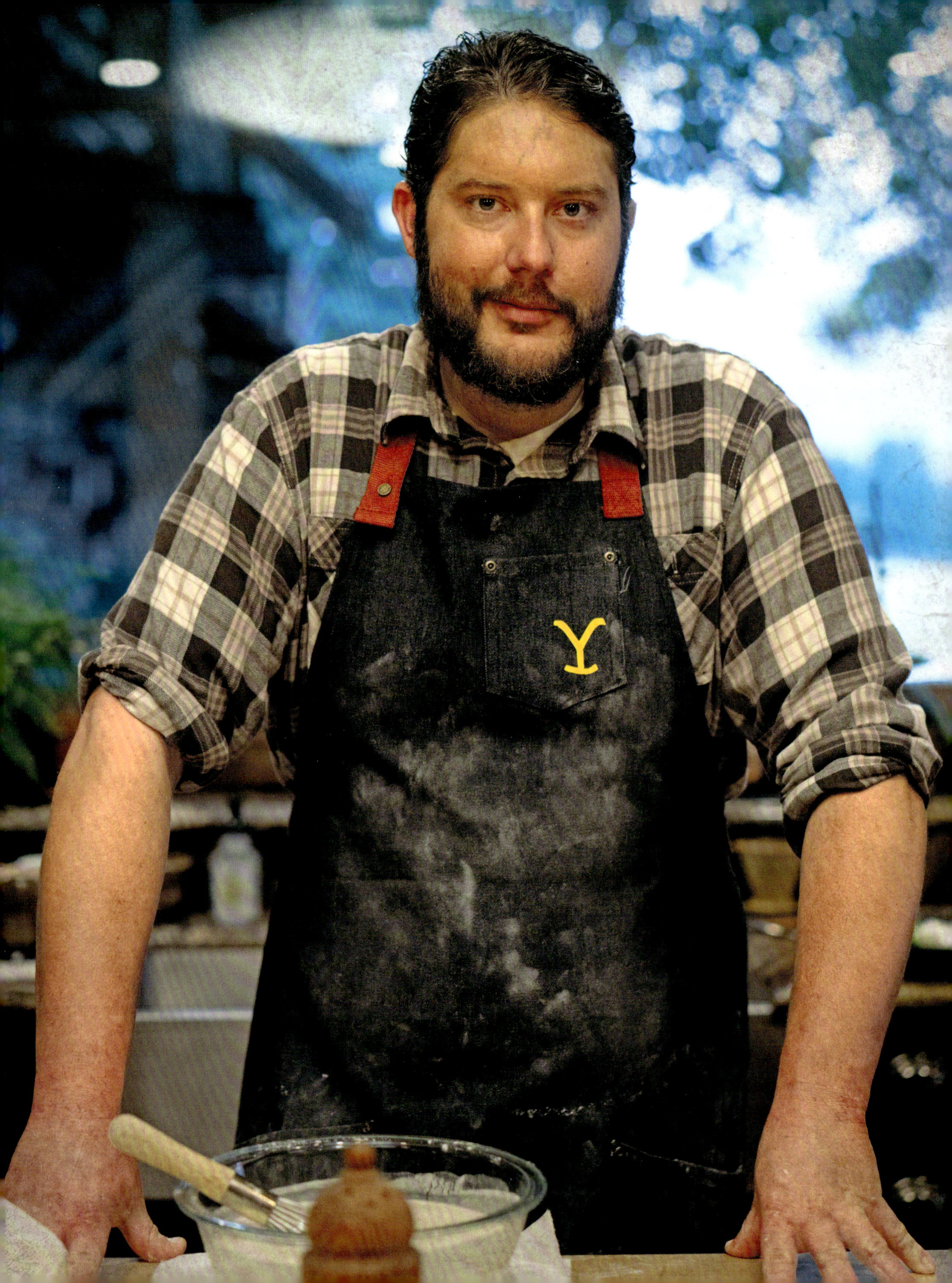

INTRODUCTION

The hit modern-day Western series *Yellowstone* portrays the epic saga of the Dutton family and the Yellowstone Dutton Ranch. Set against the sweeping vistas of Montana, the show follows the story of powerful and influential ranch owner John Dutton, played by Kevin Costner, along with his family and the community surrounding him. Written and co-created by Taylor Sheridan and John Linson, the show portrays the Dutton family's constant struggle of owning and running the largest ranch in the state of Montana, doing whatever it takes to protect their land. The stories of the bordering Broken Rock Indian Reservation, the nearby growing town, and outside developers are woven through the series with themes of corruption, ambition, preservation of a way of life, and the enduring cowboys of the American West. The tumultuous Dutton family includes sharp and scheming Beth Dutton (Kelly Reilly) and her husband and head ranch hand, Rip Wheeler (Cole Hauser), who runs the ranch; Kayce Dutton (Luke Grimes), his wife, Monica (Kelsey Asbille), and their son—John's only grandson—Tate (Brecken Merrill); and power-hungry adopted son, Jamie Dutton (Wes Bentley). Chief Thomas Rainwater (Gil Birmingham) is the chairman of the Confederated Tribes of Broken Rock and the leader of the Broken Rock Indian Reservation, who—along with his assistant, Mo, (Mo Brings Plenty) and their community members—is in a constant struggle to return the land to his tribe, the rightful owners. The ranch hands of the Yellowstone's Bunkhouse embody the "get-your-hands-dirty" cowboy life on a cattle ranch—with plenty of drama, hilarity, violence, and drinking along the way.

Putting on a show of this magnitude takes an enormous cast and supporting crew, and all those folks need to eat—both in real life and on the show itself. That's where I enter. I came on board with the *Yellowstone* team right after they started shooting the first season of the show, which premiered in 2018, and I run their craft services. That means I'm the go-to guy for all the food and drinks. Surprisingly—I certainly never expected it—my real-life role evolved into a minor character on the show, the ranch's personal cook, "Gator" (Kevin Costner wanted me to keep my real name in the show!).

So how did I end up here and come to write this cookbook? I grew up in Los Angeles, but my family is from Louisiana, and I'm of proud Cajun heritage. When I was a teenager, I decided I wanted to learn more about my heritage and how to cook, so my dad taught me how to make gumbo for a high school event, and after that, my cooking just took off. I love cooking and serving food to people, and all the care that goes into doing it right. Fast-forward a few years, and my dad—who had been in craft services for many years in the film industry in Los Angeles—had a gig in Louisiana and invited me to come and do a job in Baton Rouge. It rained and snowed; we worked eighteen-hour days in abandoned warehouses making soup because that's all the budget allowed. It was miserable . . . and I loved it! I had never felt so at home doing something.

In 2017, I received a call around midnight on a Friday. *Yellowstone* had just started filming; they were a few weeks in, and the folks doing craft services were struggling. The person who called was sitting at a table with Taylor Sheridan, and there was no food. They asked if I was interested in coming out to cook for the show. The only thing they told me was that "our director is really hungry, and you really gotta feed this guy." I didn't know the name of the show or that it was being filmed in Montana. "Can you leave right now?" they asked. I finished work, packed up everything, and left the next morning. I showed up two days later around 1 a.m.; we went shopping immediately and prepped in the parking lot at 3 a.m. We were ready with food and coffee by first call that morning. Taylor and I saw eye to eye the first time we met, and I was immediately hired to run craft services. And I've been there ever since, for all five seasons, plus the filming of *1883* and *1923*, and now the new *Bass Reeves*. Anybody who knows Taylor will tell you that he likes to eat—and wants those around him to eat too. It's very important to him, especially in the cowboy world, where three meals daily are crucial for the amount of hard work involved.

One of the reasons *Yellowstone* is so popular and that the series does so well is that everything is authentic: Montana, the horses, the cowboys, the ranching, the roping. And Taylor is adamant that things do not appear fake, and that includes the cooking on the show.

When cooking for the show's craft services, I've learned it's better to roll with the punches and not get too far ahead trying to plan—if it's Monday, don't even think about Friday. My plan is to be ready for everything. So I take it one day at a time. I'll go to my truck, make coffee for everyone, and then open the fridge and let the creative juices flow. I let the pantry talk to me and tell me what we are going to make. In Montana, I have amazing access to meat and produce as well as a terrific network of suppliers. I make all the food for the cast and crew, and a lot of the food that appears on the show. I made pretty much any prop food, dish, or drink in scenes, and anytime you see an actor or crew member, I've fed that person too. Everybody on set knows they're welcome to come to me any time they're hungry, and I will take care of them. I try to create a safe little getaway with good music, some coffee, maybe a steak, and a good story to tell . . . I try to maintain a "Gator vibe" at all times.

I cook what I know and use the bounty that surrounds us, so I make a lot of Cajun food off set—like gumbo, fried shrimp, and dirty rice—but also a lot of cowboy food on set like rib eye steaks, chili, cornbread, and baked beans. The recipes in this book reflect both worlds; they are the real dishes as well as the food I make for the cast and crew. I make a point of cooking things that folks want to eat, whether it's their favorite dish, something that feels like home, or just a warm bowl of soup on a really cold day. The dishes in this book spring from all five seasons of *Yellowstone*, so you might recognize some, like the Grilled Octopus with Lemon and Roasted Potatoes (page 93) or Beth's "Two Scoops of Ice Cream, Three Shots of Vodka" Smoothie (page 153). So, pour yourself a whiskey and get ready for a wild ride through the food of the Dutton Ranch and *Yellowstone*.

—Gabriel "Gator" Guilbeau

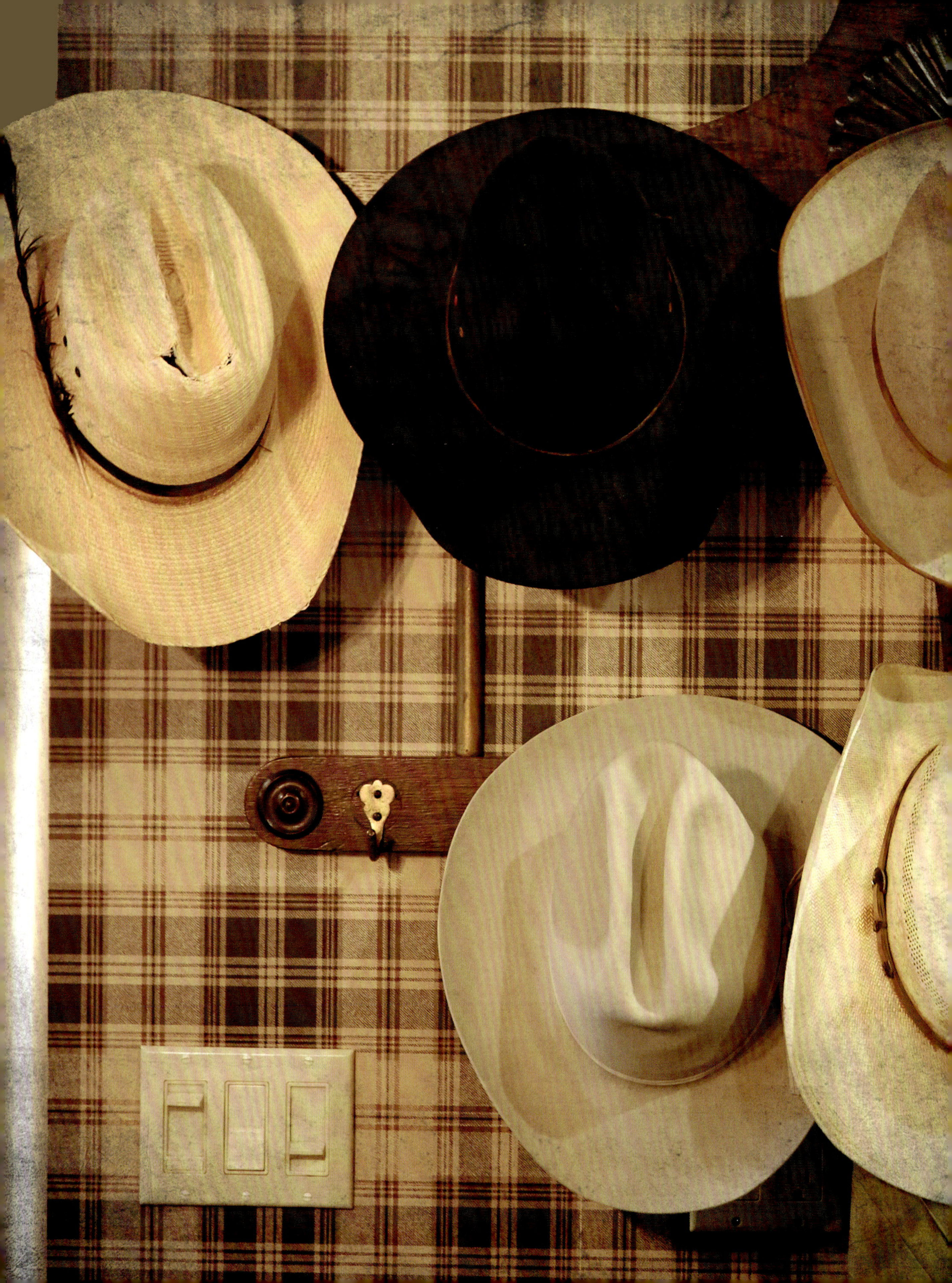

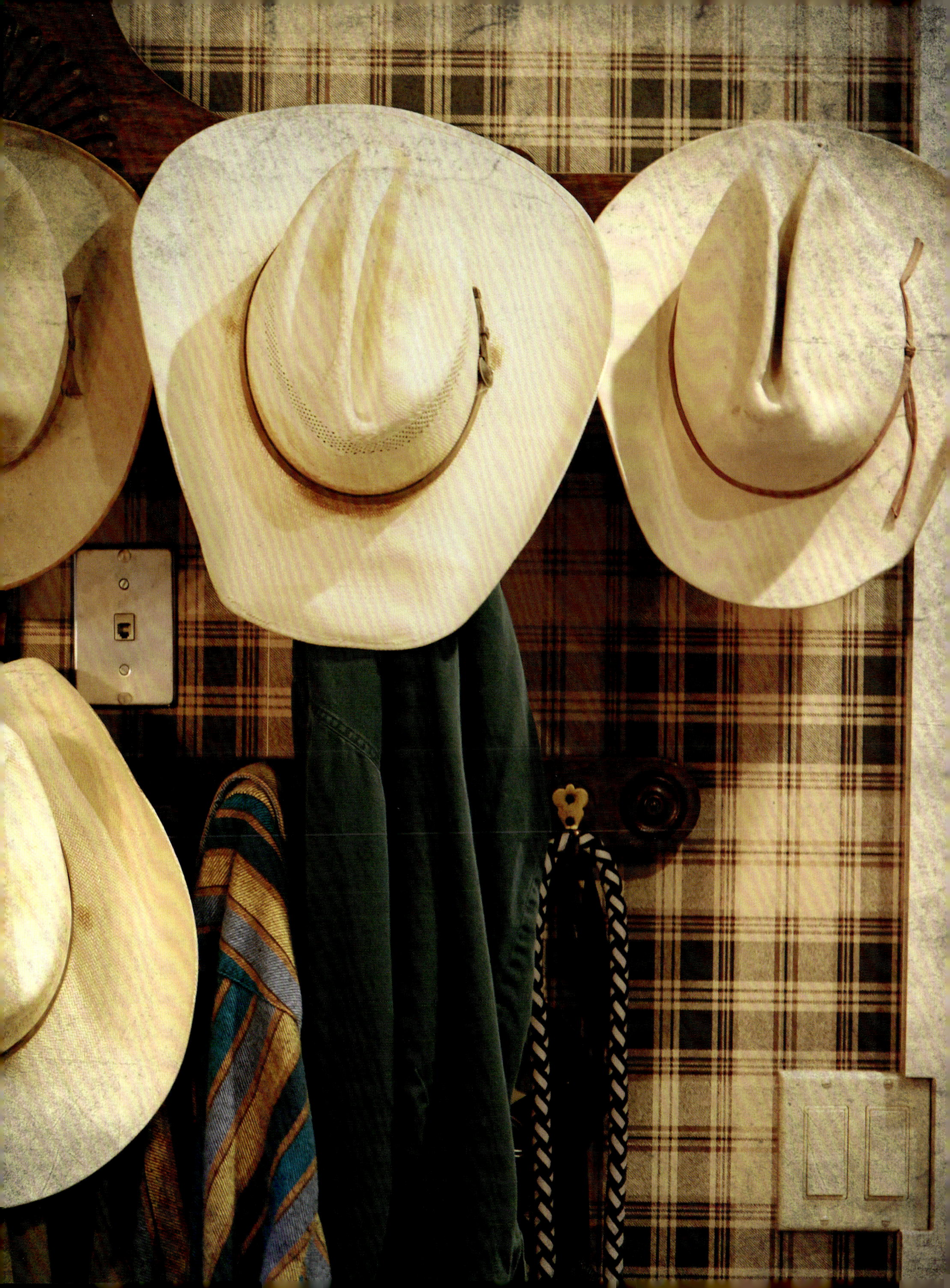

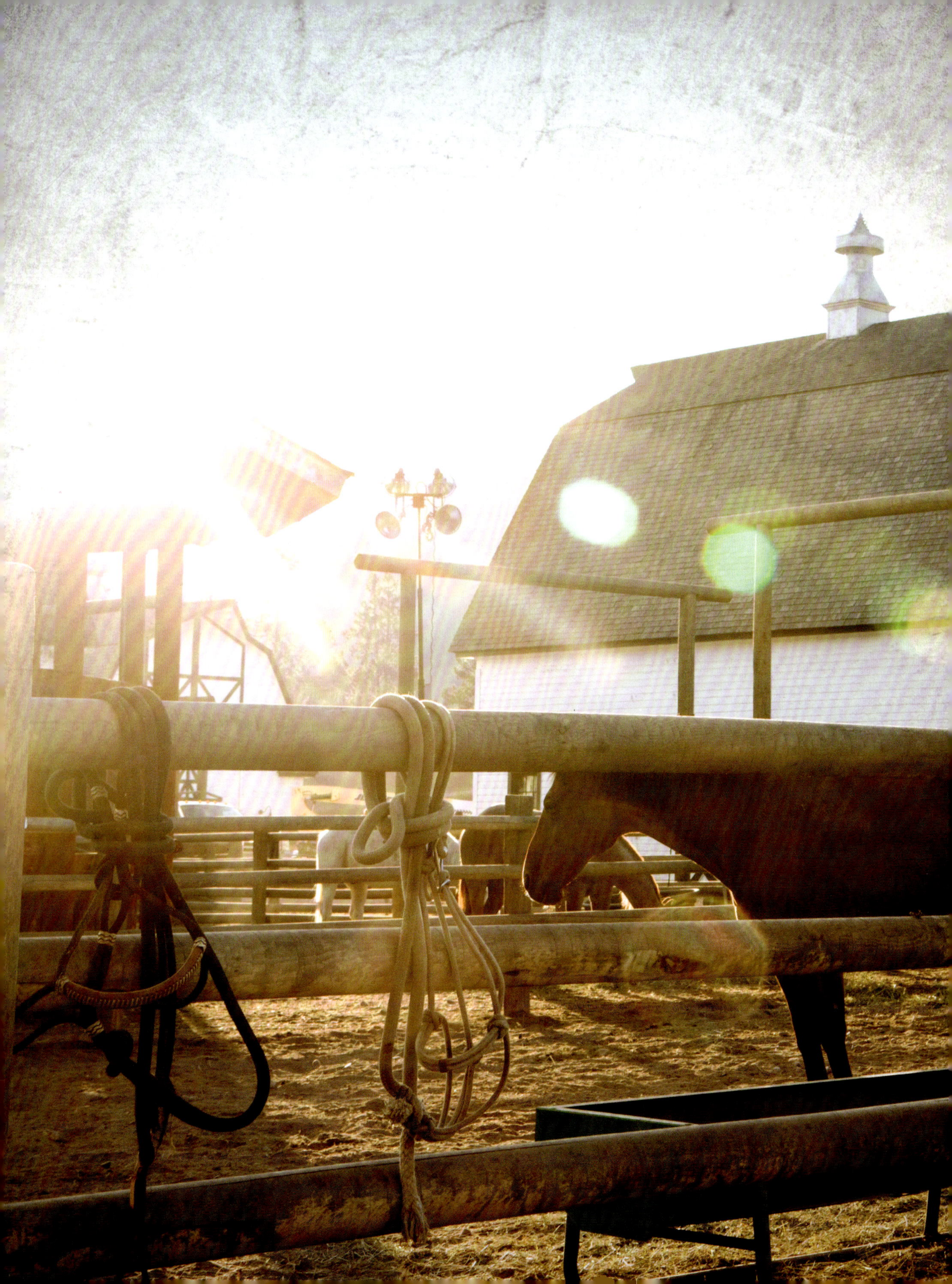

STARTERS

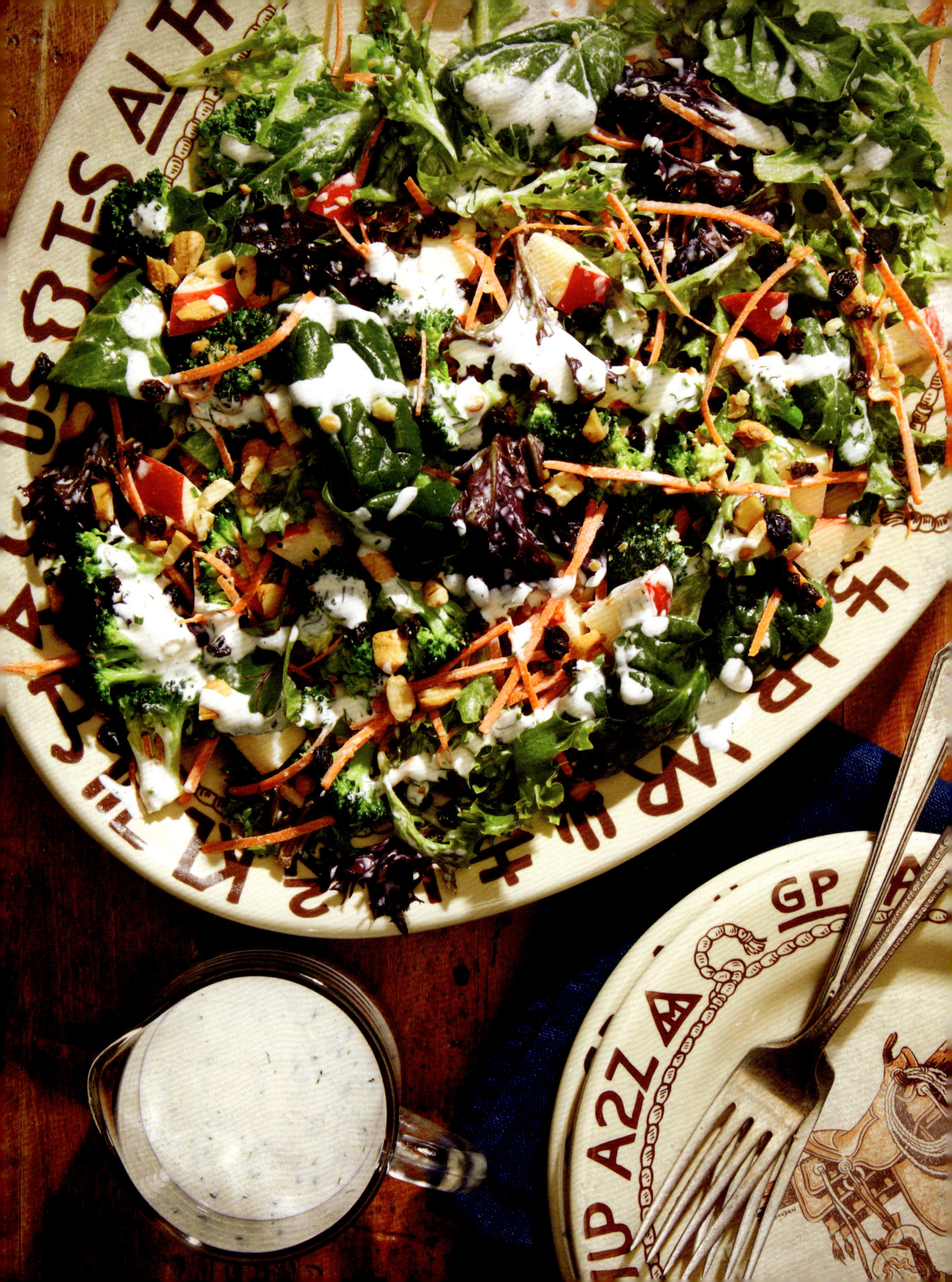

CHOPPED SALAD
with "Dutton Ranch" Dressing

In Season 1, John Dutton is diagnosed with colon cancer and, after surgery in Season 2, he appears to have beaten it. His children and ranch employees want to see their patriarch stay fit and in fighting form, which is why Beth is often chiding him to eat better. In Season 4, Beth asked me to make John a salad with fruit because, as she explains to Rip, it's good for prostate health. Trust me: this creamy ranch dressing will make anyone want to chow down on a salad, even Rip. Store it in an airtight container in the fridge for up to 1 week.

INGREDIENTS

For the "Dutton Ranch" Dressing

½ cup (120 ml) buttermilk

2 teaspoons fresh lemon juice

1 teaspoon packed minced fresh dill

1 teaspoon packed minced fresh chives

1 teaspoon packed minced fresh flat-leaf parsley

½ teaspoon onion powder

¼ teaspoon garlic powder

Kosher salt and freshly ground black pepper

¾ cup (180 ml) mayonnaise

For the Chopped Salad

Kosher salt

5 oz (150 g) chopped broccoli florets, cut into ½-inch (12-mm) pieces (about 1½ cups)

1 large apple, cored and cut into ½-inch (12-mm) pieces

1 large carrot, peeled and shredded

⅓ cup (40 g) chopped roasted salted cashews

2 tablespoons dried currants or raisins

6 cups (210 g) mixed greens

MAKES 4–6 SERVINGS; ABOUT 1¼ CUPS (300 ML) DRESSING

INSTRUCTIONS

To prepare the ranch dressing, in a bowl whisk together the buttermilk, lemon juice, herbs, onion powder, garlic powder, and ¼ teaspoon pepper until blended. Stir in the mayonnaise. Taste and season with salt, as needed. Set aside.

To prepare the salad, fill a large bowl with cold water and ice.

Fill a saucepan half full of salted water and bring to a boil over high heat. Add the broccoli to the boiling water and cook, stirring once or twice, for 1 minute, or until barely tender-crisp. Drain in a fine-mesh sieve, and then transfer to the ice water to stop the cooking. Drain again, and then pat dry with paper towels. Transfer to a salad bowl.

Add the apple, carrot, cashews, and currants or raisins to the salad bowl. Drizzle with a little ranch dressing and toss to combine. Add the mixed greens and toss again.

Serve, passing the remaining ranch dressing alongside.

POTATO CORN CHOWDER

We make a lot of soup on set. In fact, making soup is how I got started in craft services with my dad. Soup is not only economical when you're working on a tight budget, but it is also comforting and warming, especially when you make it from scratch. I pride myself on meatless soups—like this hearty chowder—that will keep you warm when it's 20°F (-6°C) outside and you have to push a wagon through a field. This soup kept the crew warm during countless takes and shooting through blizzards.

INGREDIENTS

Kosher salt and freshly ground black pepper

4 large Yukon gold potatoes, peeled and cut into ½-inch (12-mm) cubes

6 tablespoons (90 g) unsalted butter

1 cup (140 g) finely chopped yellow onion

1 cup (140 g) finely chopped green bell pepper

1 can (15 oz /425 g) creamed corn

1½ cups (350 ml) chicken broth, preferably homemade

¼ cup (15 g) chopped fresh flat-leaf parsley

Pinch of cayenne pepper

1 can (12 oz /350 ml) evaporated milk

MAKES 4 SERVINGS

INSTRUCTIONS

Fill a large pot half full of salted water and add the potatoes. Bring to a boil over high heat, and then reduce the heat to medium and boil the potatoes gently until just par-boiled, about 5 minutes. Drain, then transfer the potatoes to a cutting board and let cool slightly. Set aside.

In the pot over medium heat, melt the butter. Add the onion and bell pepper and cook, stirring until softened, about 5 minutes. Add the creamed corn, broth, reserved potatoes, parsley, 1 teaspoon salt, 1 teaspoon pepper, and the cayenne. Bring to a boil over high heat, and then reduce the heat to low and simmer, stirring occasionally, until the potatoes are very tender, about 15 minutes.

Stir in the evaporated milk until well combined. Continue to simmer just until the chowder is warmed through.

Ladle into bowls and serve at once.

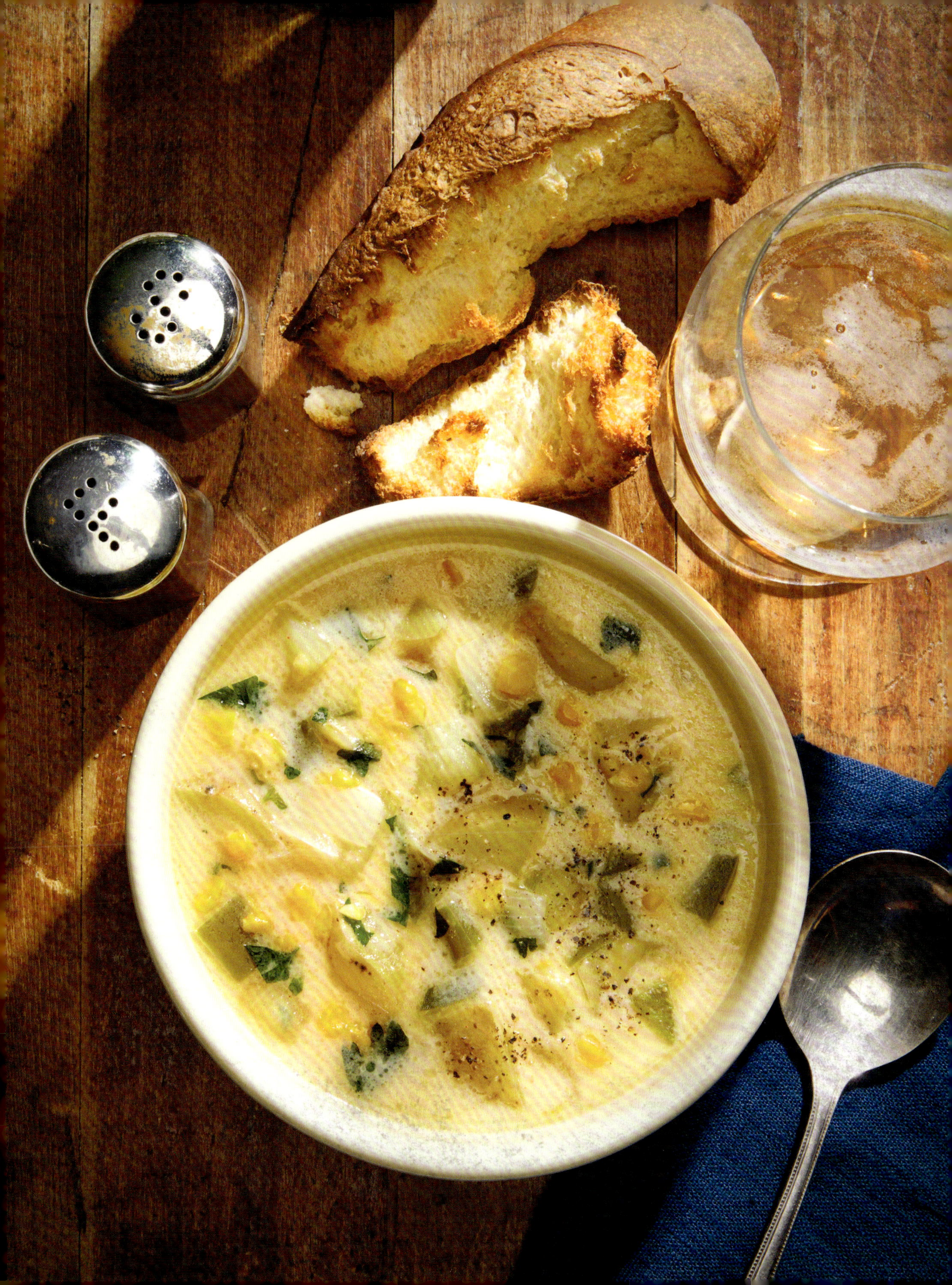

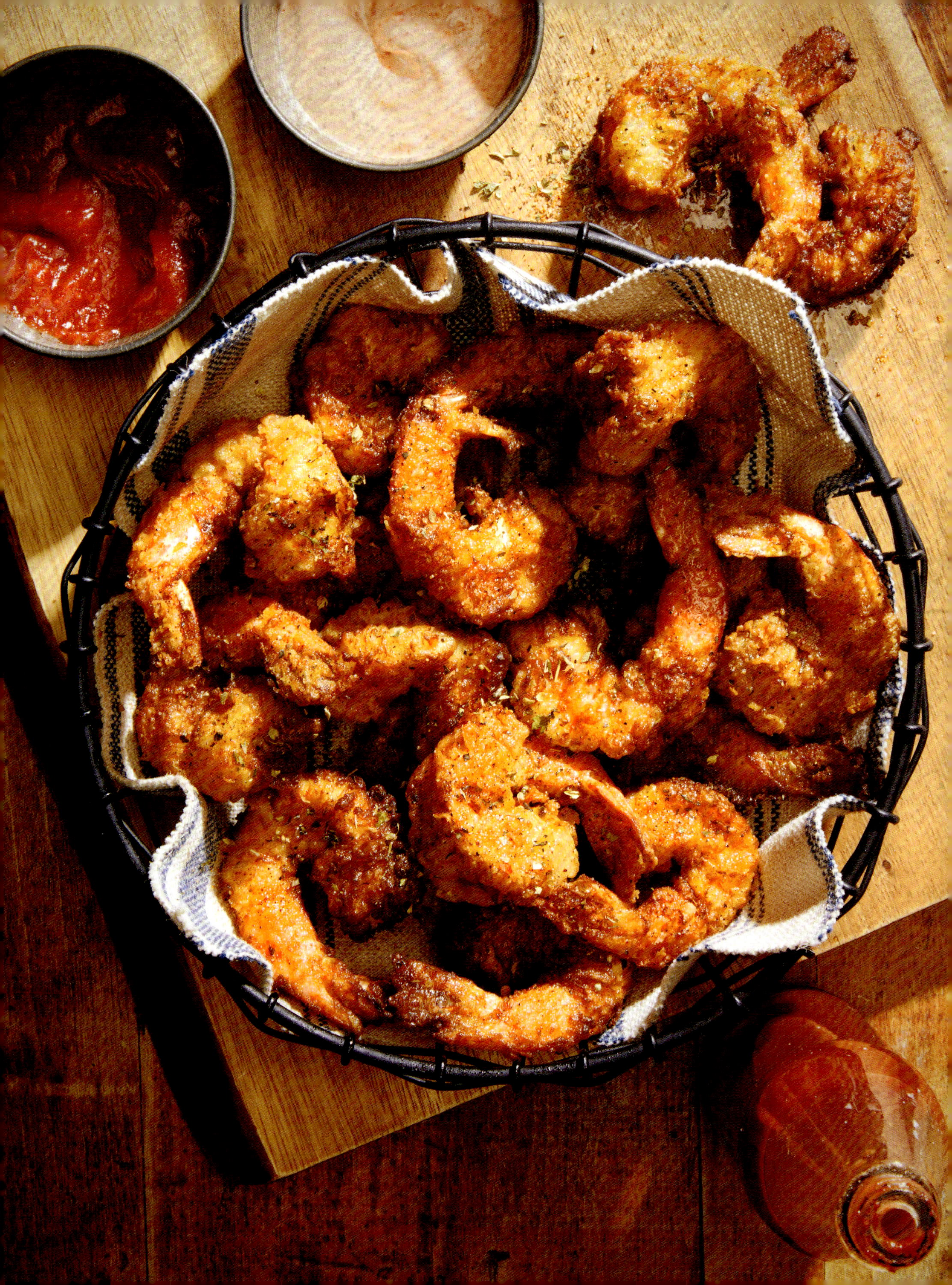

Gator's Louisiana FRIED SHRIMP

This dish is a favorite of *Yellowstone* co-creator and director Taylor Sheridan. He has an affinity for Southern foods because that's where he's from. Fried shrimp, fried catfish, and Hush Puppies (page 111) are quintessentially Southern, and they really connect you to that part of the country. This recipe is also one of my favorites. When I was a kid traveling around southern Louisiana with my dad looking for a great po'boy, fried shrimp really showed me the difference between good food and *great* food.

INGREDIENTS

2 large eggs

1 small can (5 oz /150 ml) evaporated milk

2 teaspoons distilled white vinegar

1 teaspoon Louisiana hot sauce, such as Crystal brand

1 lb (450 g) large (31–35 count) shrimp, peeled and deveined

Kosher salt and freshly ground black pepper or Cajun seasoning

Peanut oil or coconut oil for frying

1 cup (120 g) all-purpose flour

1 tablespoon baking powder

Cocktail sauce, remoulade, or your favorite dipping sauce

MAKES 4 SERVINGS

INSTRUCTIONS

In a bowl, whisk together the eggs, evaporated milk, vinegar, and hot sauce until well blended. Add the shrimp, stir gently to coat, cover, and refrigerate for 1 hour.

Using a slotted spoon, transfer the shrimp to a plate. Discard the marinade. Season the shrimp with salt and pepper.

Fill a large heavy saucepan with about 2 inches (5 cm) of the oil, but no more than half full. Heat the oil over high heat to 380°F (193°C) on a deep-frying thermometer.

In a shallow bowl, whisk together the flour and baking powder. One at a time, dredge the shrimp in the flour mixture to coat, shaking off any excess.

Fry the shrimp in batches to avoid overcrowding the pan, turning once or twice with tongs until golden brown, 1–2 minutes. Transfer to paper towels to drain. Season to taste with more salt and then serve at once, with a dipping sauce alongside.

GATOR'S TIP

You can easily turn these fried shrimp into po'boys. Just tuck the fried shrimp into some soft French bread and dress the sandwich with shredded lettuce, sliced tomatoes, pickles, and mayonnaise.

CRAWFISH CAKES
with Lime Cream

This was my grandmother's recipe and it highlights our southern-Louisiana heritage. Get real Louisiana crawfish for this if you can—it is such a wonderful protein to cook with. I love serving it to the cast and crew who may have never tried crawfish. Of course, it's a bit of a specialty item, so I cannot make it for everyone on set, but it's a treat for those who know and love it. Plus, it's a nice break from all the steak we eat. You can substitute crab for the crawfish, which I make on set fairly often as well.

INGREDIENTS

For the Lime Cream

½ cup (120 g) sour cream

2 tablespoons chopped fresh flat-leaf parsley

Finely grated zest of 1 lime

1 tablespoon fresh lime juice

¼ teaspoon kosher salt

For the Crawfish Cakes

1 lb (450 g) cooked, peeled crawfish tails

3 cups (120 g) fine fresh bread crumbs

½ cup (120 ml) mayonnaise

½ cup (45 g) chopped scallions, white and green parts

1 large egg, beaten

2 cloves garlic, minced

1 tablespoon fresh lemon juice

1 tablespoon Worcestershire sauce

1 teaspoon Cajun seasoning

¼ teaspoon cayenne pepper, or to taste

1 cup (240 ml) vegetable oil

MAKES 4–6 SERVINGS

INSTRUCTIONS

To prepare the lime cream, in a bowl stir together the ingredients until combined. Cover and refrigerate until ready to use, or up to 1 day in advance.

To prepare the crawfish cakes, line a baking sheet with parchment paper.

In a large bowl, combine the crawfish, 1 cup (40 g) of the bread crumbs, mayonnaise, scallions, egg, garlic, lemon juice, Worcestershire sauce, Cajun seasoning, and cayenne and mix gently by hand. Form the mixture into small patties, each about 2½ inches (6 cm) in diameter, and arrange on the prepared baking sheet.

Place the remaining 2 cups (80 g) bread crumbs in a shallow bowl. One at a time, coat each cake with bread crumbs on both sides, pressing the bread crumbs into the cake and letting any excess fall back into the bowl. Return the coated cake to the baking sheet.

To cook the cakes, in a large nonstick frying pan over medium-high heat, warm the oil until hot. Working in batches to avoid overcrowding the pan, carefully add the cakes to the hot oil. Cook, turning once, until golden brown on both sides, 6–8 minutes total. Transfer to paper towels to drain.

Serve hot, drizzled with the lime cream.

GATOR'S TIP

Many times, I substitute equal parts bread crumbs with crushed Ritz crackers—it's really about what I have on hand.

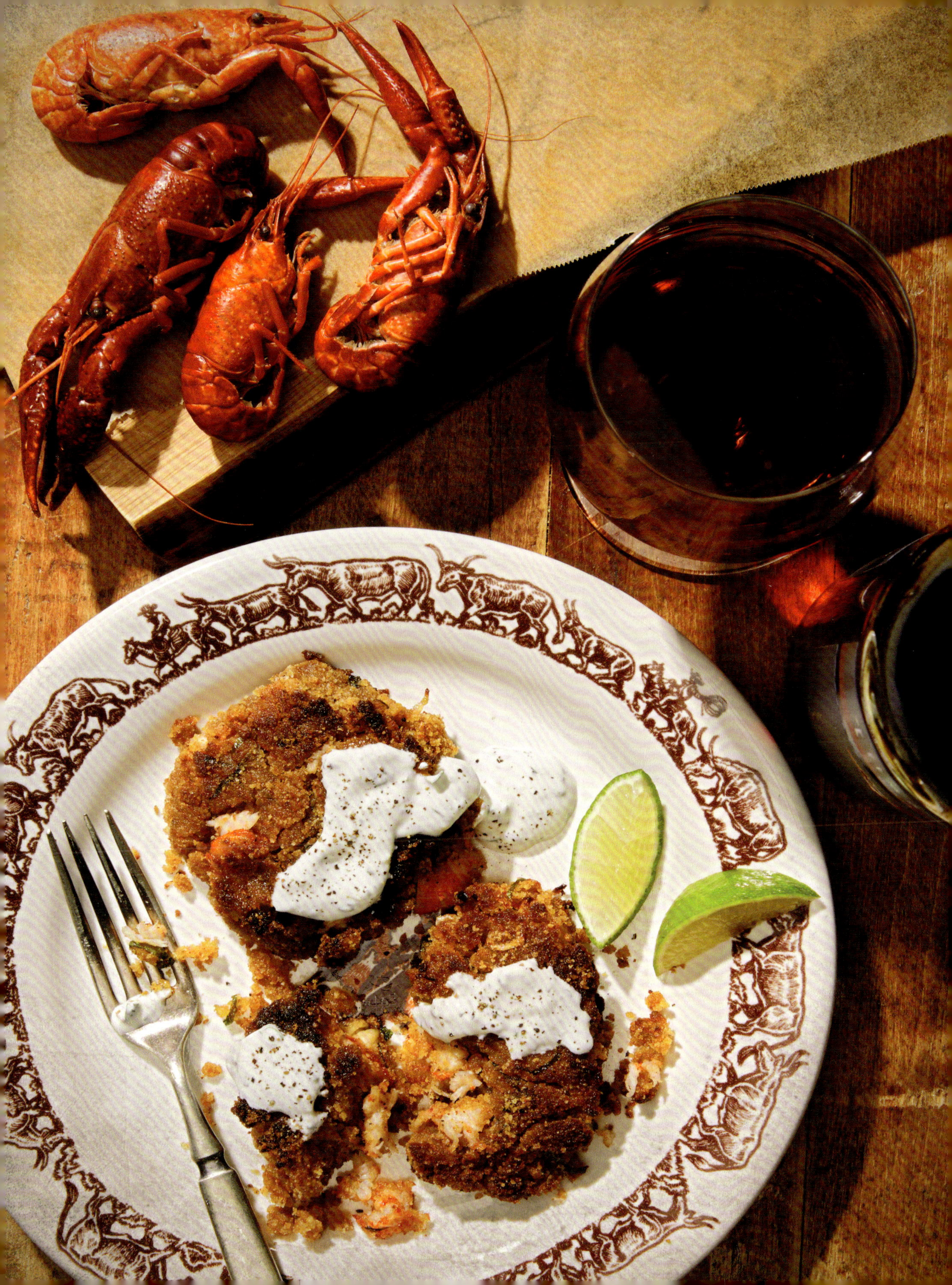

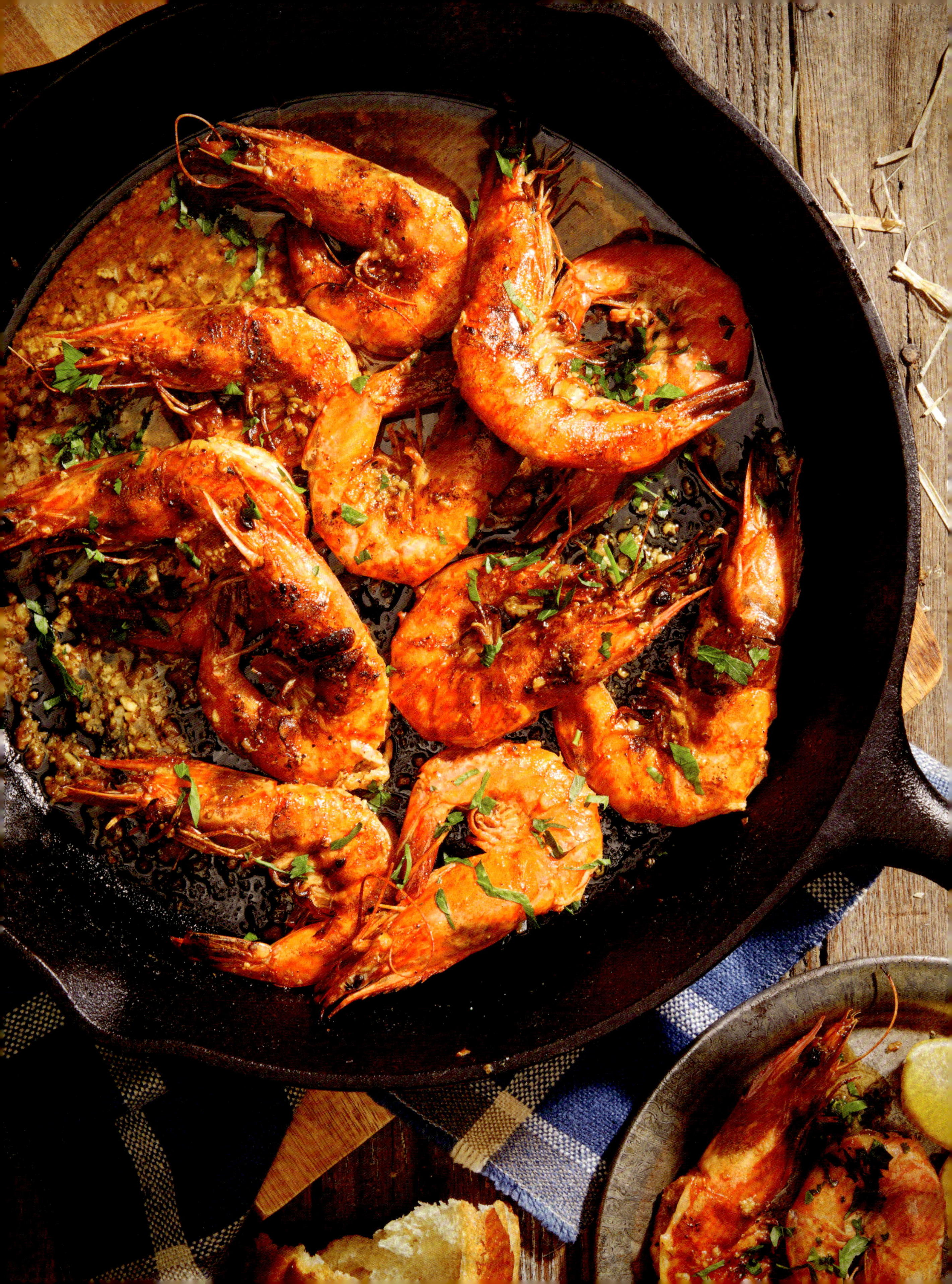

Gator's
BUTTER-ROASTED SHRIMP

This recipe is very special to me, and one that my dad and I have been making for a long time. It's based on the classic New Orleans barbecue shrimp recipe (which isn't really barbecued at all), and I'm not sure I can even explain how delicious this is. Not only is it great to eat, but it's also a real showstopper when I make it for the cast and crew. I bring out a huge pot of the biggest head-on shrimp I can find and serve it with lots of crusty French bread to sop up all the glorious buttery juices. It gets everyone excited, and even if you aren't sure about eating shrimp with the heads on, try it—you will 100 percent not regret it. Cooking the shrimp with their heads on adds a ton of flavor. You can eat the shrimp heads or suck out their contents, or not.

INGREDIENTS

½ cup (115 g) unsalted butter, cut into pieces

2 cloves garlic, minced

¼ cup (60 ml) dry white wine

1½ lb (680 g) jumbo (10–15 count) shell-on white Gulf shrimp, preferably head on and deveined

1 teaspoon cracked black peppercorns

Kosher salt

For Serving

Chopped fresh flat-leaf parsley leaves

Lemon wedges

Crusty French bread, warmed

MAKES 4–6 SERVINGS

INSTRUCTIONS

Preheat the oven to 325°F (165°C).

In a cast-iron pan over medium heat, melt the butter. Add the garlic and cook until just fragrant, about 30 seconds. Pour in the wine, bring to a simmer, and cook for about 1 minute. Add the shrimp and peppercorns and season with salt. Stir gently to combine, and then transfer the pan to the oven.

Roast, turning once halfway through, until the shrimp are just cooked through, 13–15 minutes. Remove the pan from the oven and turn the broiler to high. Place the shrimp under the broiler until the shells just start start to crackle, about 4 minutes.

To serve, garnish the shrimp with parsley and lemon wedges. Serve family-style, directly out of the cast-iron pan with plenty of crusty bread alongside for sopping up the juices.

GATOR'S TIP

If you cannot find Gulf shrimp, use any large, fresh shrimp—but it must be head on!

John, Kayce, and Tate's GLAZED VENISON MEATBALLS

In Season 2, Kayce and John take Tate deer hunting for the first time. Kayce talks Tate through the process, "Look at that. That's bigger than my first buck." "First deer," says John. "C'mon, we gotta blood ya." "What does that mean?" asks Tate. "It means, you gotta wear his blood to honor him," explains Kayce. Tate starts to cry after Kayce smears blood on his face. "It's a big deal, taking a life," says Kayce. "But everything on this earth has to do it to stay alive. Even trees." Venison is a terrific stand-in for the standard pork or beef in these flavorful meatballs. Venison is more readily available now and is a great choice for anyone who likes to hunt, which encourages a lifestyle of living off the land—very much in tune with the lifestyle on Dutton Ranch. You can serve these meatballs any way you like, but the sweet-savory sauce is really delicious with the venison. Choose a jam or jelly that isn't too chunky (or chop it into small pieces).

INGREDIENTS

For the Sauce

2 tablespoons unsalted butter

1 large shallot, finely chopped

2 tablespoons dry sherry

½ cup (120 ml) beef stock, preferably homemade

Grated zest of ½ orange

¼ cup (60 ml) fresh orange juice

½ cup (140 g) cranberry or cherry preserves, or red currant jelly

1 teaspoon Dijon mustard

¼ teaspoon cayenne pepper (optional)

For the Meatballs

Olive oil for brushing

1 tablespoon unsalted butter

½ small yellow onion, finely chopped

continued on page 30

INSTRUCTIONS

To prepare the sauce, in a saucepan over medium-low heat, melt the butter. Add the shallot and cook, stirring until lightly golden, about 3 minutes. Pour in the sherry and simmer for 1 minute. Stir in the stock, orange zest, and orange juice. Raise the heat to medium-high and bring the mixture to a boil; then reduce the heat to medium and simmer the sauce until it is reduced slightly, about 3 minutes. Stir in the preserves, mustard, and cayenne, if using, and simmer for 1 minute; then remove from the heat.

Puree the sauce with an immersion blender, or in a standard blender, and then return it to the saucepan. Continue to cook over medium heat, stirring until the sauce thickens slightly into a glaze, about 1 minute. Remove from the heat and set aside.

To prepare the meatballs, preheat the oven to 450°F (230°C). Line a baking sheet with parchment paper and brush the parchment generously with oil.

In a 10-inch (25-cm) cast-iron frying pan over medium heat, melt the butter. Add the onion and cook, stirring until tender, about 5 minutes. Transfer to a large bowl and let cool slightly. Reserve the pan.

Add the venison, bacon, egg, bread crumbs, and parsley to the bowl with the onion. Season with 1 teaspoon salt, ½ teaspoon black pepper, and a pinch of cayenne, if using. Mix gently with your hands to combine.

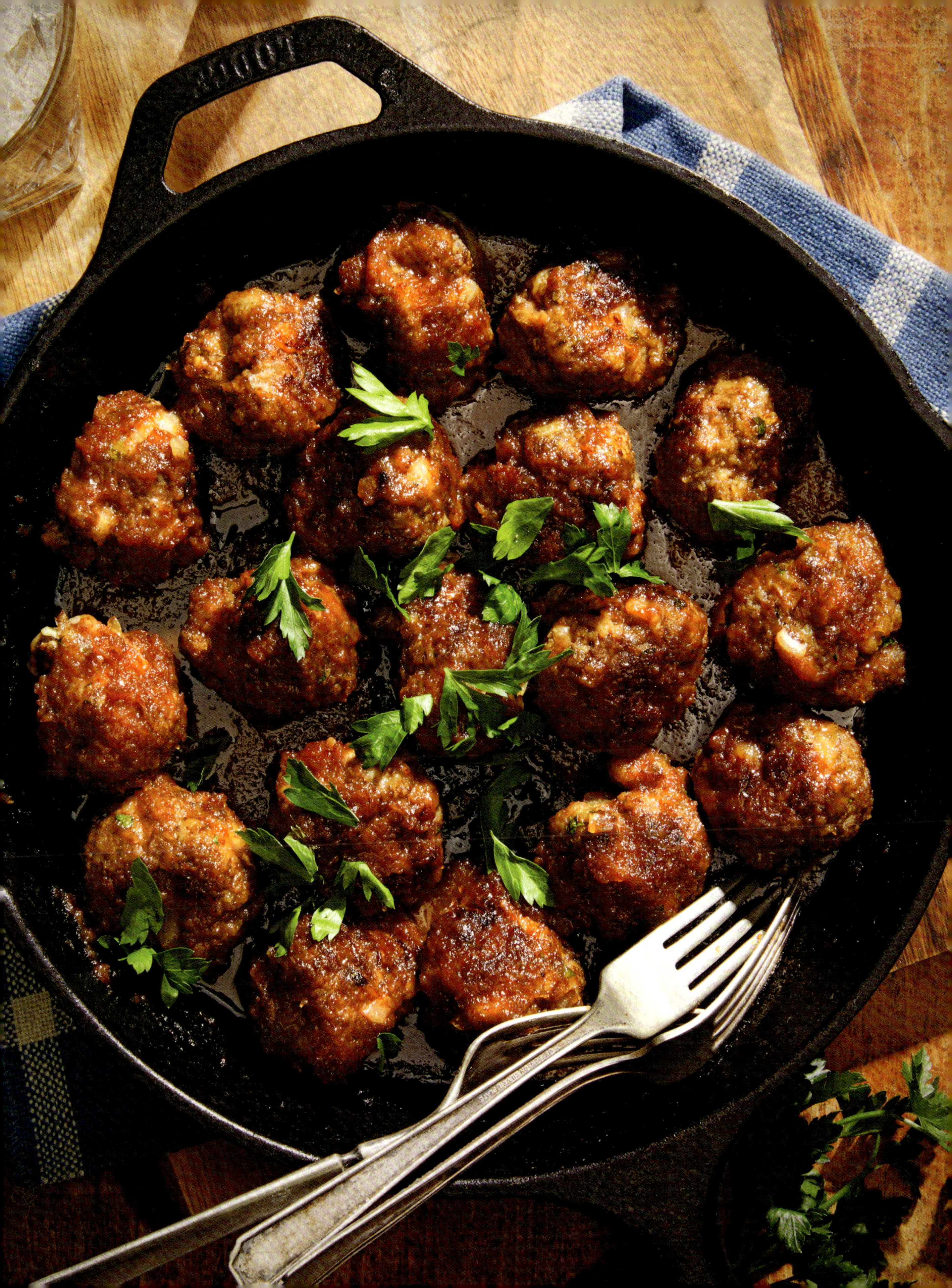

continued from page 28

1 lb (450 g) ground venison

2 slices thick-cut bacon, minced

1 large egg, beaten

1 cup (40 g) fresh white bread crumbs

2 tablespoons chopped fresh flat-leaf parsley, plus more for garnish

Kosher salt and freshly ground black pepper

Cayenne pepper (optional)

MAKES 4–6 SERVINGS

Scoop up about 2 tablespoons (1 ½ ounces /40 g) of the venison mixture, roll it into a golf-ball-size meatball, and then place on the prepared baking sheet. Be careful not to pack the mixture too tightly—just enough to hold the meat together. Repeat with the remaining venison mixture, arranging the meatballs on the prepared baking sheet with space between them. You should have 16 meatballs. Drizzle the meatballs with a little more oil.

Bake, turning once halfway through, until nicely browned and cooked through and no longer pink, about 15 minutes.

Transfer the meatballs to the reserved pan. Pour the warm sauce into the frying pan and place it over medium heat. Cook, turning the meatballs gently in the sauce, until glazed, about 2 minutes. Serve at once.

FRIED OKRA

I'll do anything to get cowboys to eat their vegetables, and frying is a surefire way to do it. Okra is terrific fried—it's like it was made for it—and this cooking method can be used for all kinds of vegetables: broccoli, green beans, onion rings, zucchini, you name it. Fried okra takes me back to my childhood, when I would watch my grandmother make it; she would put the seasoned cornmeal in a paper grocery bag, throw in the okra, and shake it all together.

INGREDIENTS

2 cups (230 g) sliced fresh okra, cut crosswise into ½-inch- (12-mm-) thick slices

1 cup (240 ml) whole milk, plus extra milk as needed

Hot-pepper sauce for seasoning (optional)

1 cup (130 g) fine cornmeal

1 teaspoon freshly ground black pepper

Vegetable oil for frying

MAKES 4–6 SERVINGS

INSTRUCTIONS

In a deep bowl, combine the okra and milk, making sure the milk covers the okra. Stir in some hot-pepper sauce, if you like. Set aside to soak at room temperature for 30 minutes.

In a shallow bowl, stir together the cornmeal and pepper. Drain the okra well. Then, in batches, toss the okra with the cornmeal mixture until coated.

Preheat the oven to 200°F (95°C). Line a baking sheet with paper towels and place it next to the stovetop.

Fill a saucepan with about 2 inches (5 cm) of the oil, but no more than half full. Heat the oil over medium-high heat to 380°F (193°C) on a deep-frying thermometer.

Working in batches to avoid overcrowding the pan, carefully transfer the okra, shaking off any excess cornmeal gently, into the hot oil. Cook the okra until golden brown, turning once with tongs or a slotted spoon, 3–5 minutes. Do not stir, as it may remove the crust.

Using a slotted spoon, transfer the okra to the prepared baking sheet to drain on the paper towels. Immediately sprinkle with salt. Repeat to cook the remaining okra.

Remove and discard the paper towels from under the okra. Then spread the okra gently into an even layer on the baking sheet. Bake until crunchy, about 30 minutes. Serve at once.

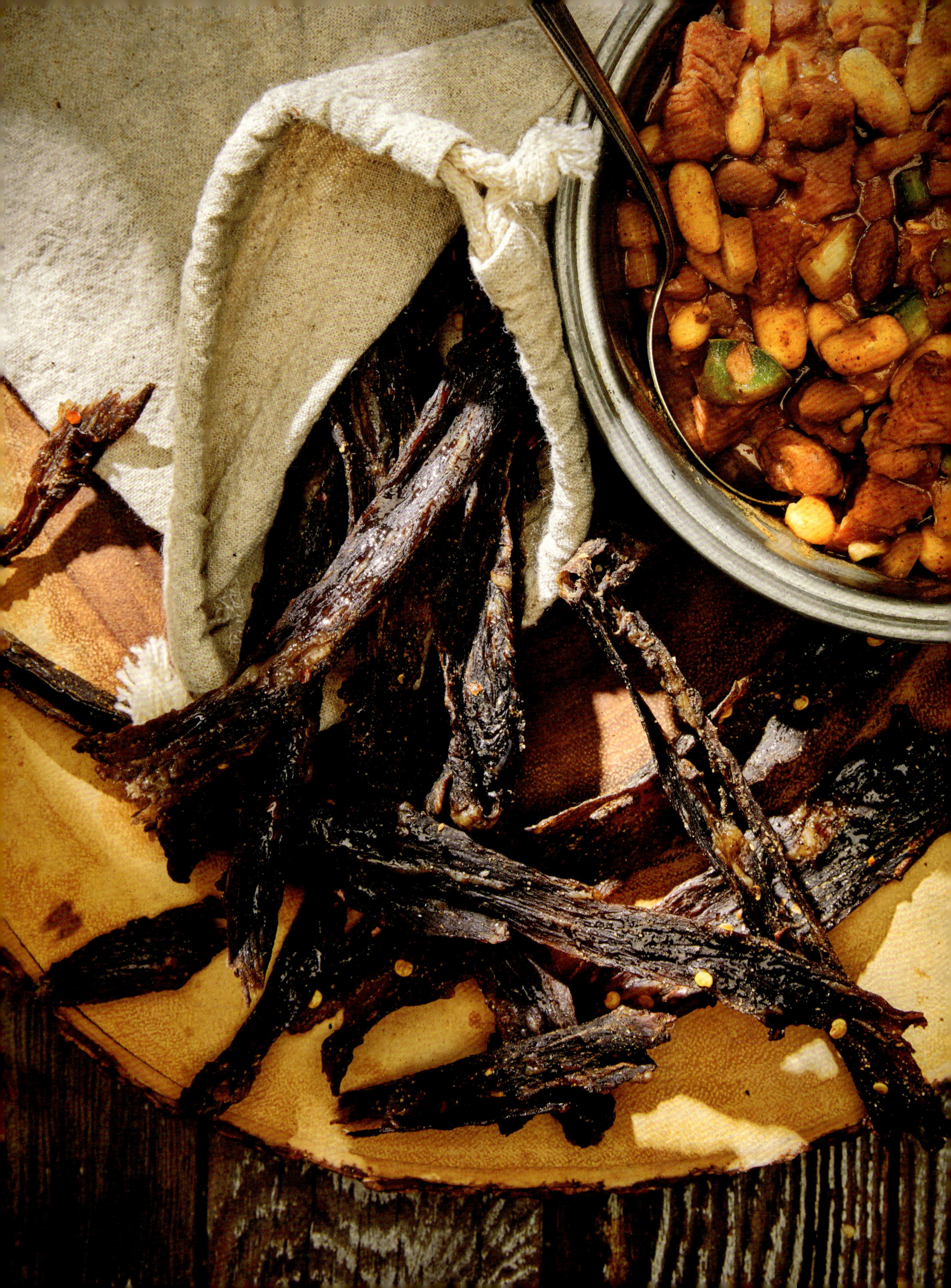

Taylor's BEEF JERKY

Jerky is another favorite of Taylor Sheridan and all the cowboys love it. Taylor is not only the co-creator of *Yellowstone*, but he also plays the role of Travis Wheatley, a horse trader and showman in the series. He is a cowboy himself in real life (and owner of the famed 6666 Ranch in Texas). We go through more beef jerky on this show than I have ever seen in my life or career. Every season, while prepping to begin filming, I start by making 100 pounds (45 kg) or so of beef jerky—and not to stockpile it, because it's pretty much gone right away. I'll divide it up and hand out big bags to the horse wranglers and the cowboys and cowgirls so they have a bunch to start the show. It blows people's minds getting that big bag. By the end of the day, maybe I'll get some too. You really cannot beat homemade beef jerky—it's well worth the time and effort to make it.

INGREDIENTS

- 1 lb (450 g) sirloin steak, trimmed of all fat
- ¼ cup (60 ml) soy sauce
- 3 tablespoons Worcestershire sauce
- 1 tablespoon firmly packed light brown sugar
- 2 teaspoons freshly ground black pepper
- 1 teaspoon red pepper flakes, or to taste
- ½ teaspoon garlic powder
- ½ teaspoon onion powder

MAKES ABOUT ¼ LB (115 G) JERKY

INSTRUCTIONS

Wrap the steak in plastic wrap and freeze for about 1 hour (this makes it easier to slice it thinly). Unwrap the steak, and using a sharp knife, cut the steak into thin slices. Transfer to a baking dish.

In a bowl, whisk together the remaining ingredients. Pour the marinade over the steak slices, cover, and refrigerate for at least 5 hours, or up to overnight.

Remove the oven racks. Line the bottom of the oven with aluminum foil.

Drain the marinade from the steak slices and transfer them onto paper towels. Blot with more paper towels (the drier it is, the quicker the jerky will dehaydrate).

Using wooden skewers, skewer 4–6 pieces of steak about ½ inch (12 mm) below the end of each strip, spacing the steak strips about 1 inch (2.5 cm) apart on each skewer. Lay one oven rack between two chairs or stools and position the skewers perpendicular to the rack so the steak strips hang down through the grates. Make sure there's space between each steak strip and the grate. Return the oven rack to the upper third of the oven.

Turn the oven to 175°F (80°C). Bake until the jerky is dried but still pliable, 1½–2 hours, depending on the size and thickness of the slices. Check the jerky often toward the end of cooking, so it doesn't overcook and become too tough. The jerky will keep, refrigerated, for up to 3 weeks.

Lee's
GARLIC BUTTER STEAK BITES

Although we may never know for sure, I'd like to imagine this dish was Lee's favorite before his untimely, and all-too-soon, tragedy in episode 1 while herding cattle with Kayce. These steak bites are seared in a cast-iron skillet and drenched in plenty of garlic butter. It's a terrific snack when you just need a quick bite to keep you going. I like to have plenty of food ready and available for the cast and crew in case they need a quick bite between takes. These are a kind of simplified (or maybe fancier?) version of "steak fingers" you see out here in Montana and in lots of Idaho restaurants—kind of like chicken-fried steak, where you dip strips of steak in batter, deep-fry them, and then serve them with ranch dressing (like "Dutton Ranch," see page 19) or barbecue sauce.

INGREDIENTS

- 2 lb (1 kg) New York strip steaks, trimmed and cut into 1-inch (2.5-cm) cubes
- Kosher salt and freshly ground black pepper
- 4 tablespoons (60 g) unsalted butter
- 4 cloves garlic, crushed
- Chopped fresh flat-leaf parsley leaves for garnish (optional)

MAKES 6–8 SERVINGS

INSTRUCTIONS

Place the steak cubes in a bowl and season all over with salt and pepper. Toss to coat.

In a large cast-iron frying pan over medium-high heat, melt half the butter. Add the steak and sear until nicely browned on one side, about 2 minutes. Flip the pieces, add the garlic, and sear the other side, 1–2 minutes longer. Add the remaining butter and stir until the steak cubes are medium-rare, 30–60 seconds longer. Transfer the steak to a plate, sprinkle with parsley, if using, and serve at once.

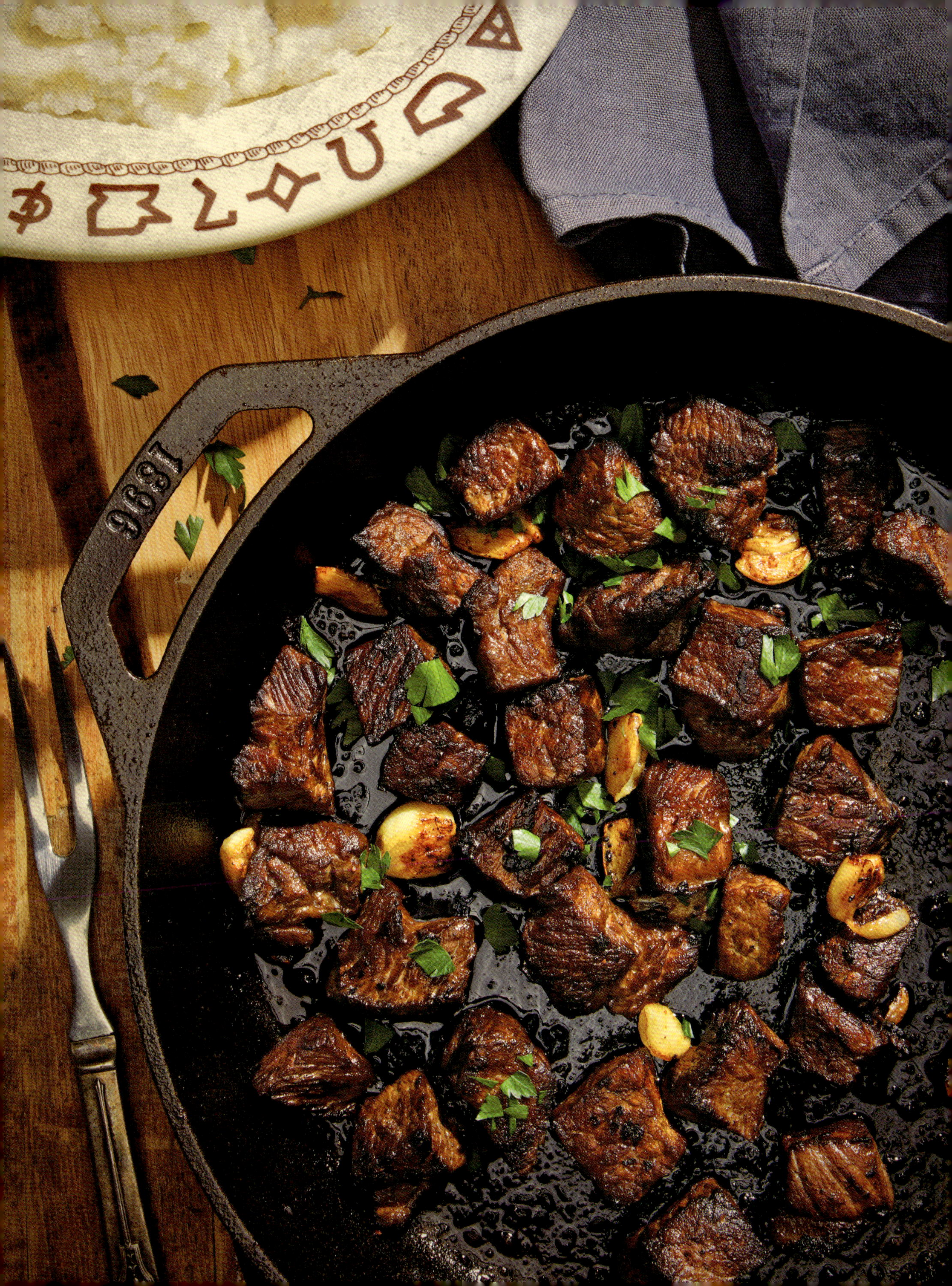
1896

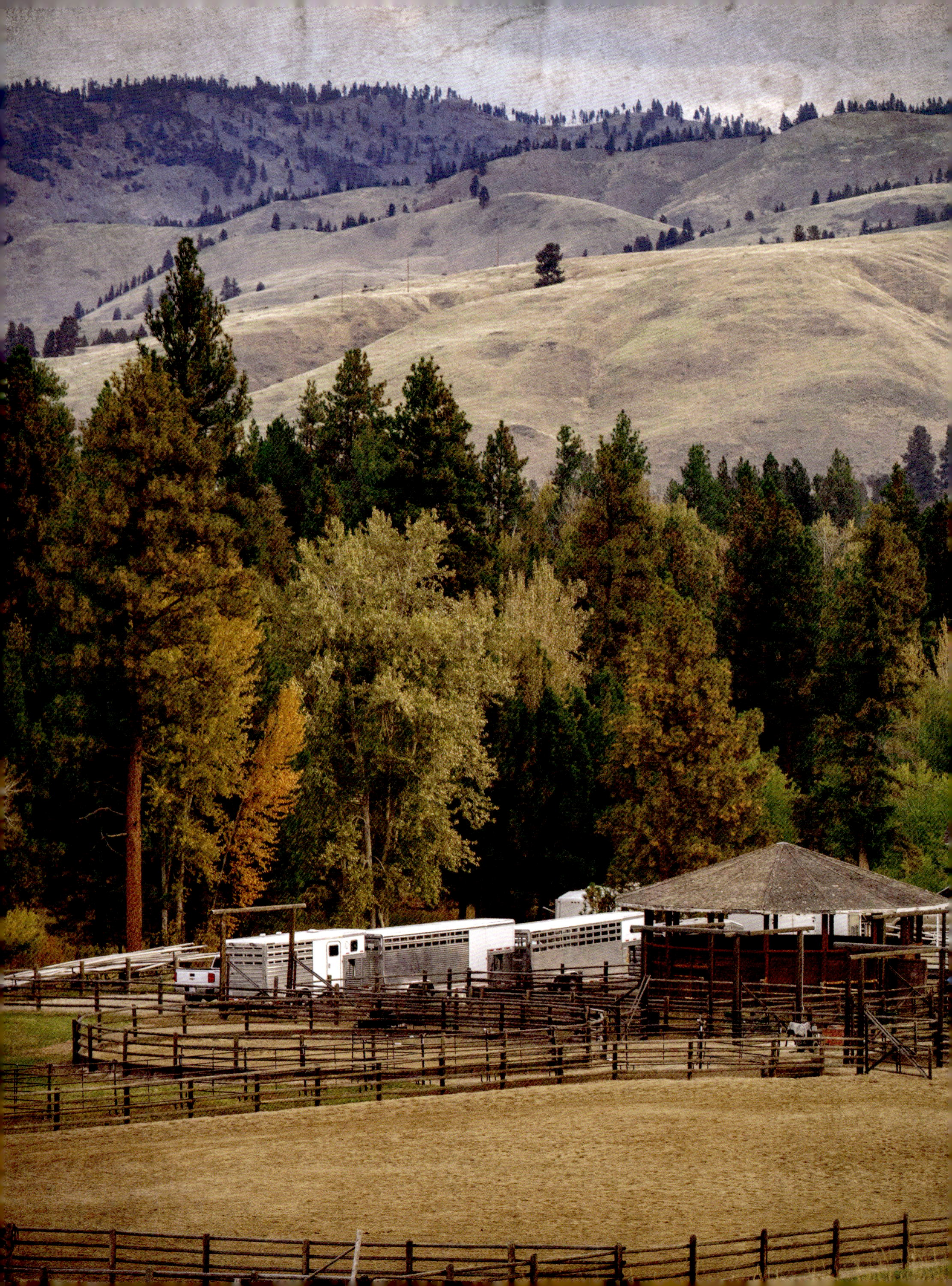

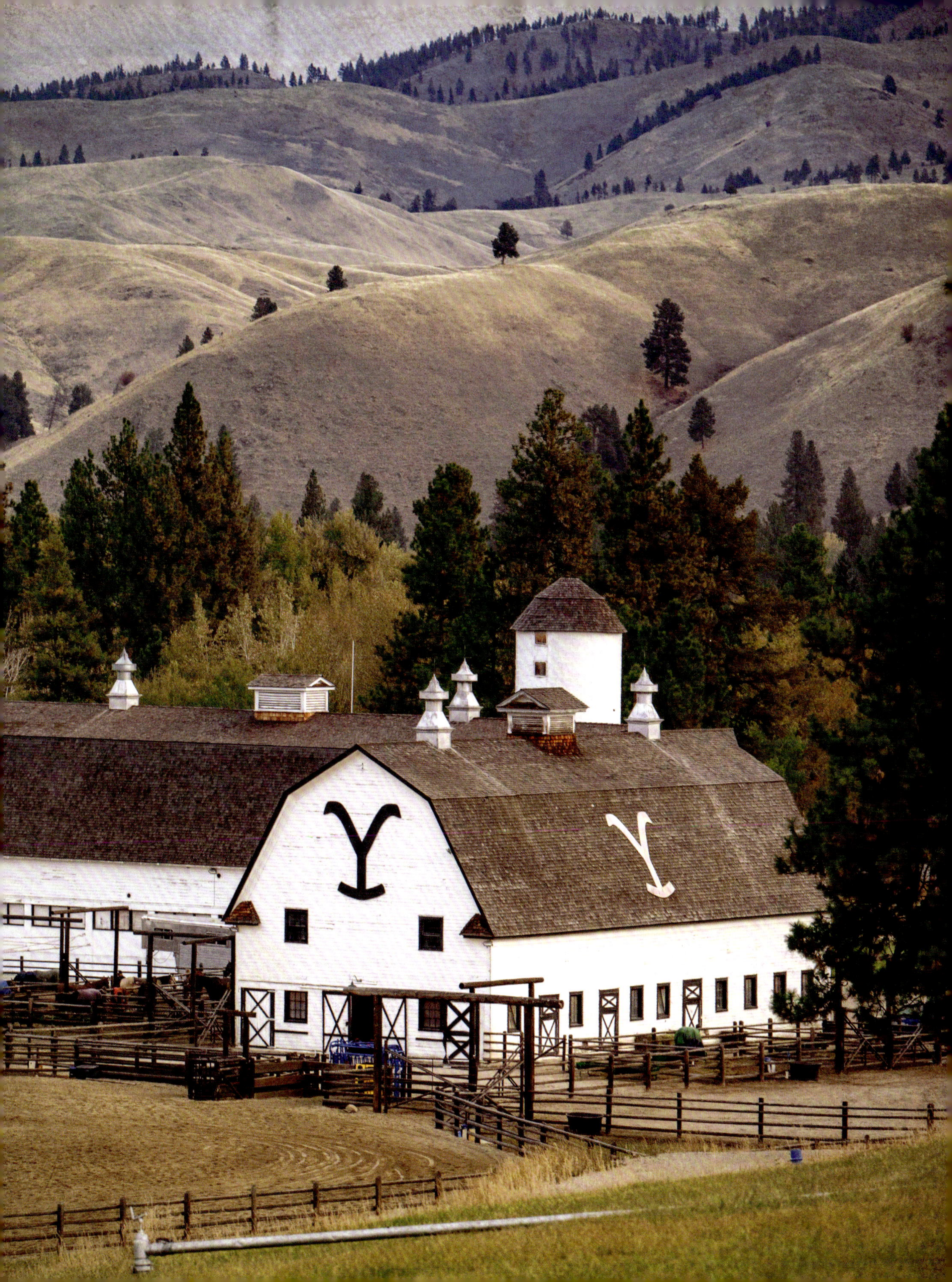

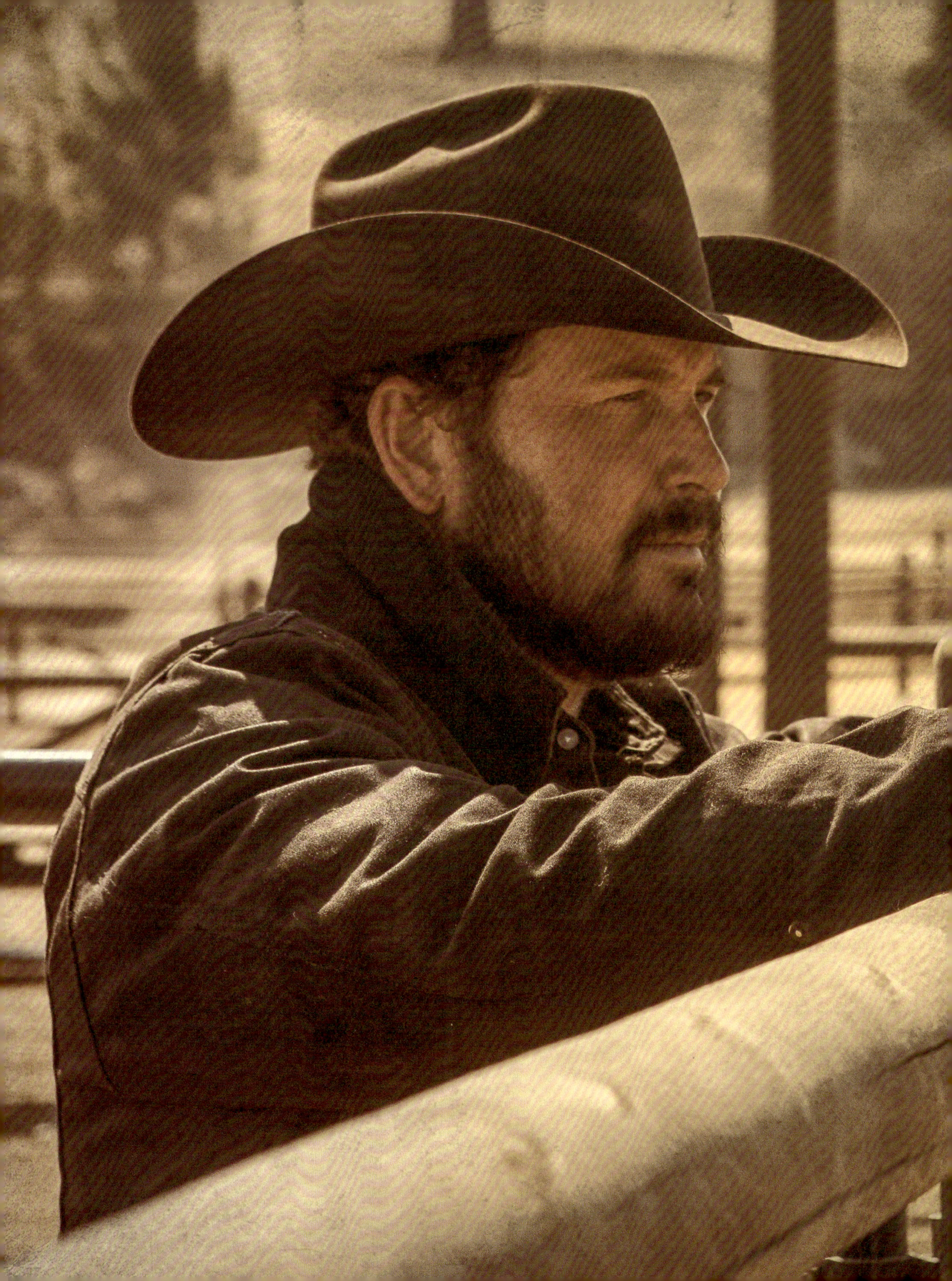

MAIN DISHES

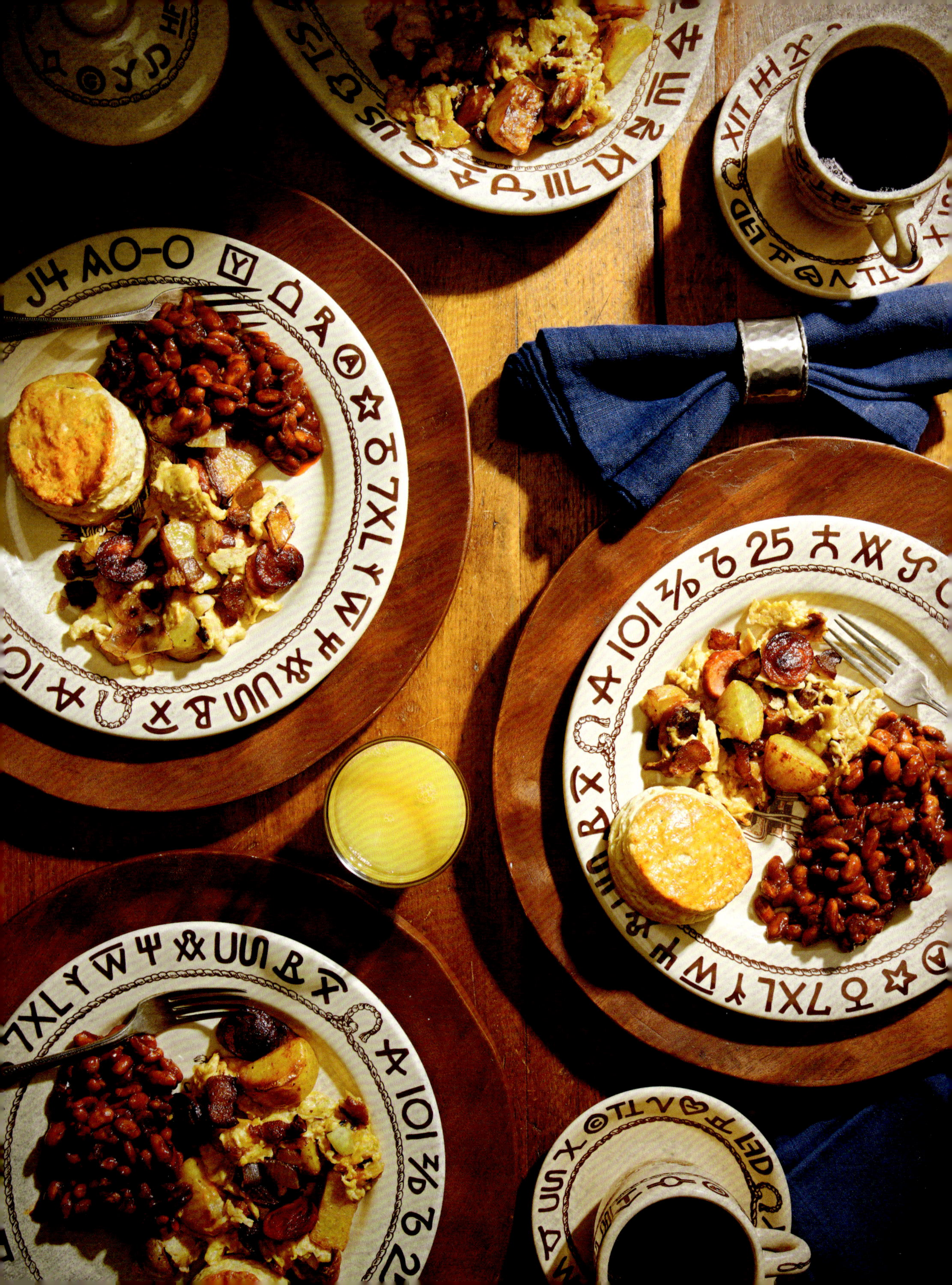

BIG RANCH BREAKFAST

Early in the morning, in the opening scene of Season 3's "Meaner Than Evil" episode, I'm in the kitchen, cooking up a big hearty breakfast. Despite that, Tate walks into the dining room of the ranch lodge and asks if he can "have some Choco Chimps." "Yeah, sure," I reply. "That sounds pretty good. How about two of those, Gator?" says John. "You don't want some tasty bacon, or I've got some elk sausage," I plead. "No, I think Choco Chimps this mornin'," says John. "This is . . . for the record . . ." I reply, while looking crestfallen. John simply looks and me and says, "It's gonna be fine, Gator." Other than that one exception, a hearty ranch breakfast is important, especially for ranch hands before a long day driving cattle or seeking revenge on enemies of the Dutton family. This big breakfast scramble has everything you need to keep going—potatoes, bacon, sausage, eggs, and cheese—plus a side of beans, biscuits, and—of course—all the coffee you want. Just don't wait to eat it, or you might not get any.

INGREDIENTS

1 lb (450 g) Yukon gold potatoes, cut into ½-inch (12-mm) pieces

Kosher salt and freshly ground black pepper

½ lb (225 g) thick-cut bacon slices, chopped

½ yellow onion, chopped

About 6 oz (170 g) smoked sausage, such as linguiça, cut into ½-inch (12-mm) pieces

10 large eggs

¼ cup (60 ml) whole milk

4 oz (115 g) Cheddar cheese, shredded (about 1 cup)

1 recipe Ranch Hand Baked Beans (page 112), warm

1 recipe This Is How You Make a F*$%ing Biscuit (page 103), warm

Plenty of strong coffee for serving

MAKES 6 SERVINGS (OR 4 REALLY BIG SERVINGS)

INSTRUCTIONS

In a saucepan, combine the potatoes, 1 tablespoon salt, and enough water to cover the potatoes by 1 inch (2.5 cm). Bring to a boil over high heat, stirring a few times; then reduce the heat to medium-low and boil gently until tender, about 10 minutes. Drain well.

Meanwhile, in a large frying pan (preferably cast iron) over medium heat, cook the bacon, stirring until crisp, about 6 minutes. Using a slotted spoon, transfer the bacon to paper towels to drain. Pour off all but 2 tablespoons of the bacon fat in the pan.

Return the frying pan to medium heat and add the onion, sausage, and potatoes. Season with salt and pepper. Cook, stirring until browned, about 5 minutes.

Meanwhile, in a large bowl, whisk together the eggs, milk, ½ teaspoon salt, and ¼ teaspoon pepper. Reduce the heat under the frying pan to low and pour the eggs into the potato and sausage mixture. Add the bacon. Cook gently, stirring every so often until the eggs start to firm up, about 1 minute. Sprinkle on the cheese and stir until melted and the eggs are done to your liking.

Serve at once, with the baked beans, biscuits, and plenty of coffee alongside.

RIP'S FRY BREAD
with Scrambled Eggs and Bacon

After Beth spends the night with Rip in his new cabin, he makes her a breakfast that includes his mother's recipe for fry bread. It's a sweet and tender moment between the two. Native American fry bread is an important part of Indigenous culture and a symbol of nourishment, perseverance, and oppression. It took its modern form when Indigenous Americans were forced to make do with government rations to survive. I like to use a little bit of honey and powdered sugar to top off my fry bread.

INGREDIENTS

For the Fry Bread

1½ cups (170 g) all-purpose flour, plus extra flour as needed

1 teaspoon baking powder

½ teaspoon kosher salt

½ cup (120 ml) warm water, plus warm water as needed

2 tablespoons canola oil, plus oil for frying

For the Scrambled Eggs and Bacon

4 slices thick-cut bacon

4 large eggs

¼ cup (60 ml) whole milk

Kosher salt and freshly ground black pepper

MAKES 2 SERVINGS

INSTRUCTIONS

To prepare the fry bread, in a bowl whisk together the flour, baking powder, and salt. Make a small well in the middle of the flour mixture and pour in the water and oil. Stir with your hands until the dough comes together, adding more warm water or flour, as needed, to make a soft dough that isn't too sticky. Knead the dough for about 2 minutes. The dough should be soft and supple, like a marshmallow. Cover the bowl with a dish towel and let the dough rest for 30 minutes at room temperature.

Lightly dust a work surface with flour. Divide the dough into 4 equal pieces, each about 2½ ounces (70 g), and, on the floured surface, pat and pull the dough balls into 6-inch (15-cm) rounds. Cover with the dish towel.

Line a baking sheet with paper towels and set aside. In a 10-inch (25-cm) cast-iron frying pan over medium heat, warm ½ inch (12 mm) of the oil to 350°F (180°C) on a deep-frying thermometer.

One at a time, fry each dough round in the hot oil, turning once or twice with tongs until the dough is crisp, golden brown, and cooked through, 1½–2 minutes. Transfer to the prepared baking sheet. Repeat to cook the remaining dough. (Keep the fry bread warm in a 200°F/95°C oven, if you like.)

To prepare the bacon and eggs, in a nonstick frying pan over medium-low heat, fry the bacon, turning, as needed, until crisp, about 6 minutes. Transfer to paper towels to drain. Pour off all but 2 tablespoons of the bacon fat in the pan.

In a bowl, whisk together the eggs and milk. Season with salt and pepper and whisk to combine. Return the nonstick frying pan to low heat and pour in the eggs. Cook, stirring gently with a rubber spatula until the eggs are cooked but still moist, or done to your liking.

To assemble, divide the fry bread between 2 plates. Top each with eggs and bacon to serve.

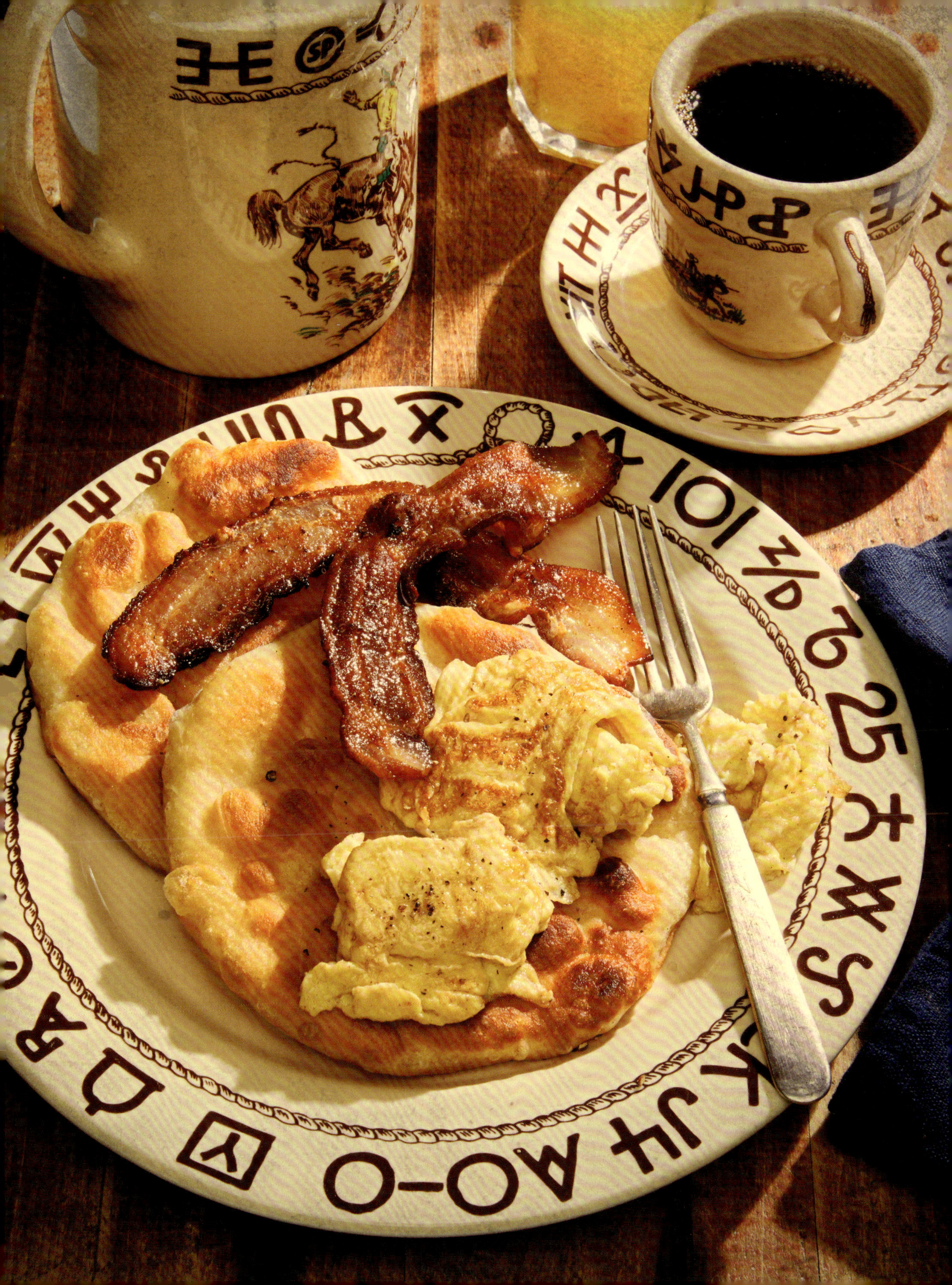

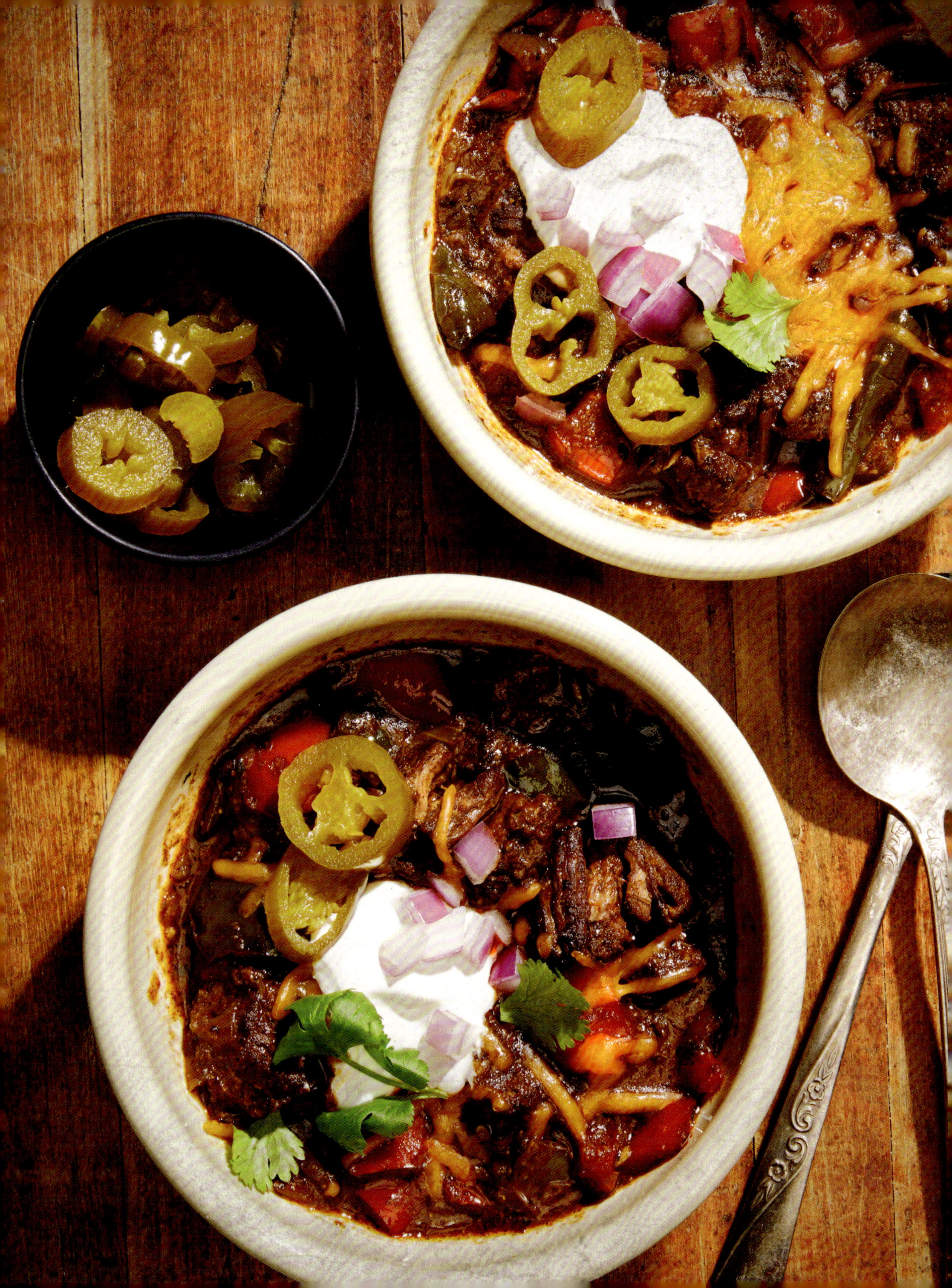

Jimmy's
COWBOY BEEF CHILI

Taylor Sheridan hails from Texas, so chili is really important around the set. I mean, when it's cold outside and we are shooting, chili is every day. In Season 4, Jimmy has very specific opinions about the correct way to prepare chili. Since there is so much access to beef all the time on set, I've made chili a hundred different ways. It's such a great way to use a lot of ingredients you might have on hand.

INGREDIENTS

4 lb (1.8 kg) boneless beef chuck roast

Kosher salt and freshly ground black pepper

3 tablespoons olive oil, plus oil as needed

1 large yellow onion, chopped

1 large red bell pepper, seeded and chopped

1 poblano chile, seeded and chopped

1 jalapeño chile, seeded and finely chopped

4 large cloves garlic, minced

3 tablespoons chili powder

2 teaspoons dried oregano

2 teaspoons ground cumin

1 bottle (12 oz /350 ml) lager beer

1 cup (240 ml) beef stock or chicken stock, preferably homemade, or water

2 tablespoons yellow cornmeal

For Serving (optional)

Shredded Cheddar or Monterey Jack cheese

Chopped red onion

Sour cream

Chopped fresh cilantro

Pickled jalapeño chiles

MAKES 8 SERVINGS

INSTRUCTIONS

Trim the beef of large pieces of fat and cut the beef into 1-inch (2.5-cm) pieces. Season the beef all over with salt and pepper.

In a heavy Dutch oven or cast-iron pot over high heat, heat 2 tablespoons of the oil until hot. In 3 or 4 batches, sear a single layer of beef cubes, without turning, until well browned on one side, about 5 minutes. Using a slotted spoon, transfer the beef to a plate. Repeat with the remaining beef, adding more oil as needed.

Reduce the heat to medium-high. Add the remaining 1 tablespoon oil to the pot; then add the onion, bell pepper, poblano, jalapeño, and garlic. Cook, stirring occasionally and scraping up the browned bits on the bottom of the pot until the vegetables soften, about 7 minutes.

Stir in the chili powder, oregano, cumin, 1 teaspoon salt, and 1 teaspoon pepper and cook until fragrant, about 30 seconds. Pour in the beer and stock and stir to combine. Bring to a boil. Return the beef and its juices to the pot and bring to a simmer. Reduce the heat to low, cover the pot partially, and simmer gently, stirring every so often until the beef is meltingly tender, about 2½ hours.

Scoop about ½ cup (120 ml) of the cooking liquid from the pot into a small bowl, add the cornmeal to it, and whisk to combine. Stir the cornmeal mixture into the chili and cook, stirring occasionally until the chili thickens slightly, about 5 minutes. Taste the chili and season with more salt and pepper, as needed. Serve hot with any toppings you like, if using.

John's PERFECT RIB EYE STEAK

A great big, perfectly seared steak is the ultimate Montana cattle ranch fare. Whether it's in the show, and John Dutton—who loves his steak—is happily chowing down on one at Ruby's Café or I'm serving it to the actors and crew, it is one of the most important recipes in this book. I cook rib eye *every single day*, and unless you are a vegetarian, it's one of the most popular items on set to eat. On our last day of shooting for Season 3, we all camped out in the middle of the ranch to film some last scenes and I had limited ingredients with which to feed everyone. I borrowed a backyard grill and cooked steaks all day long. I remember looking out at the Montana landscape as the sun was going down and it was spectacular. When I turned my attention to the crew and cast, just about everyone had a steak in their hands. Literally in their hands! Not on a plate and not using a knife and fork—just about everyone I could see was eating a steak like an apple! If that's not *Yellowstone,* I don't know what is.

INGREDIENTS

2 thick-cut boneless rib eye steaks (about 12 oz / 340 g each, and 1½ inches /4 cm thick)

Kosher salt and coarsely ground black pepper

Olive oil

Turbinado sugar for seasoning

2 tablespoons unsalted butter

3 dashes hot-pepper sauce, or to taste

Fresh thyme for serving

MAKES 2–4 SERVINGS

INSTRUCTIONS

Remove the steaks from the refrigerator 30–60 minutes before cooking to bring them to room temperature.

Season both sides of each steak generously with salt.

Heat a cast-iron frying pan large enough to hold both steaks over medium-high heat until it begins to smoke just a bit. Drizzle with enough oil just to coat the pan. Place the steaks in the hot pan and raise the heat to high. Cook until the bottoms of the steaks are deep golden brown, 2–3 minutes. Flip the steaks and cook until the other side is browned, about 2 minutes longer.

Sprinkle the steaks with a little sugar and season generously with pepper. Flip the steaks again, and then reduce the heat to medium. Add the butter to the pan, and then season the steaks with the hot-pepper sauce. Cook, swirling the pan and spooning the butter over the steaks, until the butter browns and the steaks are done to your liking, about 4 minutes for medium-rare.

Transfer the steaks to a cutting board and let rest for 5 minutes (if you can wait that long!) before slicing and serving.

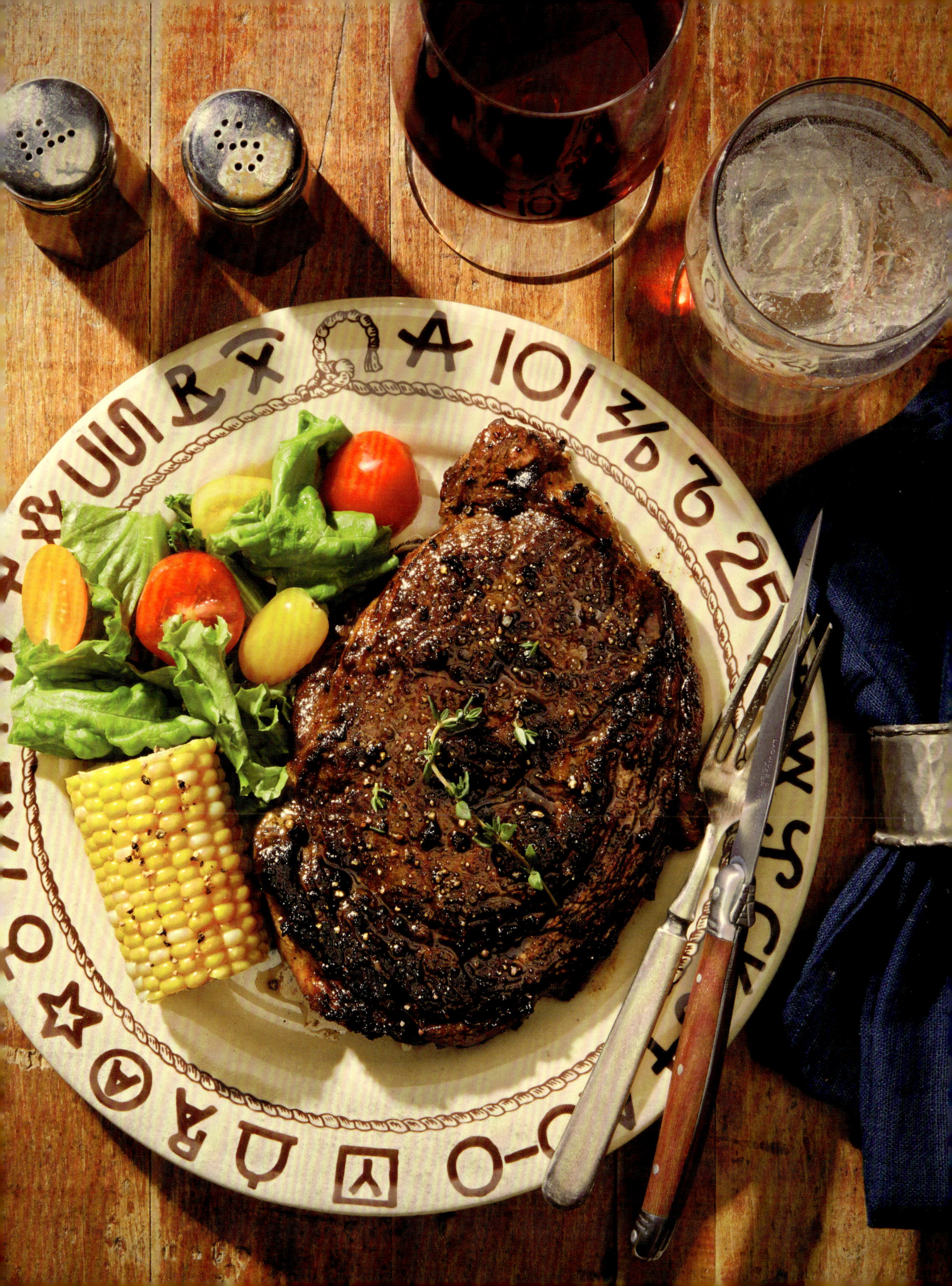

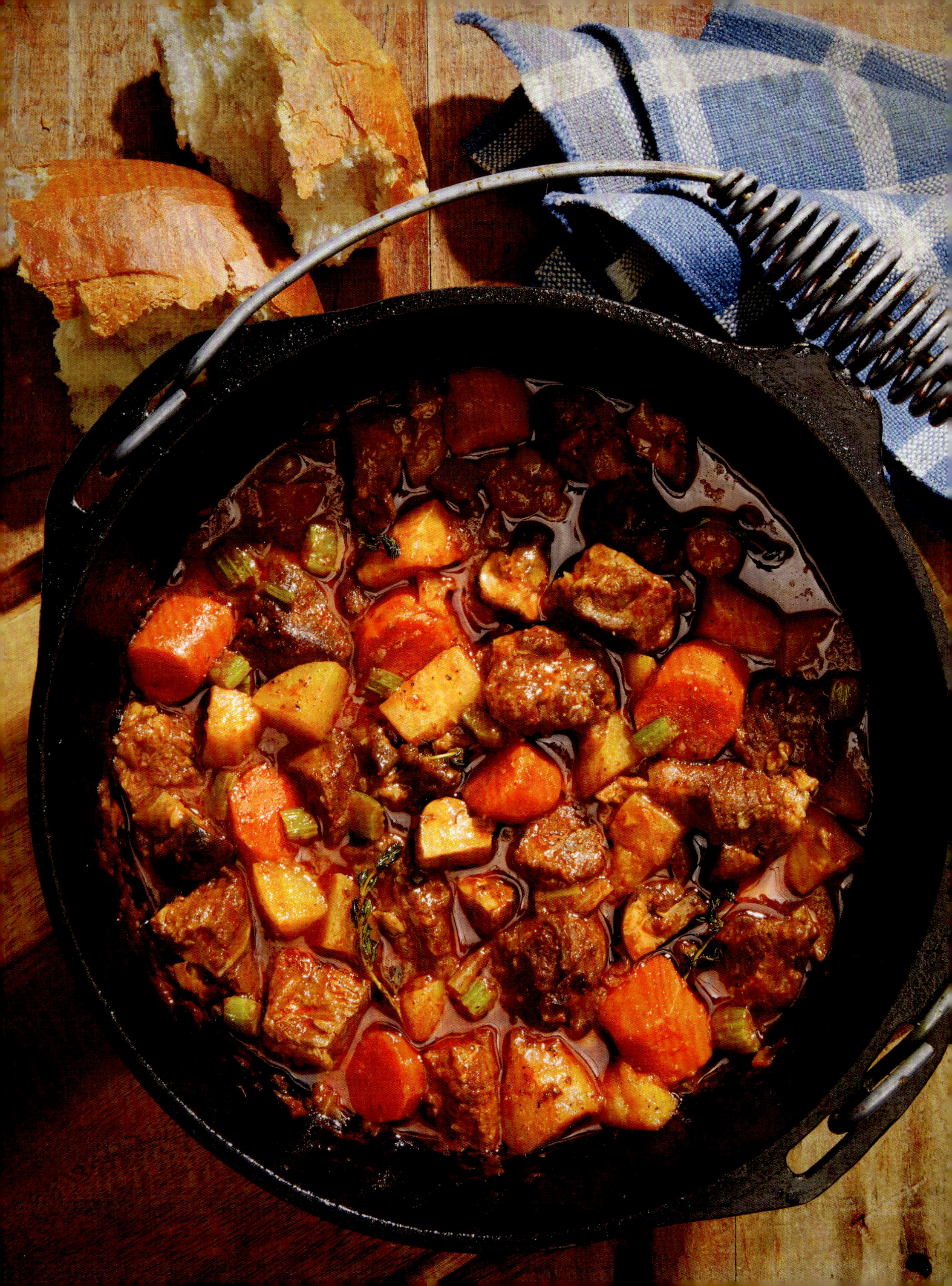

Bunkhouse
BEER-BRAISED BEEF STEW
with Root Vegetables

If there are two defining ingredients of the show, they'd have to be beer and beef. Beer plays a prominent role in Bunkhouse scenes, as well as in others, such as when Beth lures Dan Jenkins to a honky-tonk bar to seduce—and destroy—him over a bucket of beer. "Have you ever been to a place like this?" she asks Dan. "No," he says, looking around at the crowd. She eyes a cowboy and explains, "It's a real tightrope for men. If you act too meek the whole place will eat you alive, and if you act too strong the place will test ya." She flirts with and incites the cowboys as they walk along, taking beers from the bucket, while Dan gets harassed and beaten up. As Dan skulks away, she lights up a satisfied cigarette. Similarly, adding beer to beef stew imbues it with a satisfyingly malty flavor. Of course, you can also throw in some bourbon, which is just as good. Either way, the cowboys will all line up for it. Just be sure to serve it with plenty of cold beer and slices of Monica's Jalapeño-Cheddar Cornbread (page 104).

INGREDIENTS

3 tablespoons vegetable oil

2½–3 lb (1.1–1.4 kg) beef chuck stew meat

Kosher salt and freshly ground black pepper

¼ cup (30 g) all-purpose flour

1 large yellow onion, diced

2 large ribs celery, diced

4 cloves garlic, minced

3 tablespoons tomato paste

1 bottle (12 oz / 350 ml) brown ale or lager beer

2 cups (475 ml) chicken broth or beef broth, preferably homemade

2 fresh thyme sprigs

2 large carrots, peeled and cut into ¾-inch (2-cm) pieces

continued on page 50

INSTRUCTIONS

Preheat the oven to 325°F (165°C).

In a large Dutch oven over high heat, warm the oil. Put the stew meat in a bowl and season all over with salt and pepper. Dust with the flour, shaking off the excess. Add half of the stew meat to the pot, arranging the pieces in a single even layer so that they are not touching. Sear until deep golden brown on the bottom, about 4 minutes; then turn and sear the second side until deep golden brown, about 3 minutes longer. Transfer the meat to a plate. Repeat with the remaining meat.

Reduce the heat under the pot to medium and add the onion, celery, and garlic. Cook, stirring to scrape up any browned bits on the bottom of the pot until the vegetables are lightly browned and softened, about 7 minutes.

Stir in the tomato paste and cook for 1 minute, stirring. Then pour in the ale and broth and add the thyme sprigs, 1 teaspoon salt, and ½ teaspoon pepper. Stir, scraping the bottom of the pot to dislodge any browned bits.

continued from page 49

- 2 small parsnips, peeled and cut into ¾-inch (2-cm) pieces
- 12 oz (340 g) Yukon gold potatoes, cut into ¾-inch (2-cm) pieces
- 6 oz (170 g) small cremini or button mushrooms, brushed clean and quartered
- Crusty bread or cornbread for serving

MAKES 6 SERVINGS

Bring the mixture to a boil and return the stew meat to the pot. Cover tightly with the lid and place in the oven. Cook for 1 hour.

Add the carrots, parsnips, potatoes, and mushrooms and stir gently. Re-cover the pot, return to the oven, and cook until the meat is very tender and the vegetables are cooked, about 1 hour longer. Taste and season with salt and pepper, as needed.

Serve in big bowls with plenty of crusty bread.

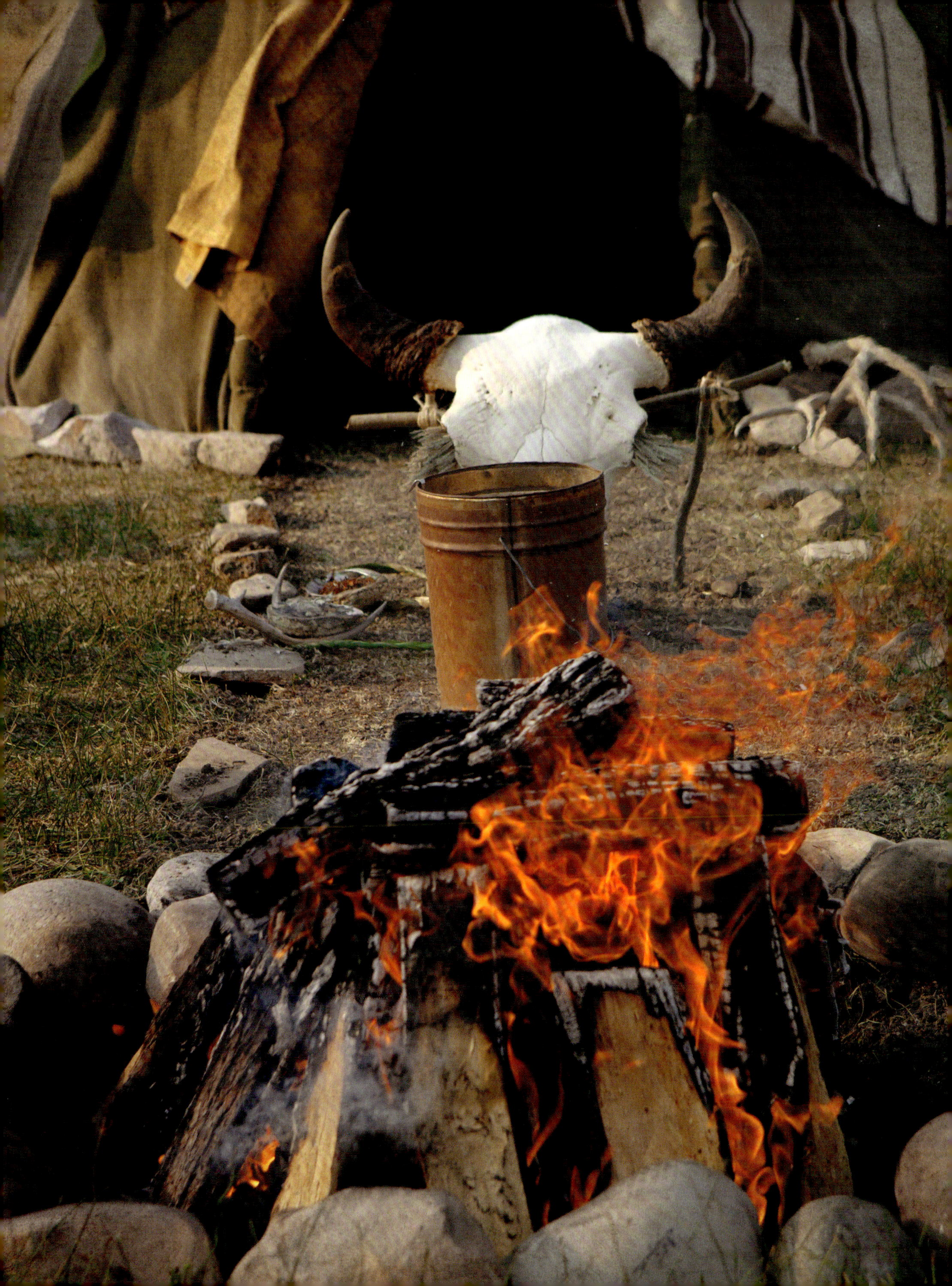

BBQ BISON BURGERS
with Maple-Bourbon Bacon

American bison (also referred to as "buffalo") make appearances throughout *Yellowstone*, from the first episode when they are being herded onto the ranch to altercations between the Duttons and nearby property owners (and old feuds) to the wranglers roping and trying to ride the buffalo in the adjoining field. For one episode we needed a bison carcass, so, of course, I made full use of it (we don't waste *any* food on *Yellowstone*). I bought a heavy-duty meat grinder and ground bison meat for more than two days. Bison meat is great, but it is really lean, so be sure to add the bacon to the ground meat so the added fat keeps it juicy. And definitely top it with more bacon. I love the smoky-sweet flavor of the barbecue sauce and this maple-bourbon glazed bacon, but you can use regular bacon if you like.

INGREDIENTS

For the Maple-Bourbon Bacon

¼ cup (60 ml) maple syrup

2 tablespoons firmly packed light brown sugar

2 tablespoons bourbon

12 slices thick-cut bacon

For the Burgers

2 lb (1 kg) ground bison

¼ cup (35 g) finely chopped yellow onion

2 tablespoons country-style Dijon mustard

1 tablespoon Worcestershire sauce

1 teaspoon kosher salt

½ teaspoon freshly ground black pepper

6 large slices Cheddar cheese

6 burger buns

Barbecue Sauce (see Maw Maw's Honey Bourbon Barbecued Ribs, page 64) for serving

MAKES 6 BURGERS

INSTRUCTIONS

Preheat the oven to 350°F (180°C).

To prepare the bacon, in a small saucepan over medium heat, stir the maple syrup, brown sugar, and bourbon together, until the sugar dissolves.

Place a wire rack on a rimmed baking sheet and lay the bacon slices in a single layer on the rack. Brush the maple-bourbon mixture on both sides of the bacon slices. Bake the bacon until crispy, 15–30 minutes (depending on the bacon's thickness). Set aside while you make the burgers.

To prepare the burgers, prepare a grill for direct cooking over high heat. Brush the grill grates clean.

In a large bowl, combine the ground bison, onion, mustard, Worcestershire sauce, salt, and pepper. Mix gently with your hands to combine, and then divide the mixture into 6 equal portions. Press each portion into a ¾-inch- (2-cm-) thick patty, about 4 inches (10 cm) in diameter.

Grill the patties over direct heat, turning once, until nicely charred on both sides and done to your liking, 4–5 minutes per side for medium. Just before the burgers are done, place a slice of cheese on each. Transfer to a baking sheet. Toast the buns on the grill, cut side down, until golden.

To assemble, place a bison patty on each bottom bun, top with barbecue sauce, and divide the bacon among the burgers. Cover with the bun tops and serve at once.

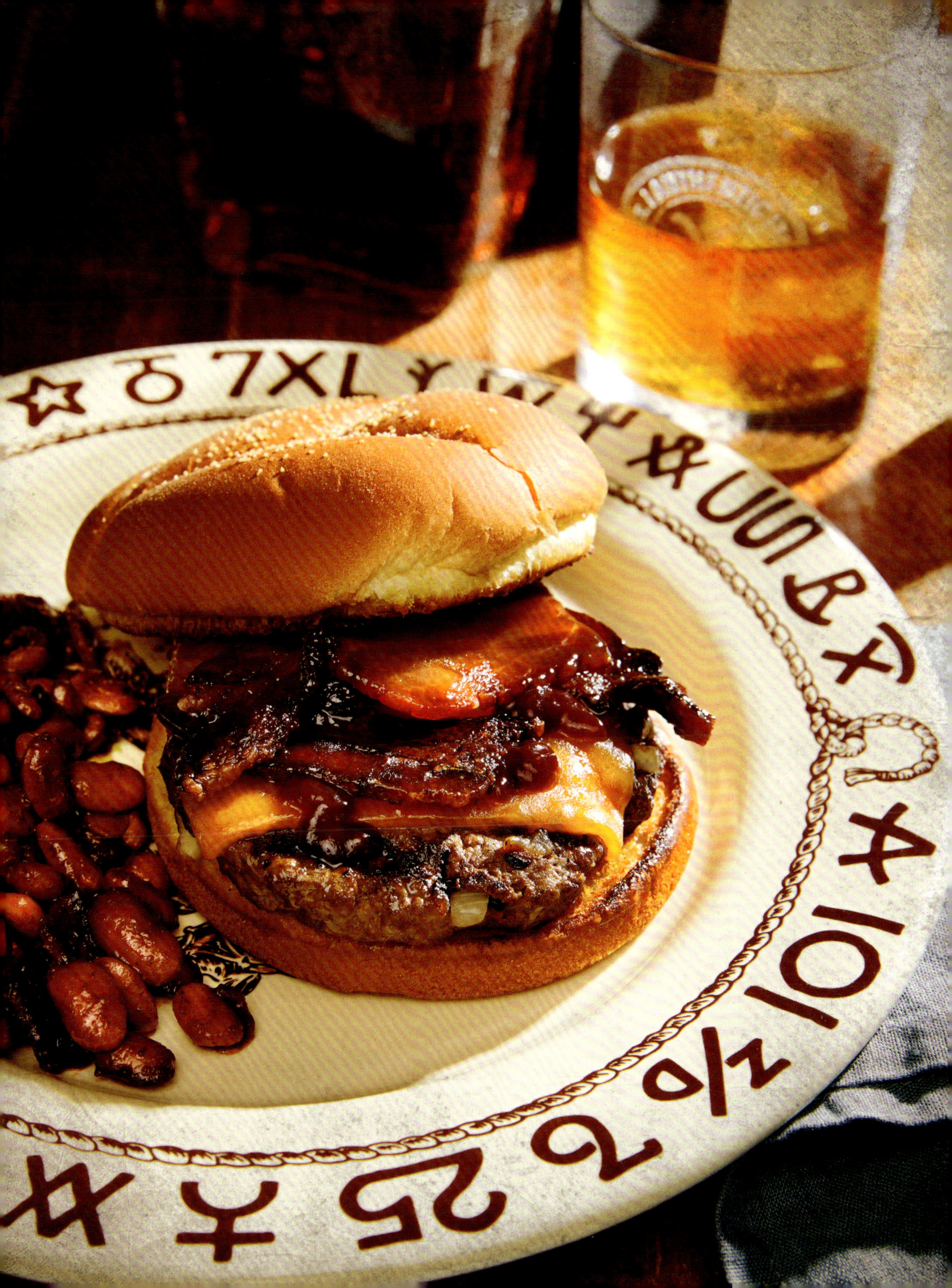

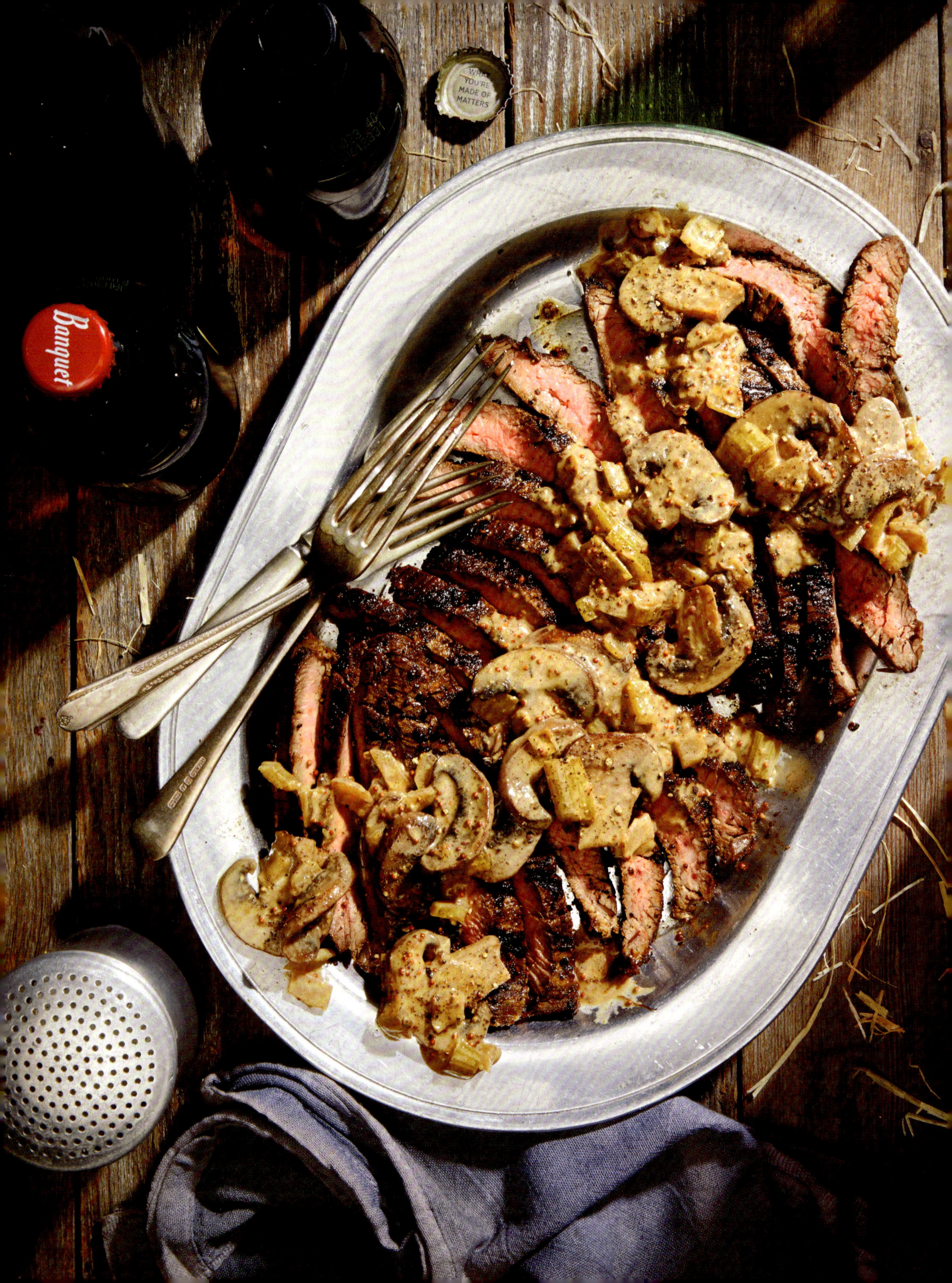
YOU'RE
MADE OF
MATTERS
Banquet

Helluva Grilled
FLANK STEAK
with Mustard-Mushroom Sauce

With the full Montana beauty as a backdrop, John and Tate go for a walk while camping in Season 3. "Ranchin's a terrible business, grandson," John tells Tate, as he goes on to explain the difficulties of cattle ranching. "Well, if ranching's so hard, how come we do it?" asks Tate. "Because it's one helluva life, Tate," explains John, "A helluva life." When you are surrounded by cattle on a cattle ranch, you are always looking for great ways to serve steak, and this mustard and mushroom sauce is a helluva way indeed. You can eat the sauce with a spoon, it's so good. It's also terrific on grilled lamb chops, which is how my grandmother used to serve it.

INGREDIENTS

1 flank steak (about 2 lb /1 kg)

Kosher salt and freshly ground pepper

Olive oil for coating

For the Sauce

4 tablespoons (60 g) unsalted butter

1 white or yellow onion, finely chopped

1 large rib celery, finely chopped

Kosher salt and freshly ground black pepper

1 lb (450 g) cremini mushrooms, brushed clean and sliced

1 teaspoon chopped fresh thyme leaves

2 tablespoons bourbon

1 cup (240 ml) beef stock or chicken stock, preferably homemade

⅓ cup (80 g) grainy mustard

½ teaspoon cayenne pepper, or to taste

¼ cup (60 ml) heavy cream

MAKES 4–6 SERVINGS

INSTRUCTIONS

Season the flank steak all over with salt and pepper, and then rub with oil to coat. Set aside at room temperature while you make the sauce.

To prepare the sauce, in a large frying pan over medium heat, melt the butter. Add the onion and celery, season with salt and pepper, and cook, stirring occasionally, until lightly browned, about 8 minutes. Add the mushrooms and thyme and cook, stirring until the mushrooms release their liquid, until tender, about 5 minutes. Pour in the bourbon and simmer for 1 minute. Pour in the stock and add the mustard and cayenne. Simmer, stirring until the liquid thickens slightly, 2–3 minutes. Reduce the heat to medium-low and stir in the cream. Simmer gently until the sauce thickens slightly, about 3 minutes. Set aside, covered to keep warm.

Prepare a grill for direct cooking over medium-high heat. Brush the grill grates clean.

Grill the steak over direct heat, turning once or twice until nicely charred on both sides and done to your liking, about 10 minutes for medium-rare. Transfer to a cutting board to rest for 10 minutes.

To serve, cut the steak across the grain into thin slices. Arrange on a platter, top with the warm sauce, and serve at once.

Mama's
BEEF POT ROAST

I swear the cast and crew have gotten hungrier and hungrier over the last few years. So, when I start noticing cowboy-sized appetites, I make pot roast in the evening to serve the next day. I put it in the oven at a really low temperature (200°F/95°C) and let it braise all night long. There is nothing better than arriving to the kitchen the next morning and being greeted with the aroma of pot roast. In fact, after I check the pot roast, I will eat it for breakfast, and without fail, about fifteen minutes later, someone else invariably smells it and asks when it's gonna be ready—and I just serve it right up. It's a nice way to start the day. Of course, you can also serve it for dinner with plenty of buttery mashed potatoes or steamed white rice and some crusty bread for mopping up all the rich beef juices.

INGREDIENTS

One 4-lb (1.8-kg) beef chuck roast

Kosher salt and freshly ground black pepper

¼ cup (60 ml) olive oil

1 large yellow onion, finely chopped

2 large carrots, finely chopped

2 ribs celery, finely chopped

4 cloves garlic, minced

1 cup (240 ml) red wine

2 cups (475 ml) beef stock or chicken stock, preferably homemade

2 tomatoes, seeded and finely chopped

2 sprigs fresh rosemary

1 small bunch chopped fresh parsley

MAKES 6–8 SERVINGS

INSTRUCTIONS

Preheat the oven to 325°F (165°C). Season the roast generously all over with salt and pepper. Heat a Dutch oven or large heavy pot over high heat. Add the oil and swirl to coat the bottom of the pan. Add the roast and sear, turning occasionally, until evenly browned on all sides, about 10 minutes. Transfer to a plate.

Pour off all but 1 tablespoon of the oil in the pot. Add the onion, carrots, and celery and cook, stirring until softened, about 5 minutes. Add the garlic and cook until fragrant, about 1 minute. Add the red wine, stirring to scrape up any browned bits on the bottom of the pot. Pour in the stock, add the tomatoes and rosemary, and bring the liquid to a boil. Return the roast to the pot, along with any juices.

Cover the pot, transfer to the oven, and braise the roast until it is fork-tender, 4–4½ hours. Transfer the roast to a cutting board and cover with aluminum foil.

Spoon off any fat from the top of the cooking juices. If the juices are too thin, bring to a boil over medium-high heat and cook until they reduce slightly. Stir half the parsley into the sauce.

To serve, cut the roast into thick slices and arrange on a platter. Top with plenty of the warm sauce. Garnish with the rest of the parsley and serve.

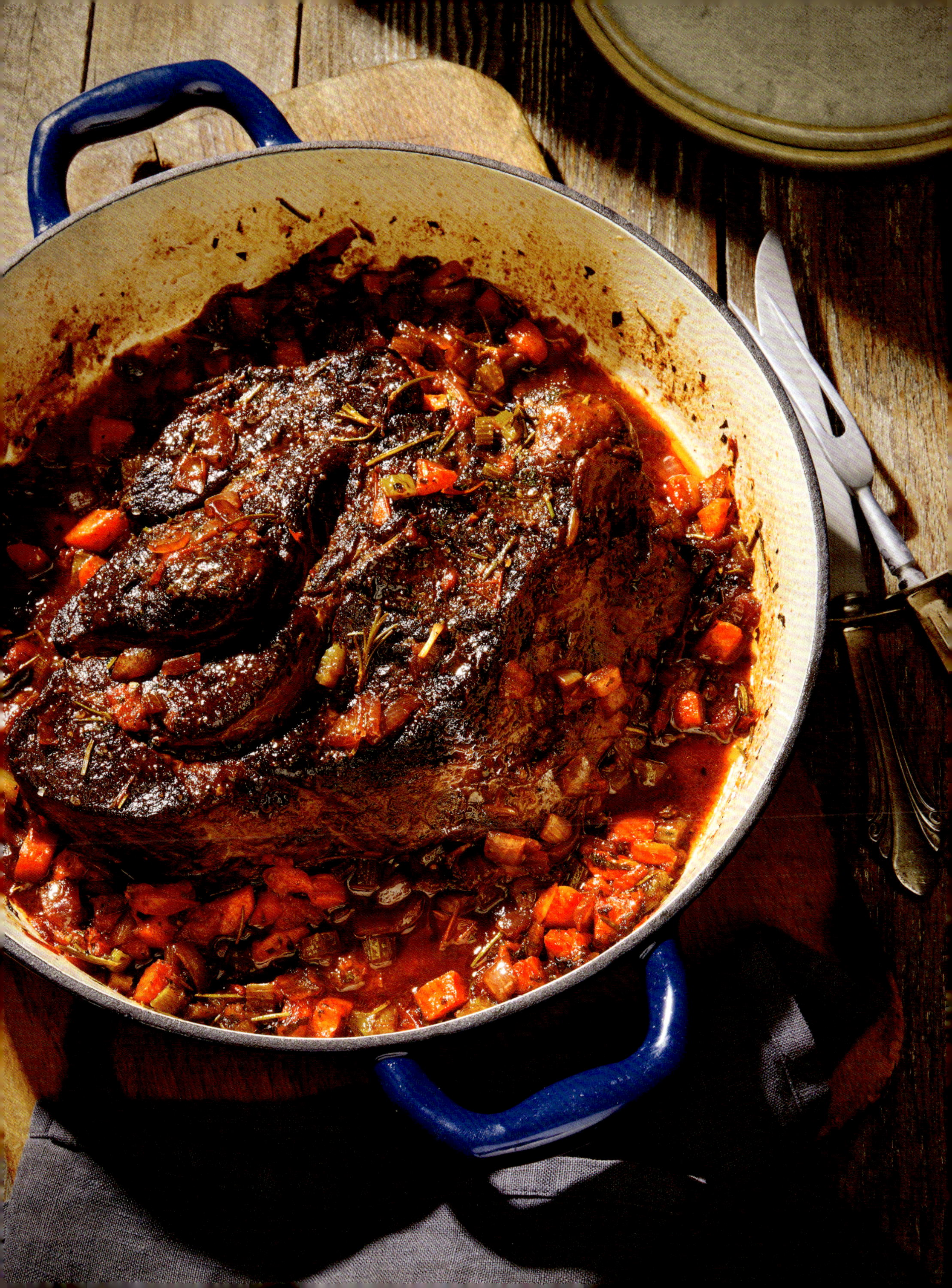

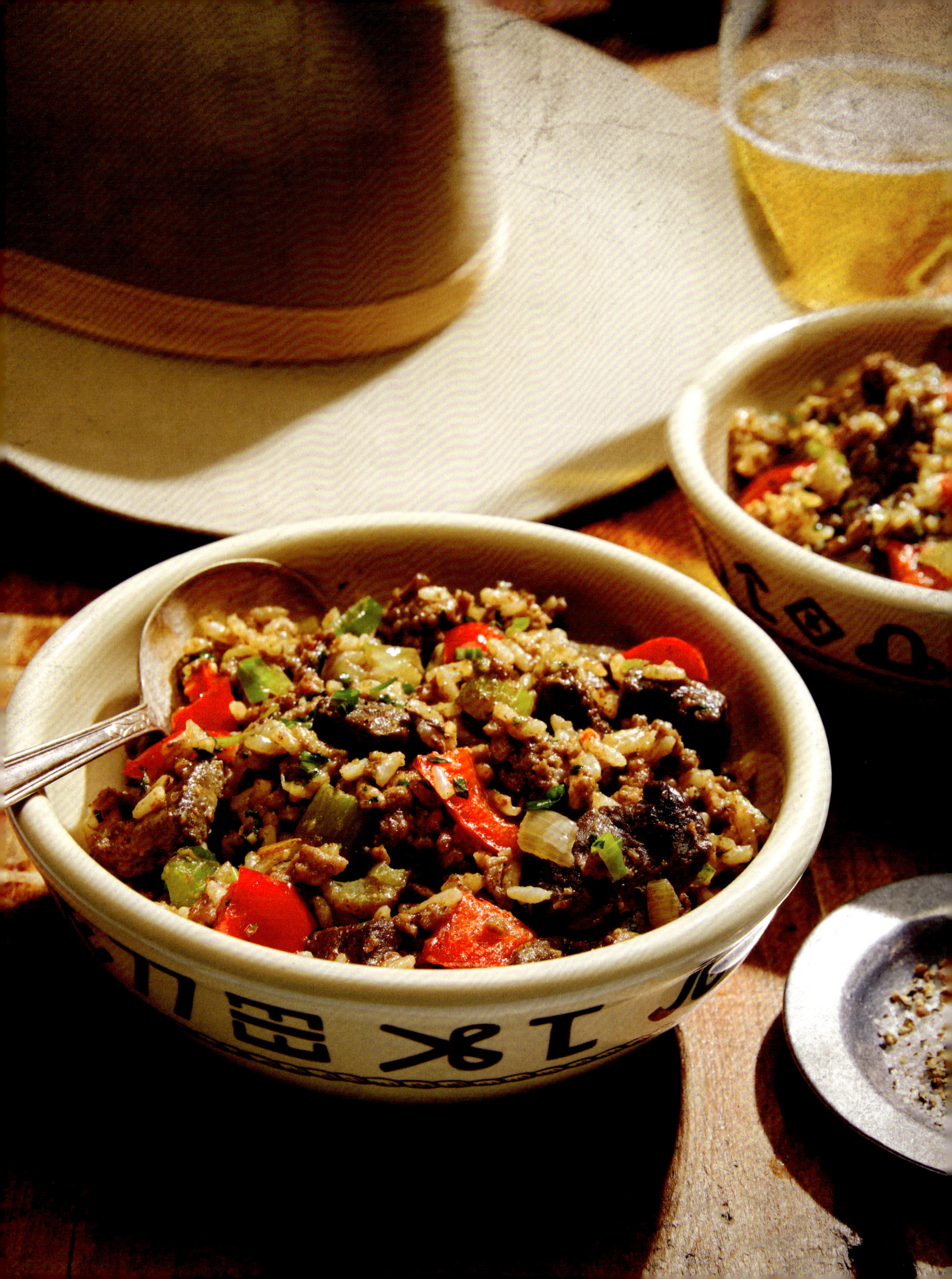

Gator's
CAJUN DIRTY RICE

This recipe is really just for me because it's one of my favorite things to eat. And it's one of the first things I remember seeing my dad cook for a movie crew when I was ten years old. I can vividly recall how he stirred the dirty rice in a pot with a big paddle while a crowd of people on the film set stood around watching him. To think that now, twenty-five years later, I'm doing the same thing my dad did, makes this recipe very sentimental. If you haven't tried it, "dirty" rice is a one-pot meal with ground meat, vegetables, liver, lots of Cajun seasoning, and rice. It's delicious.

INGREDIENTS

½ lb (225 g) ground beef

½ lb (225 g) ground pork

Kosher salt and freshly ground black pepper

3 tablespoons unsalted butter

1 white onion, finely chopped

1 red bell pepper, seeded and finely chopped

1 rib celery, finely chopped

1–3 jalapeño chiles, seeded and minced, to taste

2 cloves garlic, minced

½ lb (225 g) calf's liver or beef liver, finely chopped

¼ cup (30 g) all-purpose flour

2 teaspoons Cajun seasoning, plus seasoning as needed

1 cup (240 ml) chicken stock or beef stock, preferably homemade

4 scallions, thinly sliced, white and green parts

⅓ cup (20 g) chopped fresh flat-leaf parsley

2 cups (310 g) cooked long-grain white rice

MAKES 6–8 SERVINGS

INSTRUCTIONS

Crumble the ground beef and ground pork into a large, heavy, high-sided sauté pan or Dutch oven over medium heat. Cook, stirring occasionally, until the meat is lightly browned, about 3 minutes. Season generously with salt and pepper. Transfer the meat to a large bowl.

Return the pan to the heat and add the butter, and then the onion, bell pepper, celery, jalapeños, garlic, and liver. Season with salt and pepper. Reduce the heat to medium-low and cook, stirring occasionally until the vegetables start to soften, about 10 minutes. Return the reserved ground meat to the pan and continue to cook, stirring occasionally until the vegetables are very soft and the flavors have melded, 20–30 minutes. If the mixture starts to cook too rapidly, reduce the heat to low.

Sprinkle the flour and Cajun seasoning to taste over the meat and vegetables and stir well. Pour in the stock and stir until the mixture thickens slightly, about 1 minute. Stir in the scallions and parsley, and then simmer until the scallions soften, about 5 minutes. Add the rice and cook, stirring frequently until heated through and well blended, 3–5 minutes.

Taste and adjust the seasoning with salt, pepper, and Cajun seasoning, as needed. Transfer to a serving bowl and serve at once.

Grilled Portobello MUSHROOM BURGERS

I love mushrooms. They are so delicious and one of those things I've learned to cook really well for the cast and crew, especially for the vegetarians on set. Also, you can get great mushrooms in Montana. If you do this right, with the marinade, and then cook the mushrooms over a charcoal or wood fire on a grill, they almost taste like steak. These portobello mushrooms are great as burgers, but I also like to serve them on their own over mashed potatoes and veggies for a hearty vegetarian meal, or sliced along with other grilled vegetables as a side dish or a healthy snack.

INGREDIENTS

- 4 large portobello mushrooms, brushed clean
- 2 tablespoons olive oil
- 2 tablespoons soy sauce
- 1 tablespoon balsamic vinegar
- ½ teaspoon kosher salt
- ¼ teaspoon freshly ground black pepper
- 4 large slices Cheddar or provolone cheese (optional)
- 4 burger buns, split
- ¼ cup (60 ml) mayonnaise
- 2 tablespoons grainy mustard
- 1 recipe Pickled Onions (page 118)
- 4 thick slices ripe tomato
- 4 butter lettuce leaves

MAKES 4 BURGERS

INSTRUCTIONS

Prepare a charcoal or gas grill for direct cooking over medium-high heat (400°–450°F / 200°–230°C).

Remove the stems and scrape out and discard the black gills from the mushrooms.

In a small bowl, whisk together the oil, soy sauce, vinegar, salt, and pepper until blended. Arrange the mushrooms on a baking sheet and drizzle both sides with the marinade.

Place the mushrooms on the grill and cook, turning once halfway through until the mushrooms are tender, about 15 minutes. Top each mushroom with a slice of cheese, if using, and grill until melted. Transfer to the baking sheet. Toast the buns on the grill until golden, cut side down.

In a small bowl, stir together the mayonnaise and mustard.

To assemble, spread the cut sides of the buns with the mayo mixture. Place a mushroom on each bun bottom; then top each with pickled onions, a tomato slice, and a lettuce leaf. Cover with the bun tops and serve.

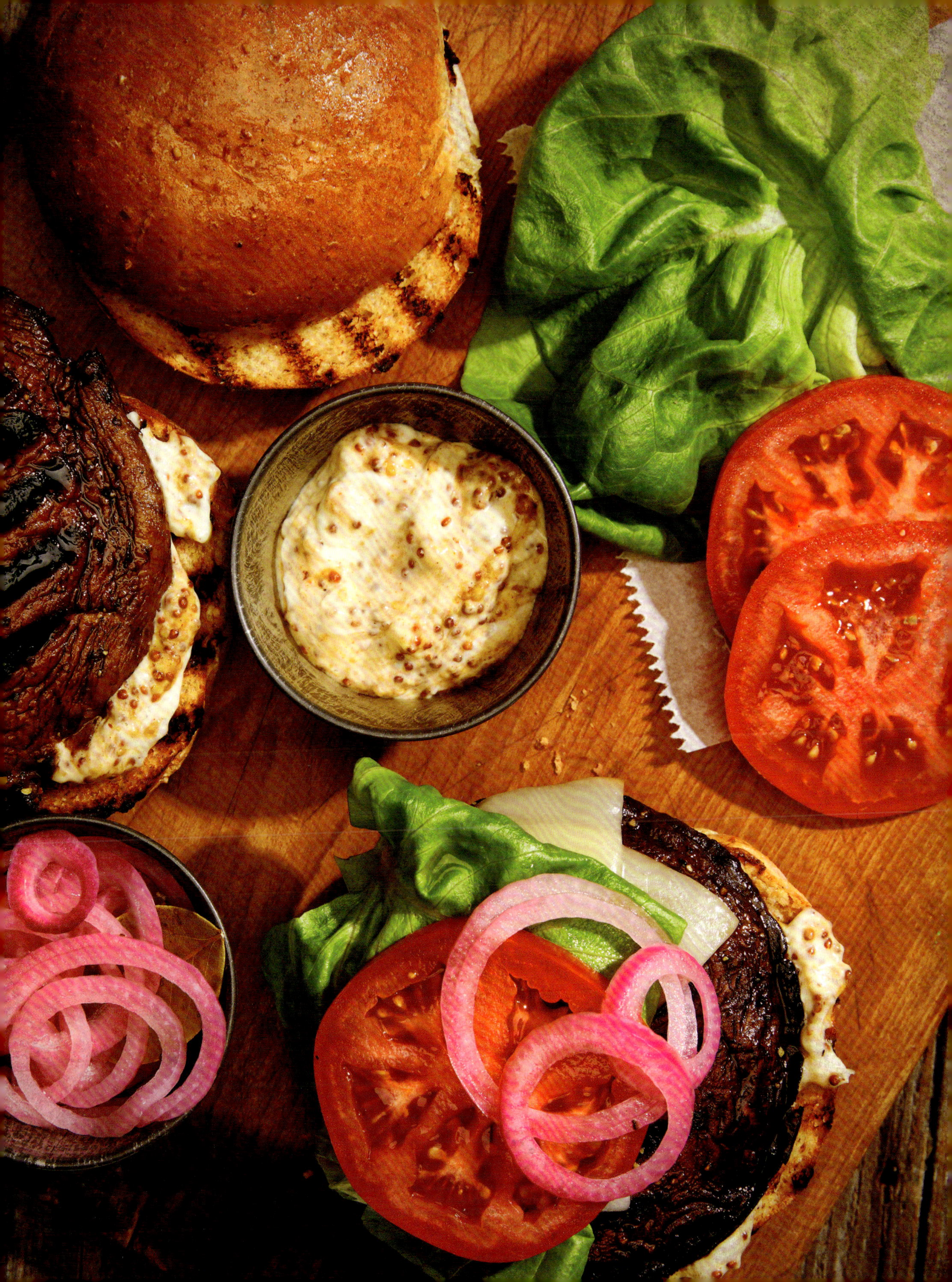

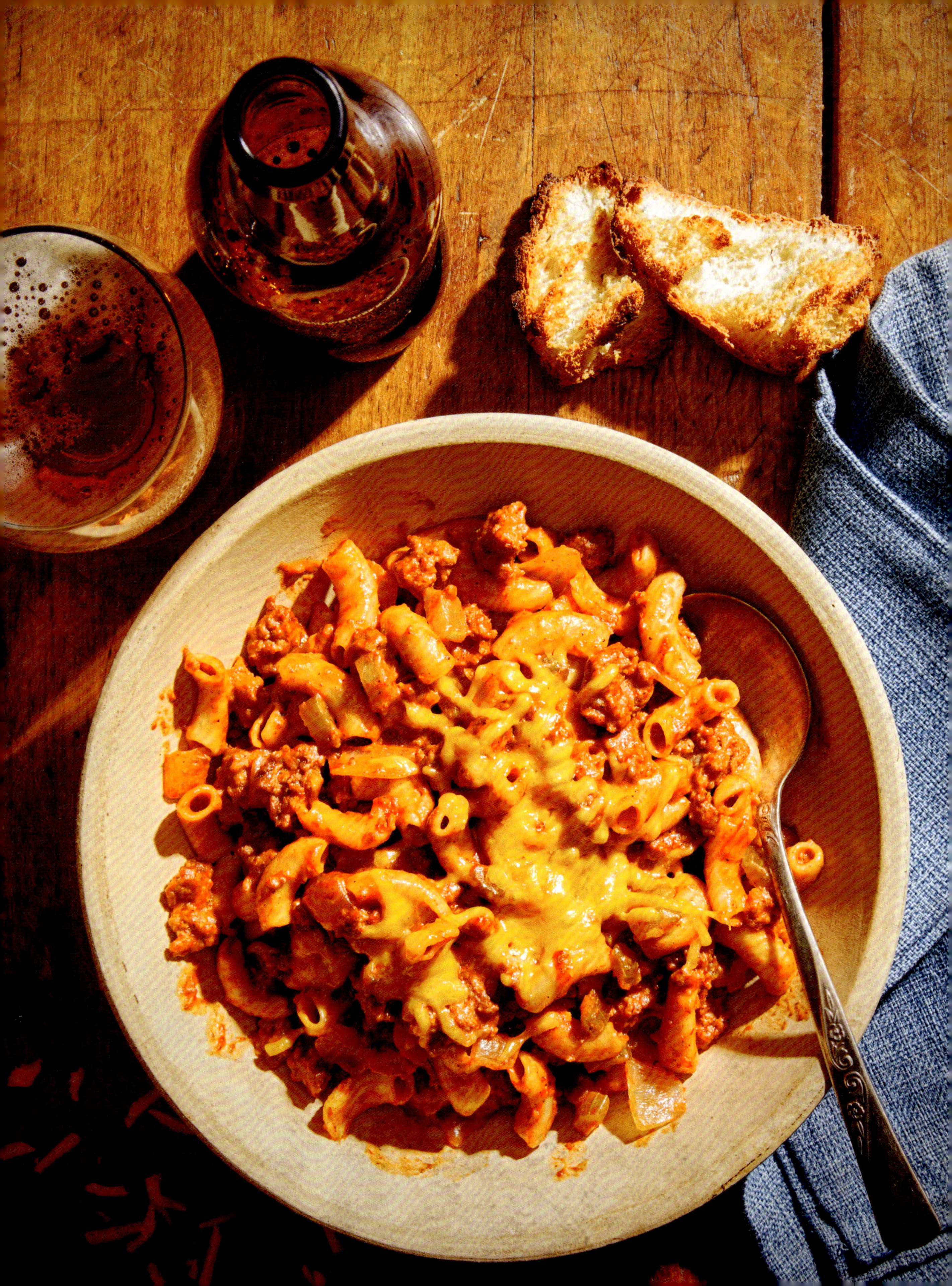

Beth's Cheesy
HAMBURGER MAC CASSEROLE

"Hello, dear," says Beth to Rip as she hands him a beer. "I made dinner." "What'd you make?" asks Rip. "Hamburger Helper, but we didn't have any hamburger so I used tuna. So, Tuna Helper," she answers. "You put tuna in the Hamburger Helper?" asks Rip. "Mmm-hmm," she agrees. "Why not just use the Tuna Helper, darling?" asks Rip. Beth looks confused, "What? They make Tuna Helper?" She tells him to try it, that her dish might surprise him. Then, he gets another surprise: Carter. "I think he might be our kid, baby," she says. "It's you, twenty years ago." This scene and the Tuna versus Hamburger Helper became a real standing joke on set. So I re-created a version for this book —but a whole lot better. It's like a big warm hug.

INGREDIENTS

2 tablespoons olive oil

1 small yellow onion, finely chopped

1 large rib celery, finely chopped

Kosher salt and freshly ground black pepper

1 lb (450 g) ground beef, preferably chuck or sirloin

¼ cup (60 g) tomato paste

1 teaspoon garlic powder

1 teaspoon chili powder

½ teaspoon cayenne pepper, or to taste

2 cups (475 ml) beef stock or chicken stock, preferably homemade, plus stock as needed

1 cup (4 oz / 110 g) elbow macaroni

3 oz (90 g) grated Cheddar cheese, plus cheese for serving (optional)

Crusty bread for serving

MAKES 4 SERVINGS

INSTRUCTIONS

In a large heavy pot or Dutch oven over medium heat, warm the oil. Add the onion, celery, and a big pinch of salt and cook, stirring, until the onion is softened, about 5 minutes. Add the ground beef and raise the heat to medium-high. Cook, stirring to break up the meat until it is no longer pink, about 4 minutes. Drain the fat from the pot, if necessary, and then return the pot to the heat.

Add the tomato paste, garlic powder, chili powder, 1 teaspoon salt, ½ teaspoon black pepper, and cayenne to taste and stir until well combined. Pour in the stock and bring to a boil.

Add the macaroni and reduce the heat to medium-low. Cover the pot and simmer, stirring every so often until the pasta is al dente, 10–13 minutes. If the mixture seems dry, add a bit more stock.

Remove from the heat and stir in the cheese. Taste and season with more salt, pepper, and cayenne, if you like. Let sit for 5 minutes before serving.

Serve in bowls with additional shredded cheese on top, if you like, and with crusty bread alongside.

Maw Maw's
HONEY BOURBON BARBECUED RIBS

When the drama of the day is put to bed, you'll often find John Dutton sitting in one of the cozy rooms of the main ranch lodge with the lights dim, sipping a bourbon or whiskey. And when ribs are paired with bourbon, well, that's when magic happens. Ribs are the perfect ranch food: hand-portable and easy to eat. You don't need a plate, and cowboys don't even need a napkin; they just wipe their hands on their pants. When filming, the cast and crew often do not have time to sit down to eat, so my meals need to be fast. This recipe is straight from my grandmother's recipe box. The ribs are easier to make than you would think, and all you cowboys (and girls) will thank me for it.

INGREDIENTS

For the Ribs

2 racks meaty baby back ribs (about 3 lb / 1.4 kg each)

1 bottle (12 oz / 350 ml) lager beer or ale

½ cup (120 ml) apple cider vinegar

¼ cup (60 ml) bourbon

1½ teaspoons kosher salt

For the Barbecue Sauce

1 cup (240 ml) ketchup

½ cup (120 ml) reduced-sodium soy sauce

½ cup (140 ml) honey

¼ cup (60 ml) bourbon

2 cloves garlic, crushed

1½ teaspoons favorite barbecue spice rub

½ teaspoon freshly ground black pepper

MAKES 4–6 SERVINGS

INSTRUCTIONS

To prepare the ribs, remove the membrane from the bone side of the rib racks. Cut the ribs into sections so they fit in a large Dutch oven, and then arrange in the Dutch oven. Pour in the beer, vinegar, and bourbon and add the salt, making sure the ribs are just covered with liquid (if not, add enough water to cover the ribs). Cover the pot, place it over medium-high heat, and bring the liquid to a simmer. Reduce the heat to low and simmer gently until the meat is very tender, about 1 hour.

While the ribs simmer, prepare the barbecue sauce. In a saucepan over low heat, stir together the ketchup, soy sauce, honey, bourbon, garlic, spice rub, and pepper. Simmer, stirring occasionally, until the flavors come together, about 45 minutes. Set aside.

When the ribs are ready, transfer them to a baking sheet and let rest for 2 minutes. Brush the ribs liberally on both sides with some of the sauce and let stand at room temperature for 30 minutes. Reserve the sauce.

Meanwhile, prepare a charcoal or gas grill for direct cooking over low heat (350°–400°F / 180°–200°C). Alternatively, heat a pellet smoker to 350°F (180°C).

Grill the ribs, bone side down, until slightly charred, 10–15 minutes. Turn and grill the meaty side of the ribs until well browned with a little char, 10–15 minutes. Turn again and brush the meaty side of the ribs with the remaining sauce. Serve at once.

NOTE: To finish the ribs in the oven, position a rack in the middle of the oven and preheat the broiler to high. Broil the ribs on the baking sheet, turning once, until nicely charred, about 10 minutes. Watch carefully so they don't burn.

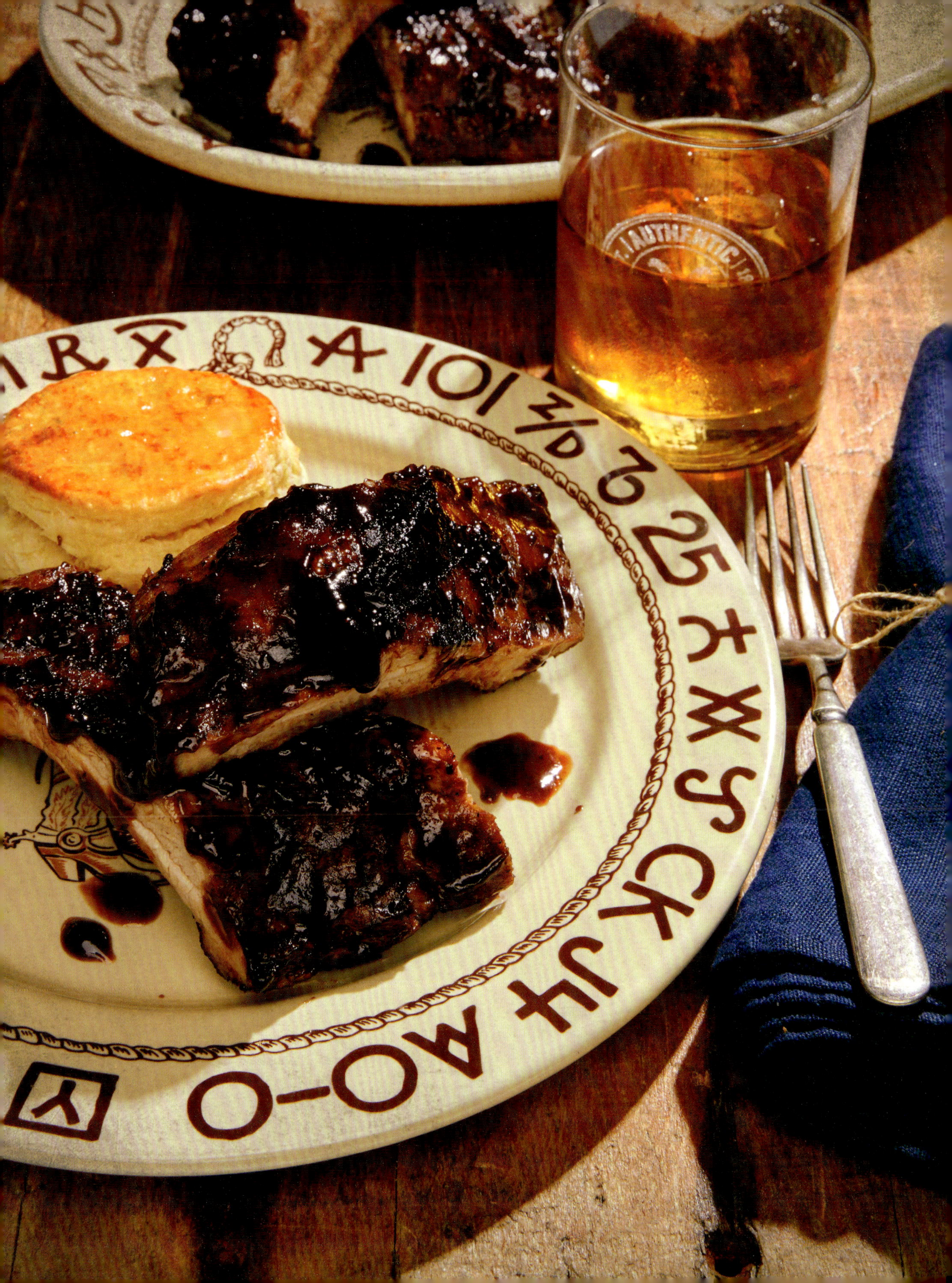
AUTHENTIC

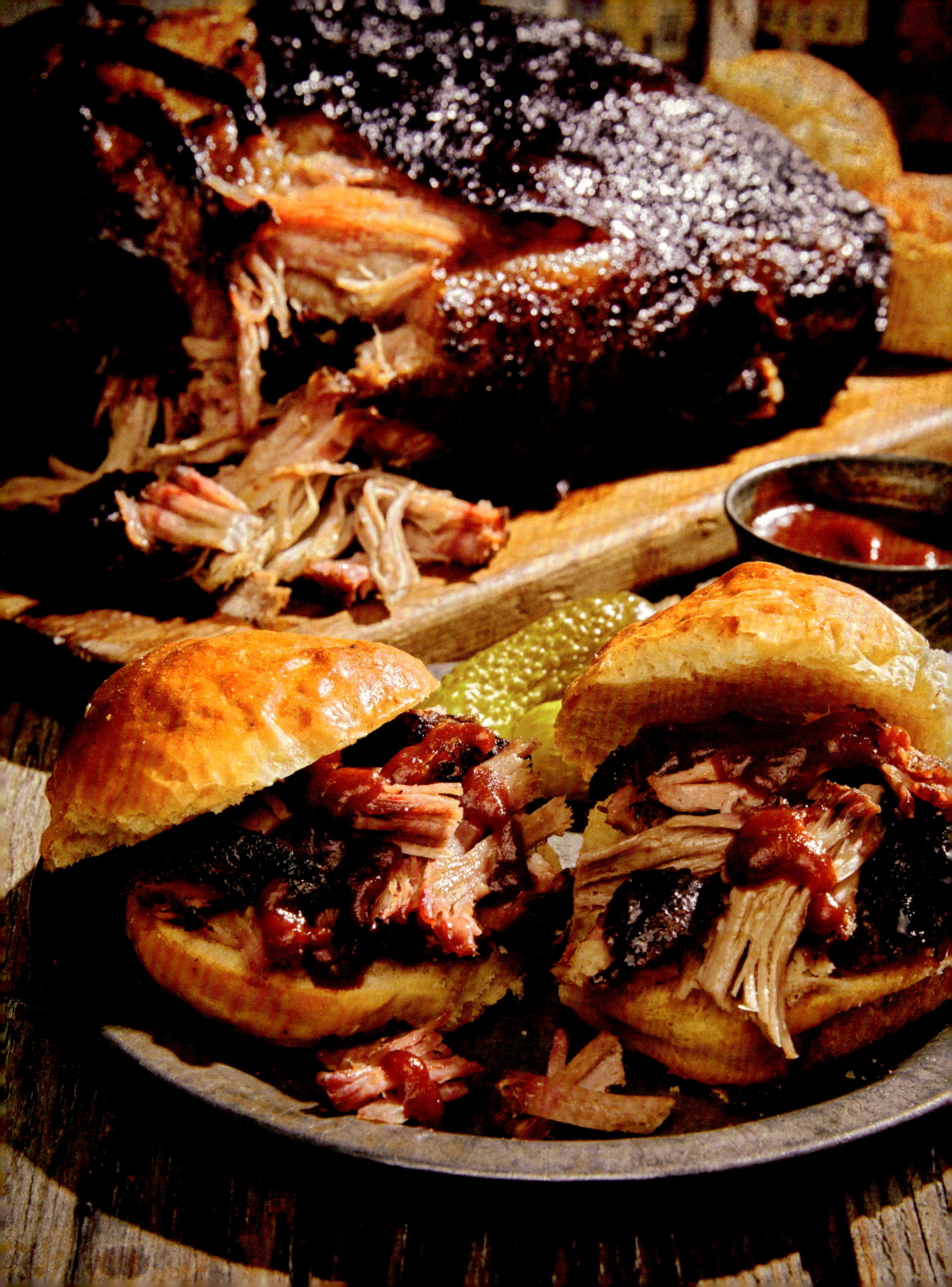

SMOKED PULLED PORK

Barbecue . . . what can I say? It's part of what has gotten me here, as the head of craft services on *Yellowstone*. I have a big smoker, and if you're gonna use it, you best fill it up. Pulled pork is one of the most quintessential dishes of Southern barbecue, and it's an easy dish to succeed at because it can withstand a bit of overcooking. And when you bite into that smoky flavor, it's just so good. Everyone on the crew—all the ranch hands—run over the second I open the smoker. Instead of the spice rub, use a mixture of salt, pepper, and chili powder.

INGREDIENTS

One 4–5 lb (1.8–2.3 kg) boneless pork butt roast

3–4 handfuls of applewood or cherrywood chips, soaked in water for 30 minutes

2 tablespoons favorite barbecue spice rub

Kosher salt and freshly ground black pepper

Olive oil for drizzling

MAKES 8–12 SERVINGS

INSTRUCTIONS

Remove the roast from the refrigerator about 1 hour before cooking so it comes to room temperature. Drain the wood chips.

Prepare a gas or charcoal grill for indirect cooking over low heat (250°–300°F / 120°–150°C). Brush the grill grates clean. Place a small aluminum foil pan half full of water off to one side of the grill grate.

Season the pork roast all over with the spice rub, salt, and pepper, and then rub with oil to coat. Add the drained wood chips directly to the coals, or place in a smoker box, if using a gas grill.

Place a cast-iron pan large enough to hold the roast and about 1 inch (2.5 cm) of fat (from the drippings) in the center of the grill grate. Place the roast in the pan, fat side up. Close the lid and cook for 4½–5 hours, checking the roast every so often and spooning the rendered fat over the top.

After 4½–5 hours, cover the cast-iron pan tightly with aluminum foil. Continue to roast for 2 hours longer, or until the roast is fork-tender. Total cooking time is about 7 hours.

Transfer the roast to a cutting board and let rest for 15 minutes. Cut away any excess fat and, using your hands or 2 forks, pull the meat into shreds.

GATOR'S TIP

For pulled pork sandwiches, drizzle the meat with Maw Maw's Honey Bourbon Barbecued Ribs sauce (page 64), stuff it into toasted burger buns, and top it with Crunchy Coleslaw (page 119), if you like.

KICKIN' CHICKEN TENDERS
with Pickled Jalapeño Sauce

Kickin' chicken is why people in New Orleans started praising my cooking and why I started traveling to do craft services. Hands down, it's the best way to eat fried chicken, and it's everyone's favorite snack on set. The crew will turn off the cameras in the middle of filming and everyone on set will come running to line up by the hundreds for my Kickin' Chicken. It's simply that good. The secret is the jalapeño sauce, which contrasts with the sweet, vinegary, salty flavors of the crispy chicken tenders. Kickin' Chicken is spectacular . . . and it's a spectacle to behold. The secret to making the best Kickin' Chicken is not being afraid to go crazy with the seasoning. Trust me: the more the better with this recipe!

INGREDIENTS

For the Pickled Jalapeño Sauce

1 cup (240 g) jarred sliced jalapeño chiles in vinegar (hot or mild), drained and chopped

2 tablespoons honey

1 tablespoon maple syrup

1 tablespoon hot-pepper sauce, or to taste

1 teaspoon Cajun seasoning

For the Chicken Tenders

1½ cups (350 ml) buttermilk

¼ cup (60 ml) Louisiana hot sauce

1½ lb (680 g) chicken breast tenderloins

2 large eggs

continued on page 71

INSTRUCTIONS

To prepare the sauce, in a bowl stir together the jalapeños, honey, maple syrup, hot-pepper sauce, and Cajun seasoning. Refrigerate until ready to use; remove from the refrigerator 1 hour before serving to bring the sauce to room temperature.

To marinate the chicken, in a large bowl whisk together the buttermilk and half of the hot-pepper sauce. Add the chicken, stir to coat, cover, and refrigerate for at least 2 hours, or up to 12 hours.

About 30 minutes before cooking, drain the chicken in a fine-mesh sieve, discarding the marinade. Set aside to bring to room temperature.

To fry the chicken, in a wide shallow bowl beat together the eggs, whole milk, and remaining hot-pepper sauce. In another wide shallow bowl, whisk together the flour, paprika, salt, black pepper, and cayenne, if using.

Fill a large, wide sauté pan or deep frying pan with ½ inch (12 mm) of the oil and heat over medium-high heat to 325°F (165°C) on a deep-frying thermometer. Set a wire rack over a baking sheet, line it with paper towels, and place it next to the stovetop.

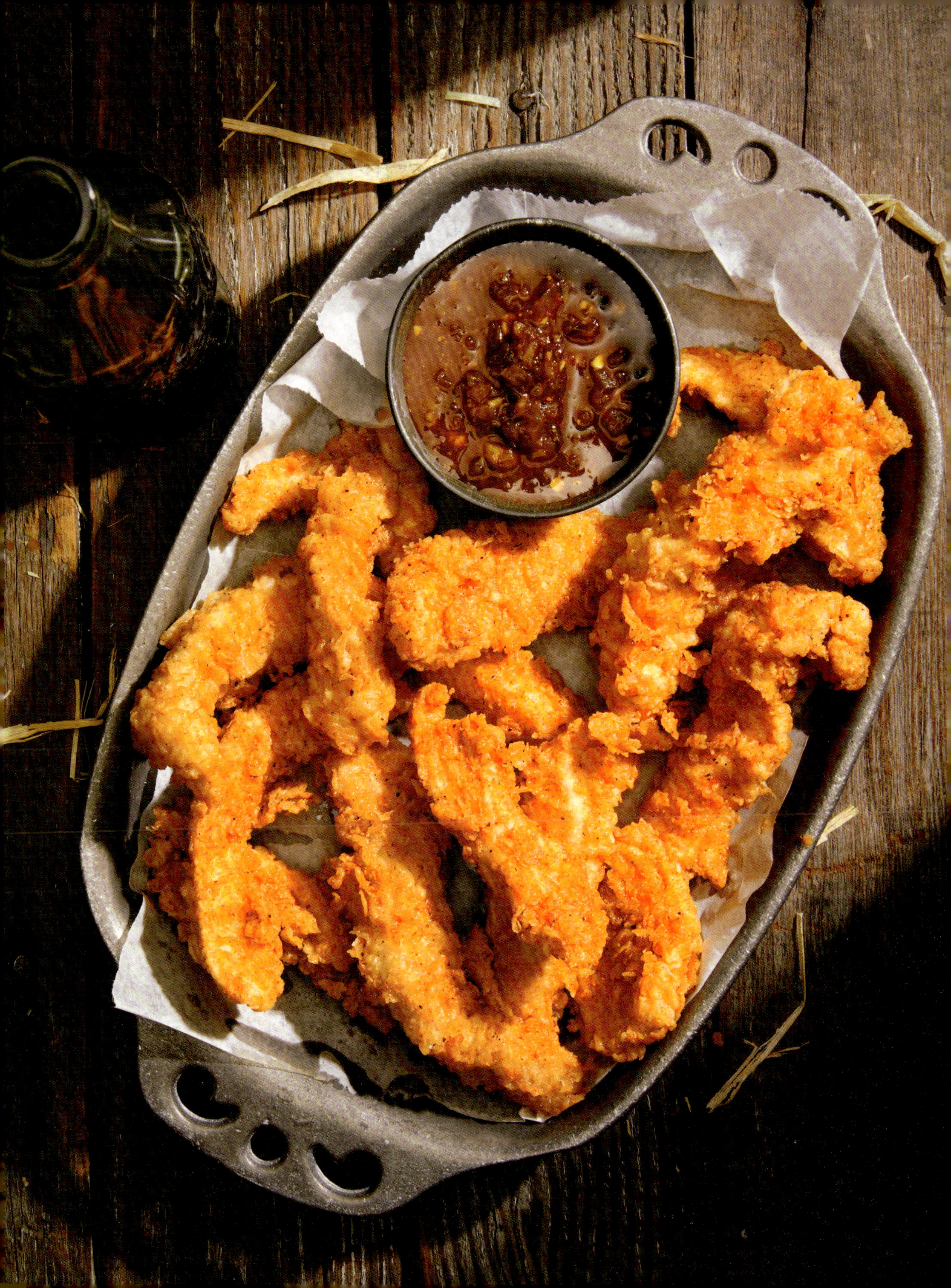

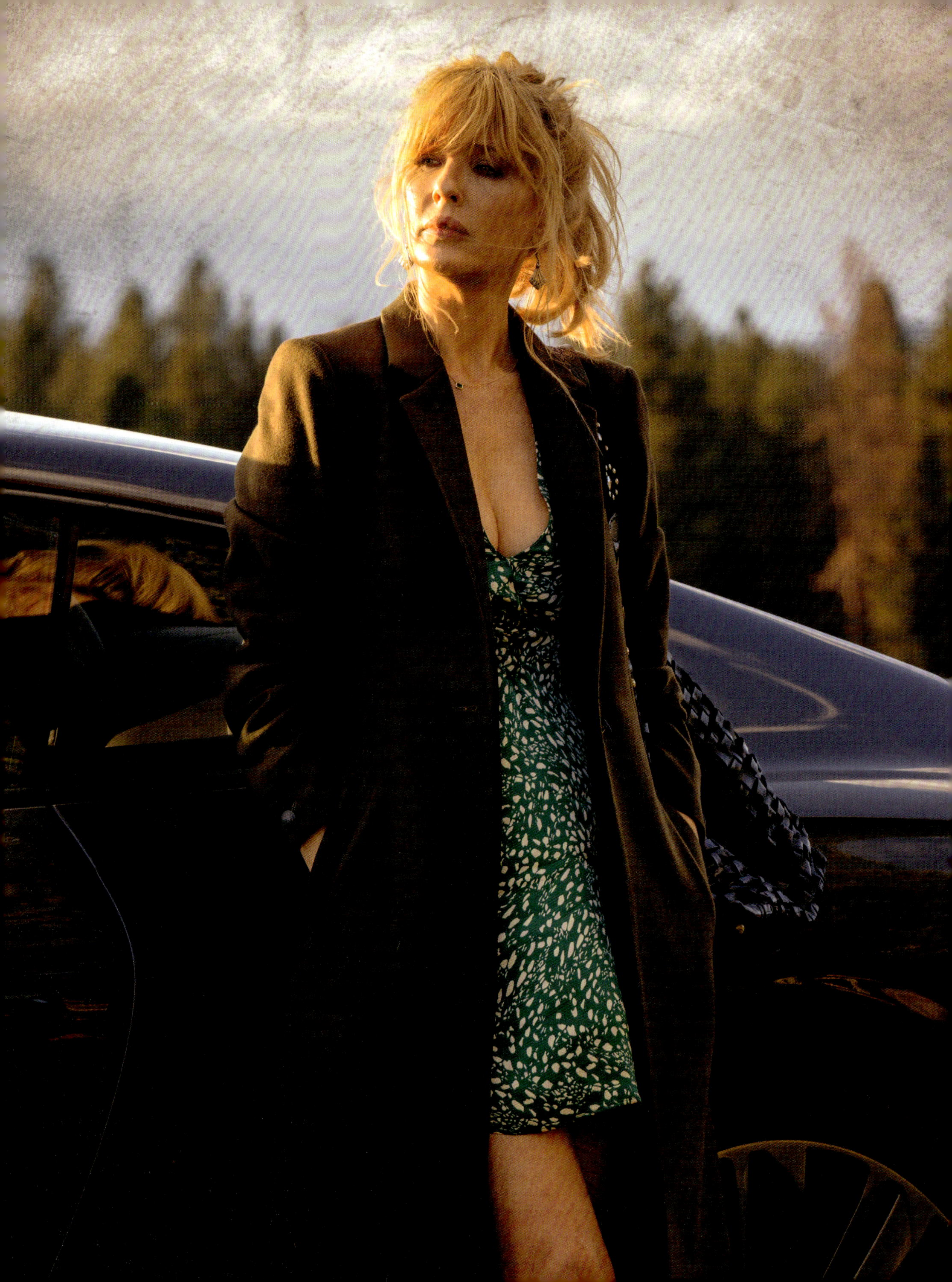

continued from page 68

- ¼ cup (60 ml) whole milk
- 2 cups (250 g) all-purpose flour
- 1 tablespoon sweet paprika
- 2 teaspoons kosher salt
- 1 teaspoon freshly ground black pepper
- 1 teaspoon cayenne pepper, or to taste (optional)
- Vegetable oil for frying

MAKES 4–6 SERVINGS

Working in batches to avoid overcrowding the pan, dip the chicken tenders in the egg mixture, letting any excess drip off; then dredge in the flour mixture, coating completely. Carefully add to the hot oil and cook, turning once or twice with tongs, until crispy, golden brown, and cooked through, about 6 minutes. Transfer to the paper towel–lined rack. Repeat to cook all the chicken tenders, letting the oil come back to temperature between batches.

Serve hot, with plenty of the pickled jalapeño sauce.

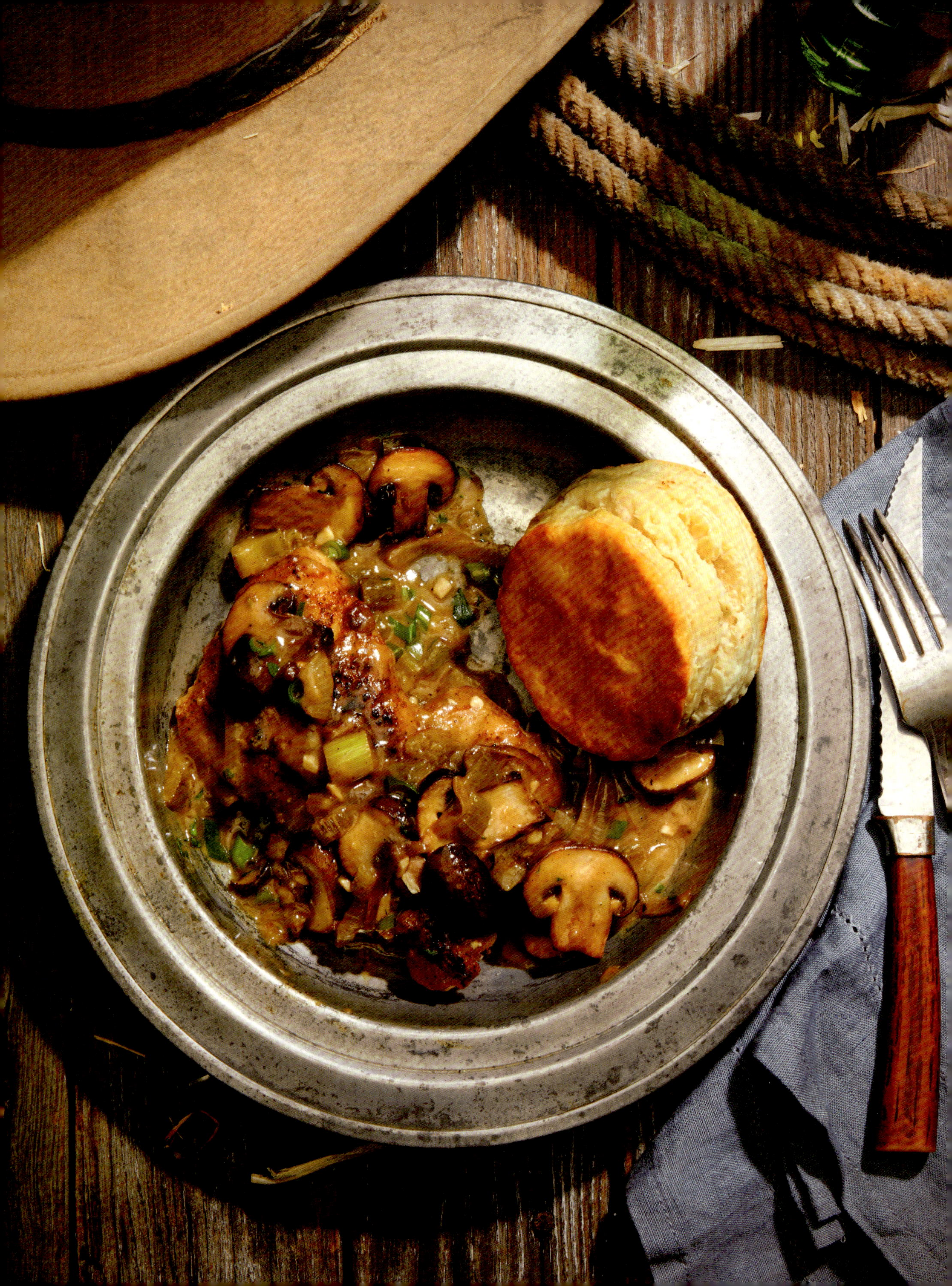

Jamie's SMOTHERED CHICKEN
in Brown Mushroom Gravy

Smothered chicken is another recipe straight out of the family cookbook, and straight-up comfort food. Although no "chicken hearts" are used in this recipe—as Beth would say about her brother Jamie—it's a hearty, home-on-the-range chicken dish that feeds a lot of people easily, and everyone loves it. I use chicken thighs because they can braise for a while without drying out, but you can use chicken breasts or even pork chops; just watch the cooking time, because you'll want to cook those lean meats a bit less. If you like, make the sauce on the stovetop, throw it in the slow cooker with the chicken thighs, and cook it low and slow so it's ready by the time the chow bell rings at suppertime.

INGREDIENTS

- 1 tablespoon Cajun seasoning, plus 2 teaspoons, or to taste
- Kosher salt and freshly ground black pepper
- 6 boneless, skinless chicken thighs (about 1½ lb /680 g)
- Olive oil for coating
- ½ cup (60 g) all-purpose flour, plus 3 tablespoons
- ¼ cup (60 ml) canola or avocado oil
- 4 tablespoons (60 g) unsalted butter
- 1½ large yellow onions, halved and thinly sliced
- 2 ribs celery, finely chopped
- 1 small green or yellow bell pepper, seeded and finely chopped
- ¾ lb (340 g) cremini or button mushrooms, brushed clean and sliced

INSTRUCTIONS

In a small bowl, stir 1 tablespoon of the Cajun seasoning and 1 teaspoon salt. Pat the chicken dry, place it on a baking sheet, and rub the chicken all over with olive oil. Sprinkle the chicken all over with the seasoned salt.

Place ½ cup (60 g) of the flour in a shallow bowl. Dredge the seasoned chicken thighs in the flour, coating them well and shaking off any excess.

In a large cast-iron frying pan over medium-high heat, heat the canola oil. Add the chicken and cook, turning once until nicely browned on both sides, about 7 minutes. Transfer the chicken to a plate.

Add the butter to the pan to melt. When melted, add the onions, celery, bell pepper, remaining 2 teaspoons Cajun seasoning, or to taste, and ½ teaspoon salt. Cook, stirring and scraping up the browned bits on the bottom of the pan until the onions are very soft and start to caramelize, about 13 minutes (if they are browning too quickly, reduce the heat).

Reduce the heat to medium and add the mushrooms. Continue to cook, stirring until the mushrooms are tender, about 3 minutes. Add the remaining 3 tablespoons flour, the garlic, ½ teaspoon salt, and cayenne to taste, if using, and stir to coat the vegetables. Stir in the broth until the gravy is smooth and bring to a boil.

continued on page 74

continued from page 73

3 cloves garlic, minced

Cayenne pepper (optional)

2 cups (475 ml) chicken broth, preferably homemade

3 scallions, finely chopped, white and green parts

¼ cup (15 g) chopped fresh flat-leaf parsley

Steamed white rice or mashed potatoes for serving

MAKES 6 SERVINGS

Return the chicken to the pan and reduce the heat to low. Cover the pan and simmer gently until the chicken is cooked through, about 30 minutes. Stir in the scallions and parsley and warm through gently.

Serve at once, over plenty of rice or mashed potatoes.

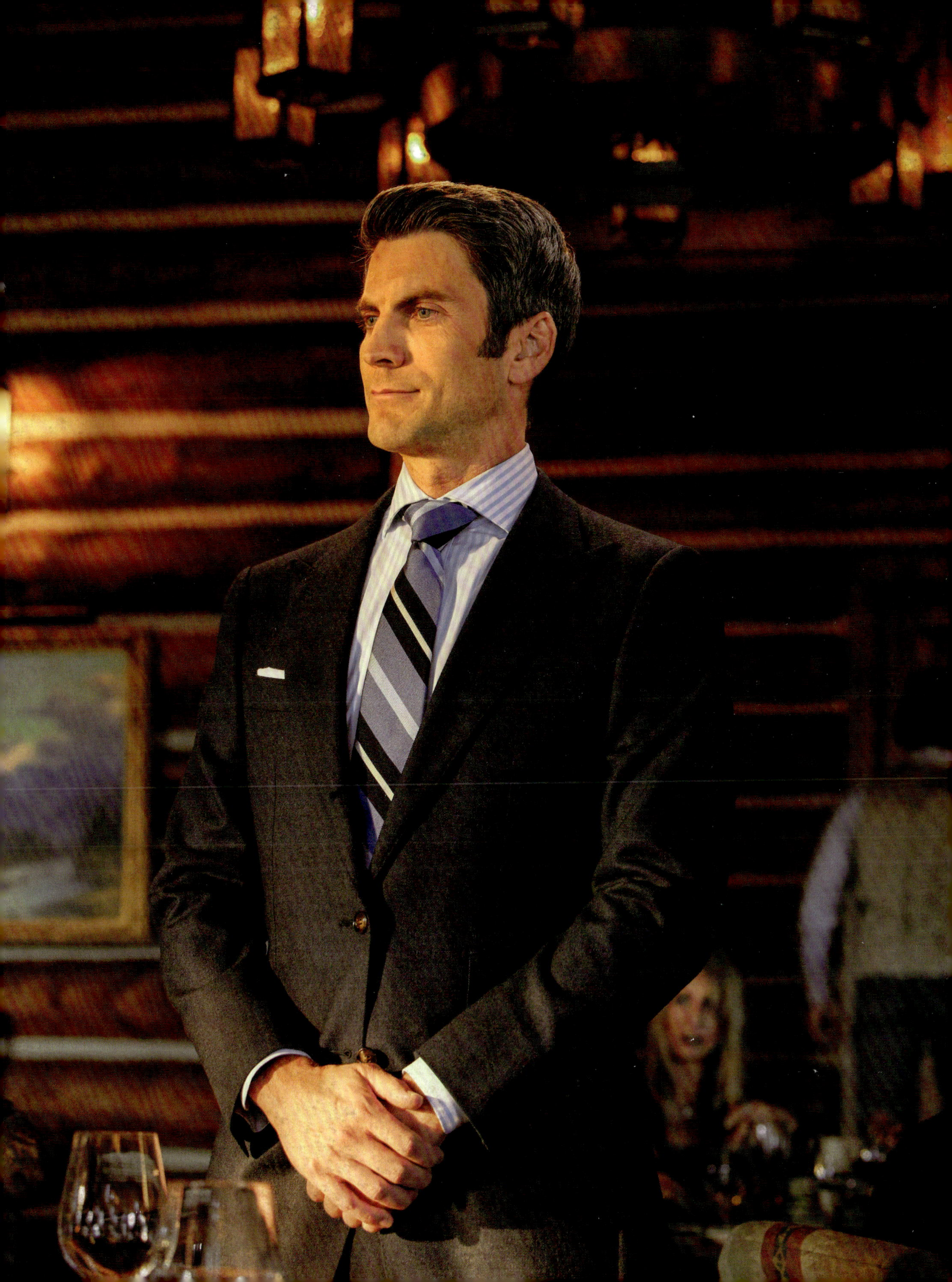

Gator's Cajun
CHICKEN AND SAUSAGE GUMBO

I was about thirteen when I decided I wanted to learn how to make the food of my Cajun heritage, and I asked my dad to teach me to make gumbo. A lot of people make seafood gumbo, but not everyone likes it. However, I want everyone to *love* gumbo, so I use chicken and andouille sausage. The roux is a very important part of making gumbo and should smell like toast when it is ready. Don't rush this step.

INGREDIENTS

- 2 tablespoons vegetable oil, plus ½ cup (120 ml)
- 6 boneless, skinless chicken thighs, cut into 2-inch (5-cm) pieces (about 2 lb / 1 kg)
- Kosher salt and freshly ground black pepper
- 3 teaspoons Cajun seasoning
- 12 oz (340 g) andouille or other spicy smoked sausage, cut into ½-inch- (12-mm-) thick slices
- ½ cup (60 g) all-purpose flour
- 1 large yellow onion, chopped
- 3 ribs celery, chopped
- 1 green bell pepper, seeded and chopped
- 1 red bell pepper, seeded and chopped
- 3 jalapeño chiles, seeded and finely chopped
- 4 cups (950 ml) chicken broth, preferably homemade, plus extra broth as needed
- 2 bay leaves
- ¼ cup (15 g) chopped fresh flat-leaf parsley
- 1 tablespoon Cajun hot-pepper sauce
- Steamed white rice for serving

MAKES 6–8 SERVINGS

INSTRUCTIONS

In a large Dutch oven or stockpot over medium-high heat, warm 2 tablespoons of the oil. Season the chicken pieces all over with salt, pepper, and 1 teaspoon of the Cajun seasoning. Working in 2 batches, add the chicken to the Dutch oven and sear until nicely browned on one side, 4–5 minutes. Transfer to a plate. Add the sausage pieces and cook until well browned on one side, about 4 minutes. Transfer to the plate with the chicken.

Add the remaining ½ cup (120 ml) oil to the Dutch oven and reduce the heat to low. Add the flour and whisk until smooth. Cook, stirring until the roux is dark brown in color, 30–45 minutes.

Add the onion, celery, bell peppers, jalapeños, and 1 teaspoon salt to the pot with the roux. Raise the heat to medium and cook, stirring until tender, about 7 minutes. Pour in the broth slowly, stirring until well combined. Add the reserved chicken and sausage, along with the bay leaves and remaining 2 teaspoons Cajun seasoning. Raise the heat to medium-high and bring to a gentle boil; then reduce the heat to low and simmer, stirring every so often until the gumbo is thickened and flavorful, 1½–2 hours. If the gumbo starts to get too thick, partially cover the pot. Add a bit more broth to get to the consistency you like.

Stir in the parsley and hot-pepper sauce and serve at once over warm rice.

GATOR'S TIP

If you really want to give this a kick, add a couple of minced habanero peppers along with the jalapeños.

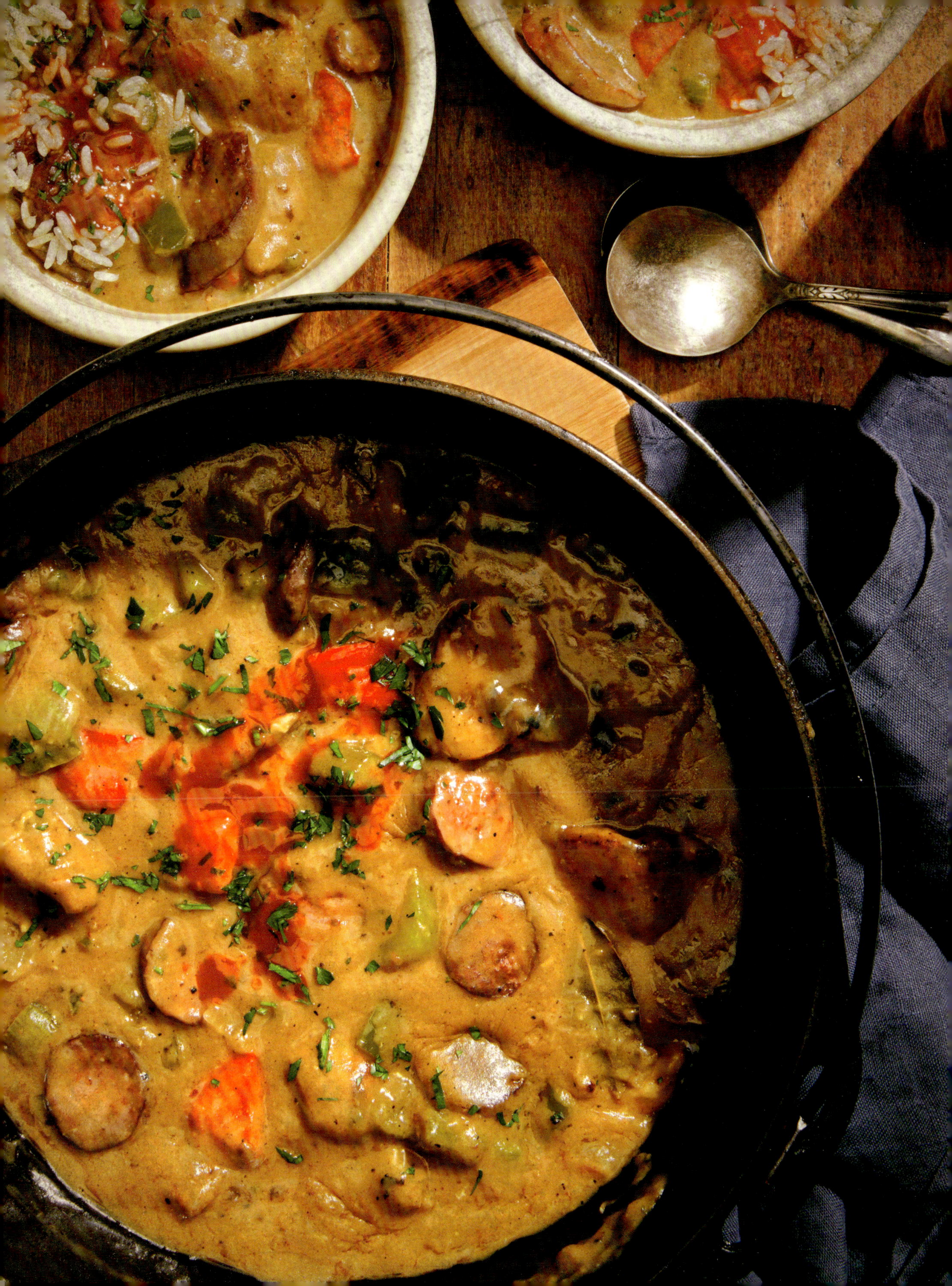

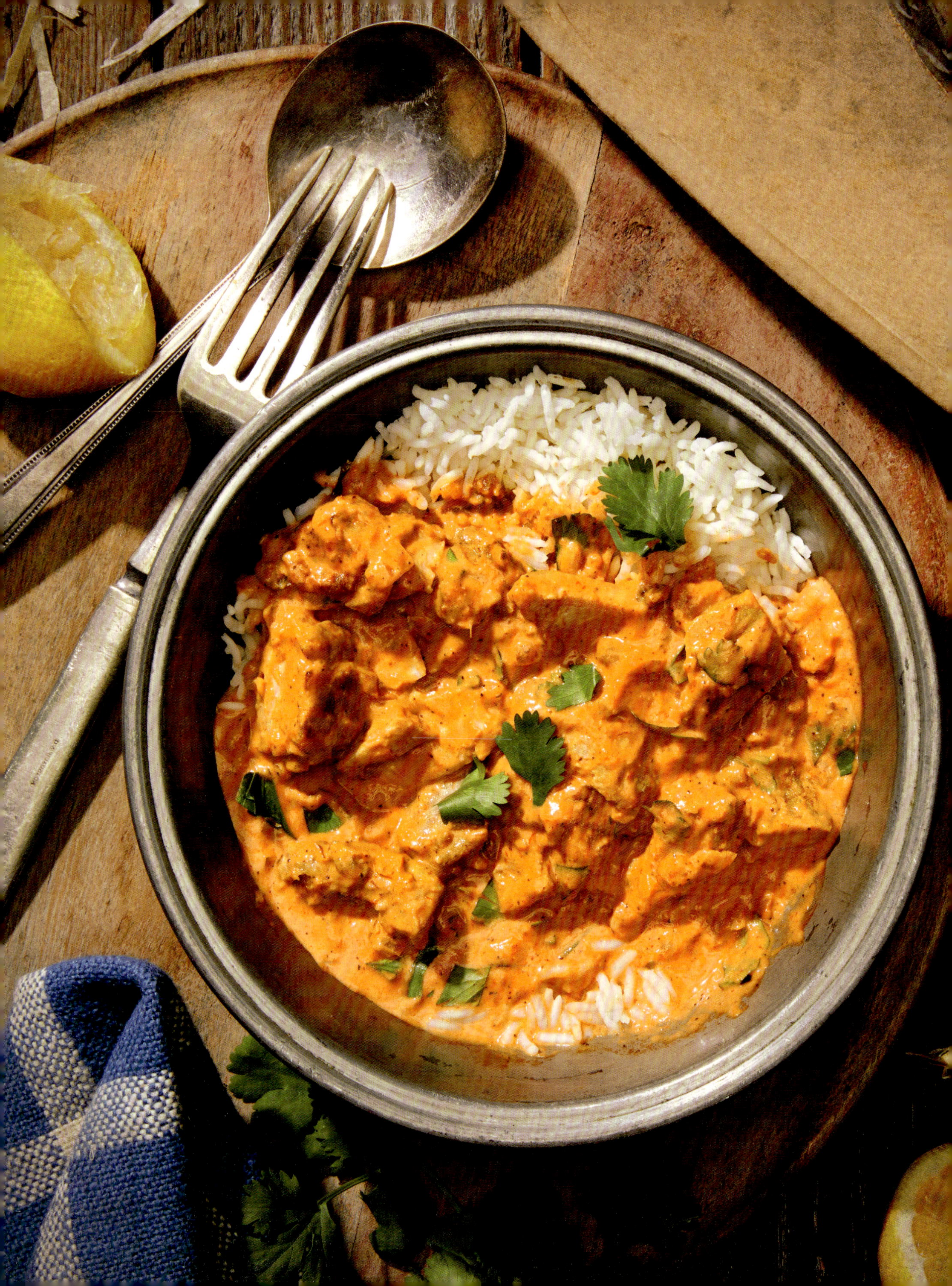

Western BUTTER CHICKEN with Rice

The first time I made butter chicken we were filming in a big field of grass late on a Friday night. It was a long and extremely hot day and people were tired. We had been grilling food for a few days and needed something that was a little more luxurious to eat—it's important to change things up to maintain good morale on set—so I made this recipe and took it out to the crew. There was an audible chatter as I approached and set up the table. I told the crew, "Everything's gonna be okay" and served the butter chicken on a croissant as a sandwich with a bit of pot roast on top. When I looked around, all I could see was everyone's greasy faces in the moonlight as they all ate . . . very quietly. That's how my butter chicken started, and now I make it on set regularly. It's decadent and really good.

INGREDIENTS

For the Marinated Chicken

- ½ cup (125 g) plain yogurt
- 3 cloves garlic, minced
- 1 tablespoon grated peeled fresh ginger
- 1 teaspoon curry powder
- 1 teaspoon garam masala
- 1 teaspoon kosher salt
- ½ teaspoon freshly ground black pepper
- Pinch of ground cinnamon
- 6 boneless, skinless chicken thighs (about 1½ lb / 680 g)

For the Sauce

- 6 tablespoons (90 g) unsalted butter
- 1 small yellow onion, finely chopped
- 1 jalapeño chile, seeded and minced

continued on page 80

INSTRUCTIONS

To prepare the marinated chicken, in a large bowl whisk together the yogurt, garlic, ginger, curry powder, garam masala, salt, pepper, and cinnamon to blend. Add the chicken and stir to coat evenly. Cover and refrigerate for at least 4 hours, or preferably overnight.

Position a rack in the upper third of the oven and preheat the oven to 425°F (220°C).

Remove the chicken from the marinade, shaking off any excess; discard the marinade. Spread the chicken onto a large, rimmed baking sheet in a single even layer. Bake until cooked through and lightly browned, about 25 minutes.

While the chicken cooks, prepare the sauce. In a saucepan over medium heat, melt 4 tablespoons (60 g) of the butter. Add the onion and jalapeño and cook, stirring occasionally until tender, about 5 minutes. Add the garlic and ginger and cook, stirring until fragrant, about 30 seconds. Add the chile powder, cumin, and garam masala and cook, stirring until fragrant, about 10 seconds. Add the tomato paste and cook, stirring until the paste darkens and the mixture is well combined, about 1 minute. Reduce the heat to low and pour in the cream and water; stir to combine. Let simmer for about 3 minutes. Remove from the heat.

continued from page 79

- 2 cloves garlic, minced
- 1 teaspoon grated peeled fresh ginger
- 1 teaspoon pure chile powder, such as ancho
- 1 teaspoon ground cumin
- 1 teaspoon garam masala
- ½ cup (115 g) tomato paste
- 1 cup (240 ml) heavy cream
- ½ cup (120 ml) water, plus more as needed
- 1 tablespoon fresh lemon juice, or to taste
- ¼ cup (15 g) chopped fresh cilantro
- Kosher salt and freshly ground black pepper
- Steamed basmati rice for serving

MAKES 4–6 SERVINGS

When the chicken is ready, transfer to a cutting board and let cool slightly. Cut into bite-size pieces, and then add the chicken and any juices to the saucepan with the sauce. Stir in the lemon juice and cilantro. Taste and season with salt and pepper, as needed. Add a little more water to thin the sauce if you like. Rewarm over low heat until steaming; then add the remaining 2 tablespoons butter, cut into pieces. Stir until melted.

Serve over basmati rice.

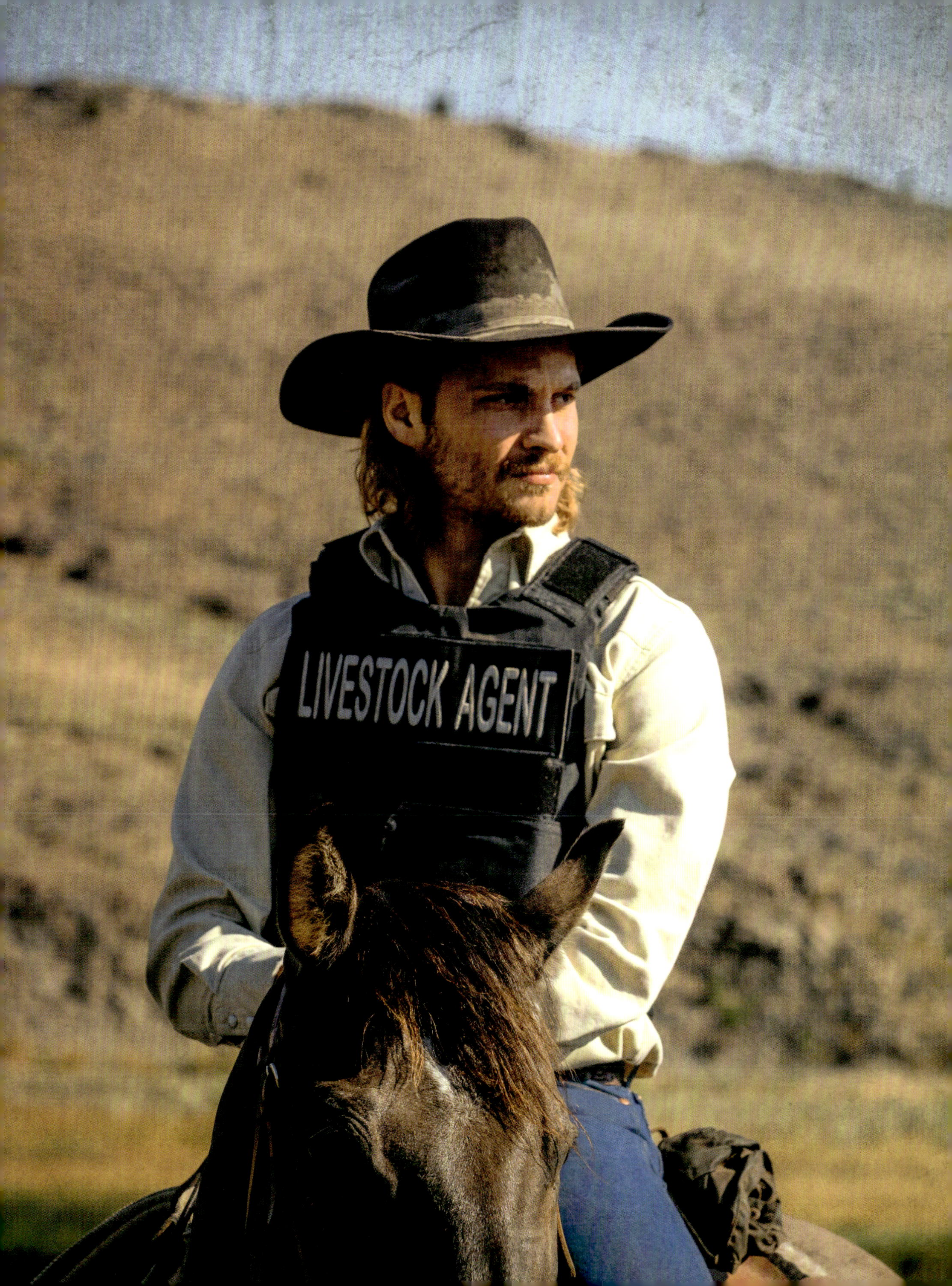
LIVESTOCK AGENT

Rancher's
CHICKEN AND BISCUIT DUMPLINGS

This hearty, warm chicken stew is the ultimate ranch-style comfort food. It's what I make when I'm homesick and I miss my family, so that's why I started making it for the crew. This is one dish that hits plenty of people hard, especially anyone from the Midwest or Oklahoma. It tastes like home. And it's pretty simple to make, whether you use fresh biscuits or pop 'em out of a can. Beware: you cannot make enough of this recipe. Once, while filming in the freezing cold, I couldn't make it fast enough. I think I made 30 gallons (114 l) of stew, and in nine minutes it was gone! Then, all of a sudden, someone came along with a slice of bread and wiped the pot clean. Serve this to anyone who looks cold—and eat it the same day you make it (trust me, everyone does and will). It's great for a crowd, or a bunch of ranch hands.

INGREDIENTS

- 2 lb (1 kg) boneless, skinless chicken breasts (about 4 small breasts), halved lengthwise
- Kosher salt and freshly ground black pepper
- 4 tablespoons (60 g) unsalted butter, plus 2 tablespoons (optional), at room temperature
- 2 tablespoons olive oil
- 1 large yellow onion, finely chopped
- 3 carrots, peeled and diced
- 2 large ribs celery, thinly sliced
- 1 red bell pepper, seeded and diced
- ¾ lb (340 g) Yukon gold potatoes (about 2 large) unpeeled, cut into ½-inch (12-mm) cubes

continued on page 85

INSTRUCTIONS

Season the chicken all over with salt and pepper. In a large Dutch oven or heavy pot over medium-high heat, melt 2 tablespoons of the butter with 1 tablespoon of the oil. Add half the chicken breasts and sear on one side until golden brown, about 4 minutes. Transfer to a cutting board. Repeat with the remaining chicken. Cut the chicken into 1-inch (2.5-cm) pieces. (The chicken will be undercooked, but will finish cooking in the stew.) Set aside.

Reduce the heat under the pot to medium. Add the remaining 2 tablespoons butter and remaining 1 tablespoon oil to the pot, along with the onion, carrots, celery, bell pepper, and potatoes. Season with salt. Cook, stirring until the vegetables soften, about 7 minutes.

Sprinkle the vegetables with 3 tablespoons of the flour and the cayenne and cook, stirring for about 1 minute. While stirring constantly, gradually pour in 5 cups (1.2 l) of the stock. Bring to a boil, and then reduce the heat to low. Add the reserved chicken and simmer gently until the vegetables are tender and the chicken is cooked through, about 10 minutes. (Don't let the stew boil or the chicken will get tough.)

Position a rack in the upper third of the oven and preheat the oven to 450°F (230°C). Line a baking sheet with parchment paper.

If you like your stew a bit thinner, add the remaining 1 cup (240 ml) stock; if you like your stew a bit thicker, in a small bowl stir together the remaining 2 tablespoons butter and 2 tablespoons flour to make a slurry; then stir it into the stew and let simmer for a few minutes until thickened.

82

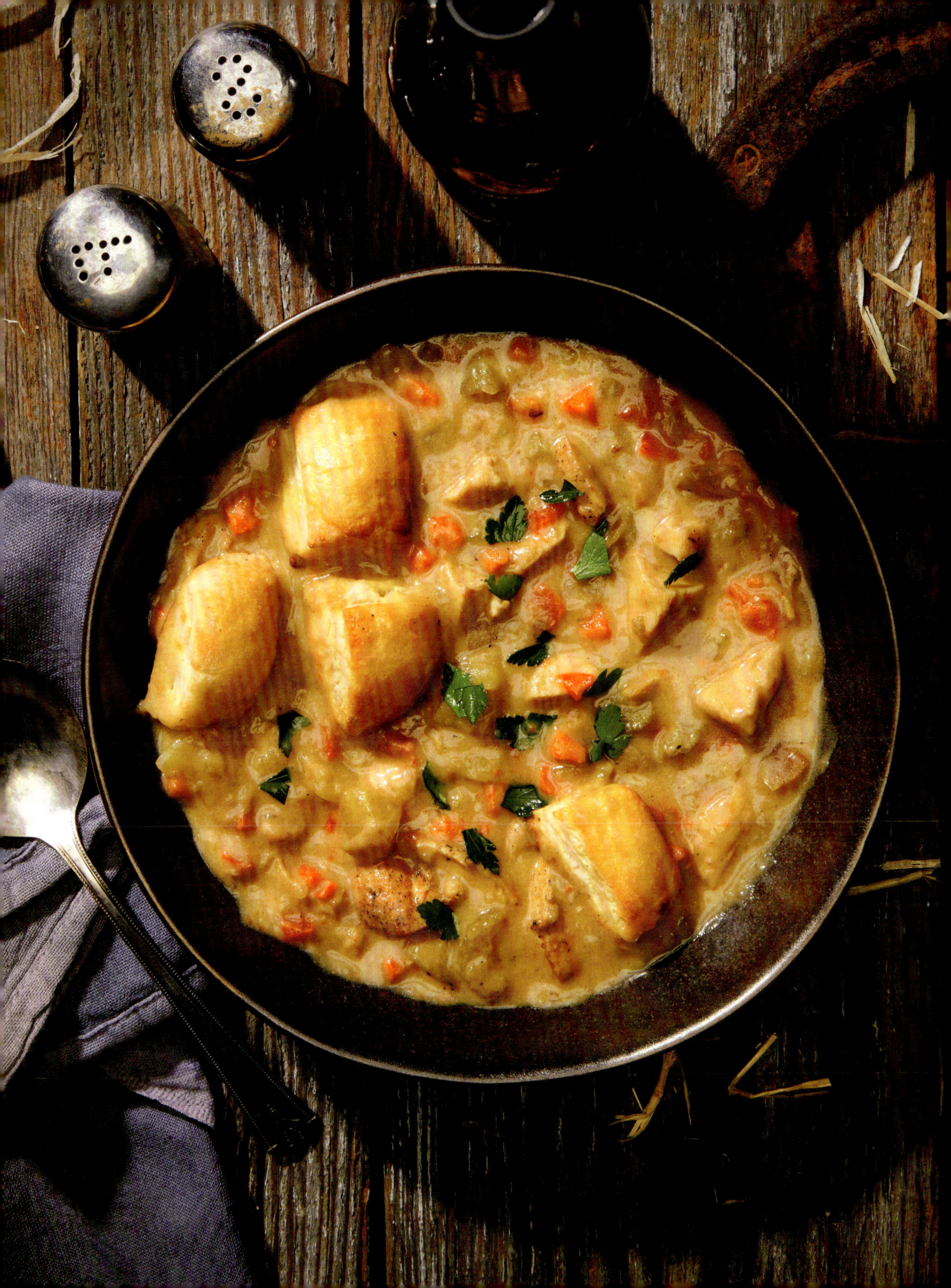

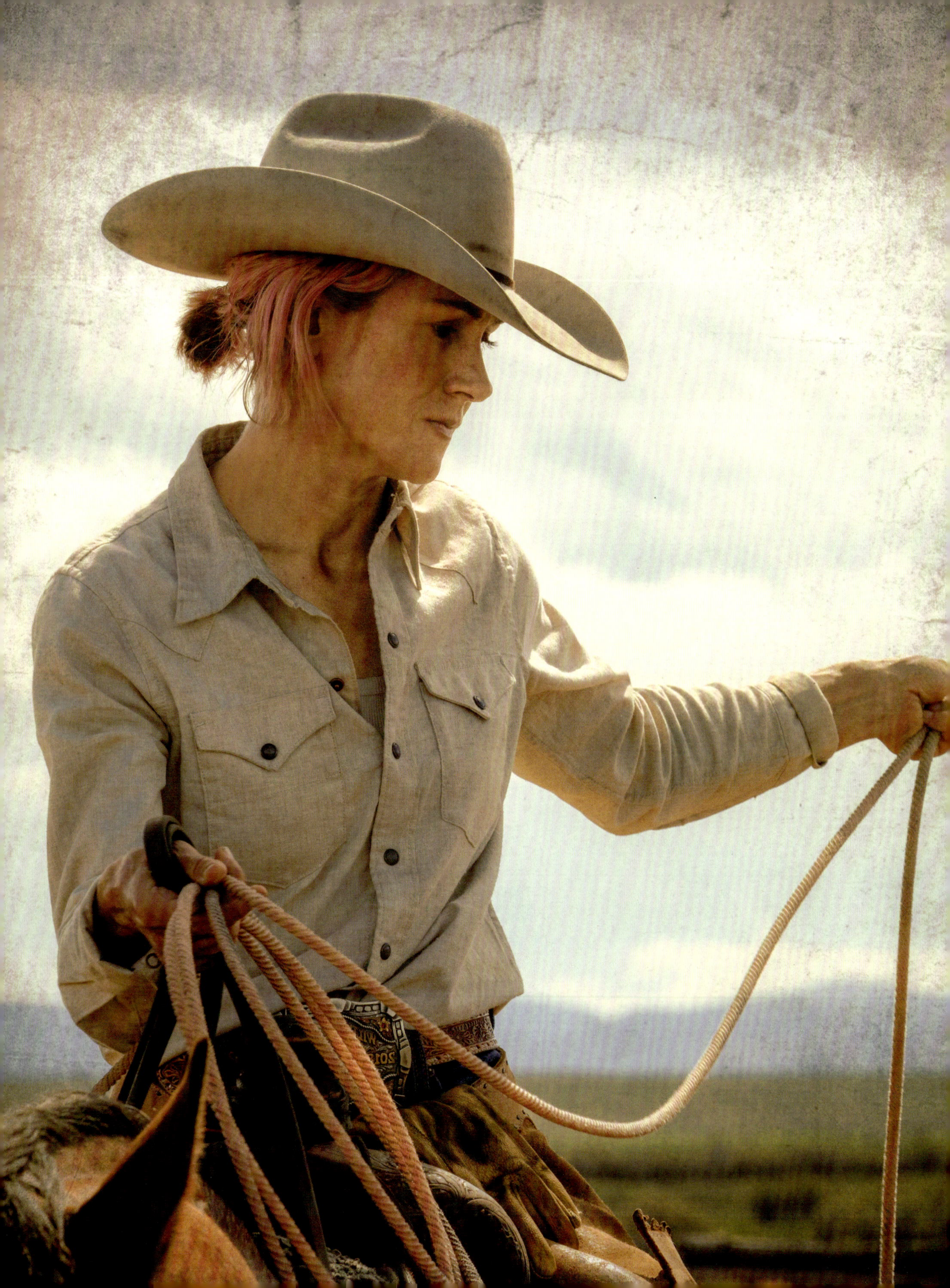

continued from page 82

3 tablespoons all-purpose flour, plus 2 tablespoons (optional), plus flour for dusting

Pinch of cayenne pepper

5–6 cups (1.2–1.4 l) chicken stock, preferably homemade

1 recipe This Is How You Make a F*$%ing Biscuit dough (page 103)

¼ cup (60 ml) half-and-half (optional)

Chopped fresh parsley for serving

MAKES 8–10 SERVINGS

Cover the pot and remove from the heat while you prepare the biscuits.

Lightly dust a work surface with flour and place the biscuit dough on it. Pat the dough into a ½-inch- (12-mm-) thick rectangle, and then cut it into 1½–2-inch (4–5-cm) pieces; you should have 20–22 pieces. Arrange the biscuits on the prepared baking sheet. Bake until puffed and lightly golden but not cooked through, about 8 minutes. Leave the oven on.

While the biscuits partially cook, return the pot to medium heat and bring the stew to a simmer. Stir in the half-and-half, if using.

Arrange the biscuit pieces on top of the stew. Transfer the pot to the oven and bake until the biscuits are cooked through, 7–10 minutes.

Sprinkle with parsley and serve.

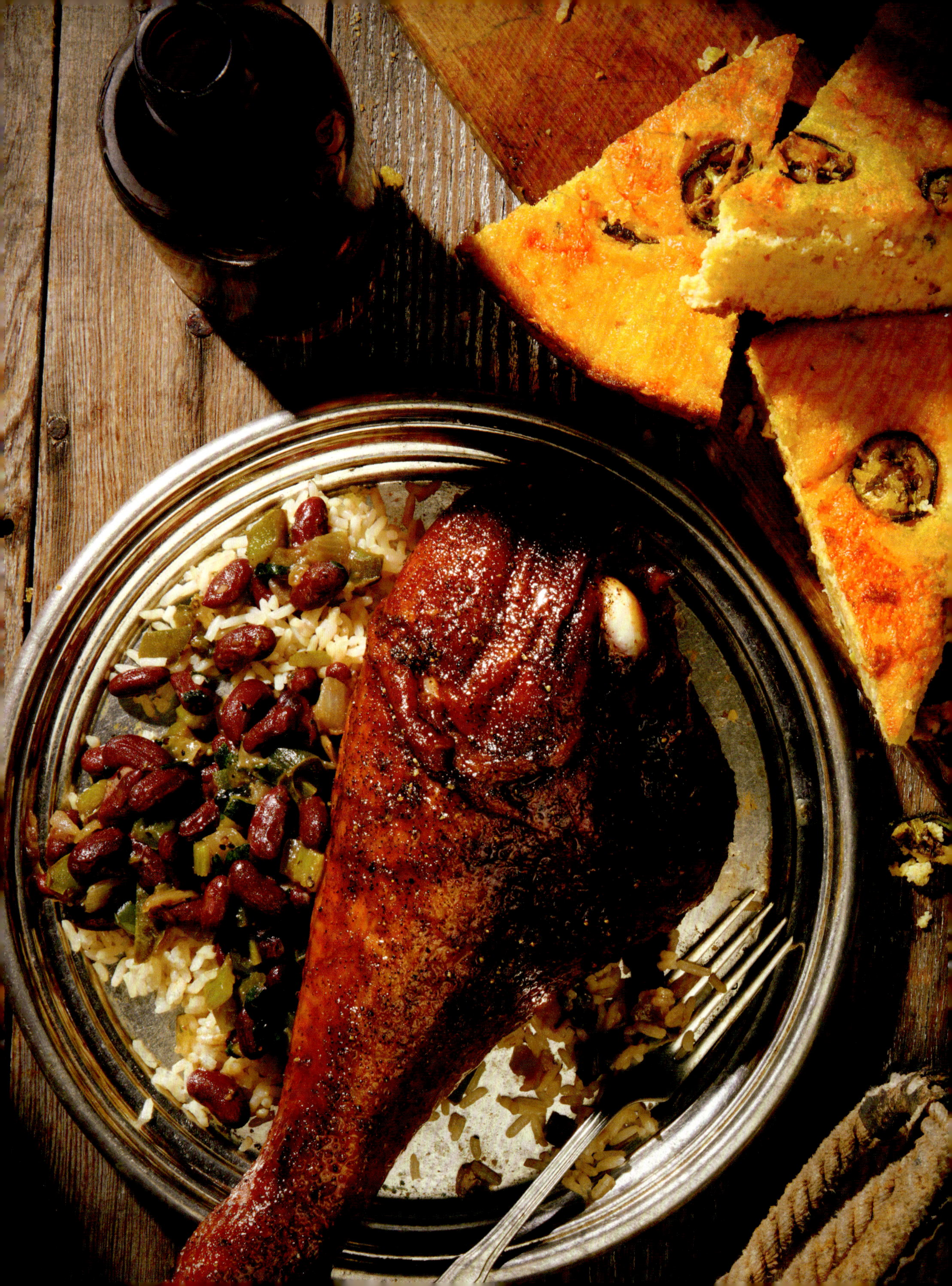

Smoked
TURKEY LEGS
with Red Beans and Rice

When I was growing up, we would eat red beans and rice every Monday. Although ham hocks are commonly used, I don't particularly care for them, so I use smoked turkey legs instead and they are just as delicious. On set, they are easy to grab and eat. It's fun to watch people walk away with food like that. This recipe also gets people hyped—once someone walks on set with a big turkey leg, a mad dash ensues. And the best part of this recipe is that it's really two recipes in one, so if all you want are the beans and rice, you're still winning! Take the time to brine the turkey legs for twenty-four hours before you smoke them—it gives them so much flavor and helps them soak up the smoke. And be sure to serve them with Monica's Jalapeño-Cheddar Cornbread (page 104).

INGREDIENTS

For the Smoked Turkey Legs

2 qt (2 l) cold water

⅓ cup (50 g) kosher salt

¼ cup (60 g) firmly packed light brown sugar

1 tablespoon garlic powder

1 tablespoon onion powder

1 tablespoon ground sage

2 teaspoons sweet paprika

2 teaspoons freshly ground black pepper

6 turkey legs

Few handfuls of applewood or cherrywood chips

For the Red Beans and Rice

¼ cup (60 ml) olive oil

1 white onion, finely chopped

1 green bell pepper, seeded and finely chopped

2 ribs celery, finely chopped

2–4 jalapeño chiles, seeded and finely chopped

continued on page 88

INSTRUCTIONS

To prepare the smoked turkey legs, in a large saucepan combine 1 qt (1 l) of the cold water, the salt, brown sugar, garlic powder, onion powder, sage, paprika, and pepper. Cook over medium heat, stirring until the sugar dissolves. Remove from the heat and add the remaining quart (liter) cold water. Set aside to cool completely.

Arrange the turkey legs in a container that will just fit the legs and brine, while keeping the legs submerged in the brine. Pour in the brine. Cover and refrigerate for 24 hours.

Soak the wood chips in cold water for 30 minutes. Drain the chips and wrap in a piece of aluminum foil; pierce the foil a few times with a paring knife.

Remove the turkey legs from the brine and discard the brine. Place the turkey legs on a baking sheet and pat dry with paper towels. Let stand at room temperature while you prepare the grill.

Prepare a gas or charcoal grill for indirect cooking over low heat (about 300°F / 150°C), or prepare a smoker. When the grill is ready, place the packet of wood chips directly on the coals, or in the smoker box, if using a gas grill. When the grill is smoking, arrange the turkey legs on the grill grate over indirect heat. Cook, periodically checking and turning the legs and maintaining a low grill temperature until the legs are dark brown and cooked through, about 3 hours, or until the deepest section of the turkey legs reaches an internal temperature of 165°F (75°C) on an instant-read thermometer.

continued from page 87

- 3 large cloves garlic, minced
- 4 tablespoons (60 g) unsalted butter
- 6 cups (1.5 l) chicken stock, preferably homemade
- 2 bay leaves
- 1 teaspoon ground sage
- 1 lb (450 g) dried red kidney beans, soaked overnight in cold water
- Kosher salt and freshly ground black pepper
- Cajun hot-pepper sauce for seasoning
- ⅓ cup (20 g) minced fresh flat-leaf parsley
- Steamed white rice for serving

MAKES 6 SERVINGS

While the turkey legs smoke, prepare the beans. In a large Dutch oven over medium heat, warm the oil. Add the onion, bell pepper, celery, and jalapeños. Cook, stirring occasionally until softened, about 6 minutes. Add the garlic and cook until fragrant, about 1 minute. Add the butter to melt. When melted, pour in the stock and add the bay leaves and sage. Drain the beans, rinse, drain again, and add to the pot. Raise the heat to high and bring to a boil. Reduce the heat to low and simmer, stirring every so often until the beans are very tender but not falling apart, about 1 hour 30 minutes.

Taste the beans and season with salt, pepper, and hot-pepper sauce, as needed. Remove the bay leaves and stir in the parsley just before serving. Cover to keep warm, if the turkey legs are still smoking.

Serve the beans over the rice with a turkey leg alongside.

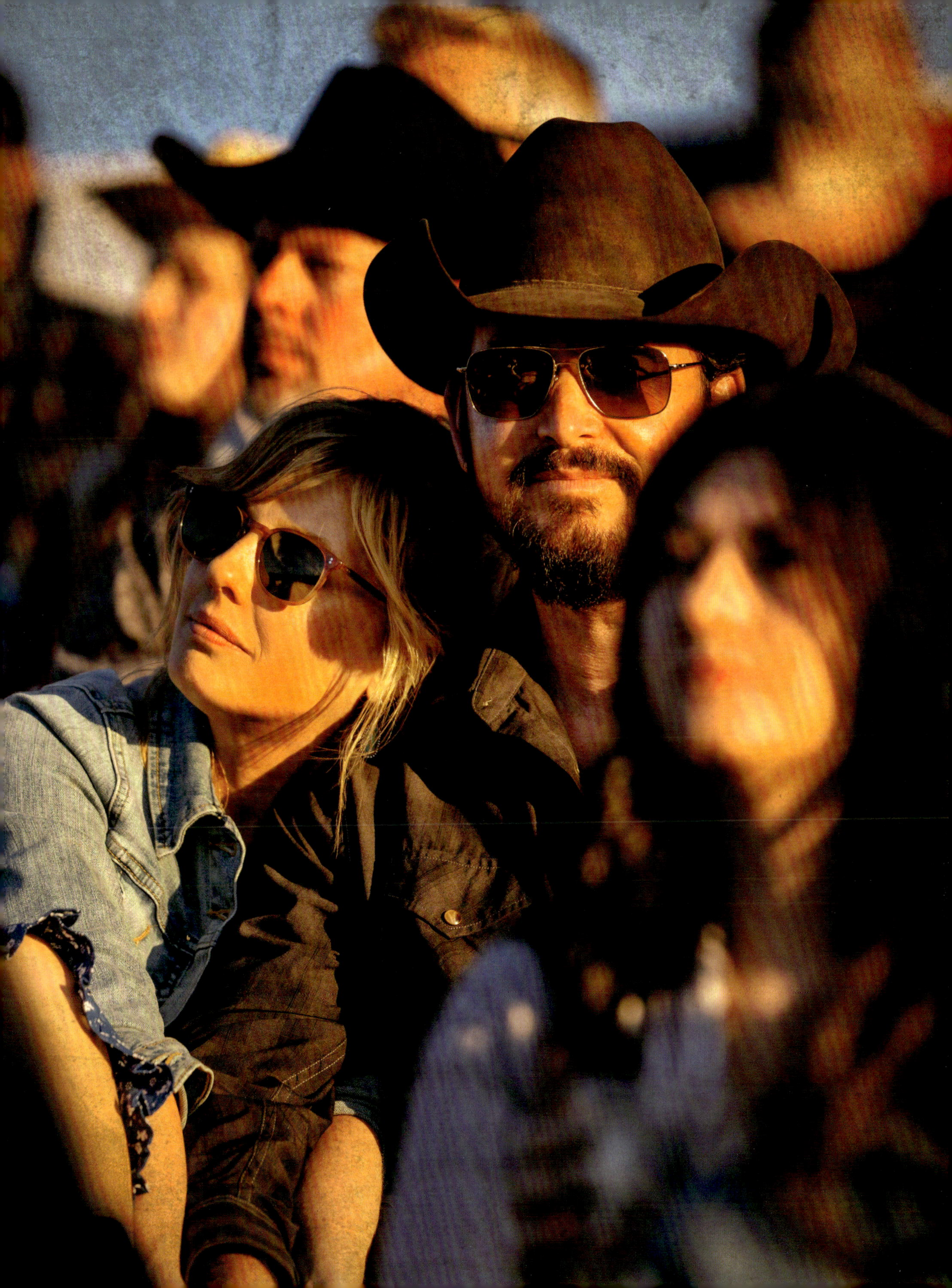

John and Tate's
PAN-ROASTED WALLEYE

When the cowboys head out to camp for the summer and "babysit" the cattle, John decides that being under the stars with them might help his grandson, Tate, get over the trauma of his kidnapping. Tate sleeps for the first time in a long while without having nightmares and wakes up the next morning ready to go fishing. When he asks his grandfather if he woke too late for fishing, John answers, "Trout are like bankers. They never do a damn thing in the morning." He then turns to Tate and says, "You should bring the net if you plan on a big one." Tate is excited to make his fresh-caught fish, using just a squeeze of lemon from the chuck wagon. This recipe is about as simple as that, but trust me, it's delicious. And it works well on almost any meaty fish, such as pike or cod, but I tend to use walleye because it's a great fish that is common in Montana.

INGREDIENTS

¼ cup (60 ml) mayonnaise

2 tablespoons fresh lemon juice

1 teaspoon finely grated lemon zest

1 teaspoon sweet or hot paprika

½ teaspoon kosher salt

½ teaspoon freshly ground black pepper

4 white fish fillets (4–6 oz / 115–170 g each), such as walleye, pike, or cod

1 tablespoon olive oil

MAKES 4 SERVINGS

INSTRUCTIONS

In a small bowl, whisk together the mayonnaise, lemon juice, lemon zest, paprika, salt, and pepper until blended. Spread the mixture all over the fish fillets.

In a large cast-iron or other heavy frying pan over medium-high heat, warm the oil. Add the fish in a single layer and cook, turning once until golden brown on both sides and just opaque throughout, 3–6 minutes, depending on the type of fish. Serve at once.

GATOR'S TIP

I use a similar recipe for seared tuna but substitute 2 tablespoons soy sauce for the salt and 2 limes for the lemon.

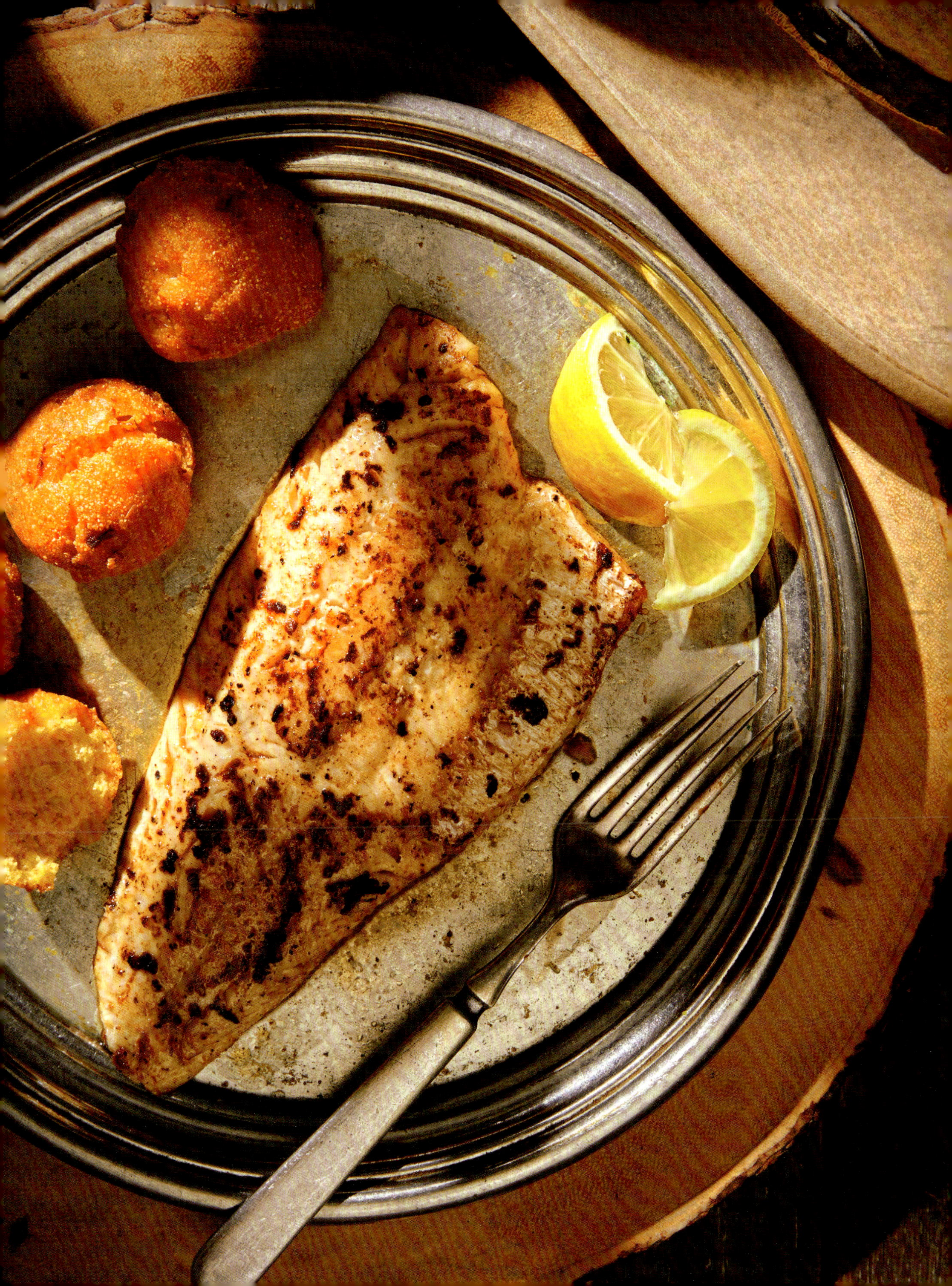

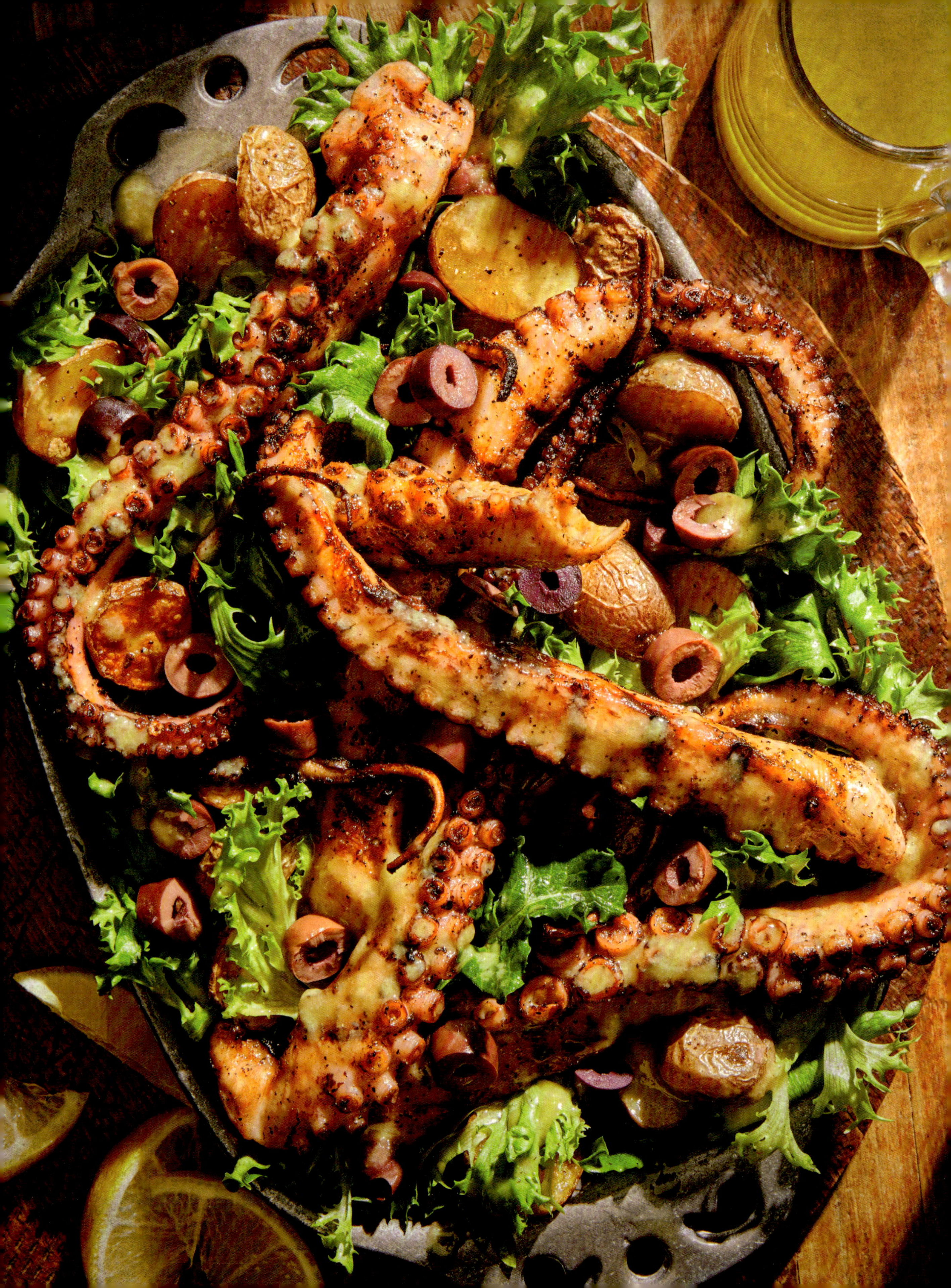

GRILLED OCTOPUS
with Lemon and Roasted Potatoes

The first time I did a scene with Kevin Costner, in Season 2, Taylor took me by surprise, only telling me the night before that I was to have a speaking scene the next day. I had to serve char-grilled octopus to John, Kayce, and Beth in the lodge dining room. We ended up using a flamethrower to get it charred enough to look good on camera. That was also the day that Kevin decided to call my character on the show by my name. When I brought out the octopus, I vividly remember the look Kevin gave me; he was really taken aback by the fact that I set this in front of him, and the line he says was really what he was thinking. If you do like octopus, this is the best way to eat it. Don't start with a whole octopus, but seek out pre-cooked frozen octopus—you'll have much better results.

INGREDIENTS

For the Lemon Vinaigrette

⅓ cup (80 ml) olive oil

3 tablespoons fresh lemon juice

1 tablespoon Dijon mustard

Kosher salt and freshly ground black pepper

For the Roasted Potatoes

1½ lb (680 g) small red potatoes, halved

Olive oil for drizzling

Kosher salt and freshly ground black pepper

For the Octopus

2 lb (1 kg) cooked octopus tentacles, thawed, if frozen

Olive oil for coating

Kosher salt and freshly ground black pepper

1 head frisée lettuce, torn into leaves

⅓ cup (50 g) pitted, sliced Kalamata olives (optional)

Roughly chopped fresh flat-leaf parsley leaves for garnish

Lemon wedges for serving

MAKES 4–6 SERVINGS

INSTRUCTIONS

To prepare the vinaigrette, in a jar with a tight-fitting lid combine the oil, lemon juice, and mustard. Season with salt and pepper. Cover the jar and shake vigorously until the dressing is emulsified. Set aside.

Preheat the oven to 425°F (220°C). Prepare a gas or charcoal grill for direct cooking over medium-high heat.

To prepare the potatoes, place the potatoes on a rimmed baking sheet and drizzle with oil. Season with salt and pepper and toss to coat. Spread into an even layer. Roast until tender, stirring once or twice, about 25 minutes. Set aside.

To prepare the octopus, rub the octopus all over with oil and season with salt and pepper. Place the octopus on the grill and cook, without turning, until crisp and browned on one side, about 4 minutes. Turn the octopus and grill until the other side is nicely browned, about 4 minutes longer.

In a large bowl, toss the frisée with some of the vinaigrette. Spread on a platter. Top with the octopus and potatoes. Sprinkle with the olives, if using, and parsley. Drizzle with more vinaigrette. Arrange the lemon wedges around the octopus.

Serve, passing more vinaigrette alongside.

Lee, Jamie, and Kayce's
FIRE-GRILLED WILD TROUT
with Chimichurri

It's a sweet moment when all three Dutton brothers—Lee, Jamie, and Kayce—take Tate fishing (while riding horses!) in the river. It's the same day that Kayce returns to the ranch in Season 1 to tell his father he can spend more time with his grandson. As they cook the trout over a fire, Jamie and Lee question Kayce about why he plans to raise Tate on a reservation. "People do it every day," says Kayce. And Jamie responds, "Cause they have no choice, Kayce." Tate pipes in, "It's a good day!" Still, the brothers start to argue, and when Lee throws a stick at Kayce, Tate stands up and throws his entire fish at Lee, yelling, "Hey! Don't throw things at my dad!" Kayce assures him, "It's okay, buddy, we're just brothers arguing. Nobody's mad." Lee laughs and responds, "You're gonna tell me there's no fight in that blood?" Jamie, laughing, replies, "He's right, though, it is a good day." This grilled trout can make any day end up a good one too.

INGREDIENTS

For the Chimichurri

1 cup (60 g) chopped fresh flat-leaf parsley

1 cup (60 g) chopped fresh cilantro

⅓ cup (80 ml) olive oil

3 cloves garlic, chopped

2 tablespoons chopped yellow onion

1 teaspoon kosher salt

½ teaspoon dried oregano

½ teaspoon red pepper flakes, or to taste

3 tablespoons sherry vinegar

continued on page 97

INSTRUCTIONS

To prepare the chimichurri, in a food processor combine all the ingredients, except the vinegar, and process until finely chopped, stopping to scrape down the sides of the bowl once. Transfer to a serving bowl. Stir in the vinegar just before serving. (To store, don't add the vinegar; transfer to a jar with a tight-fitting lid and refrigerate for up to 2 days and stir in the vinegar just before serving.)

Line a baking sheet with parchment paper.

To prepare the trout, place the trout on the prepared baking sheet. Rub the fish all over with oil, and then season generously with salt and pepper. If using whole trout, stuff the cavities of the trout with the thyme sprigs, dividing them equally among the fish. If using fillets, sprinkle the meaty side with the thyme leaves.

Prepare a grill for direct grilling over medium-high heat (450°F / 230°C). Brush the grill grates clean, and then brush them with oil.

Arrange the fish on the grill directly over the heat, meaty side down if using fillets. Grill, turning once, until nicely charred and cooked through, about 4 minutes per side for whole fish and about 3 minutes total for fillets.

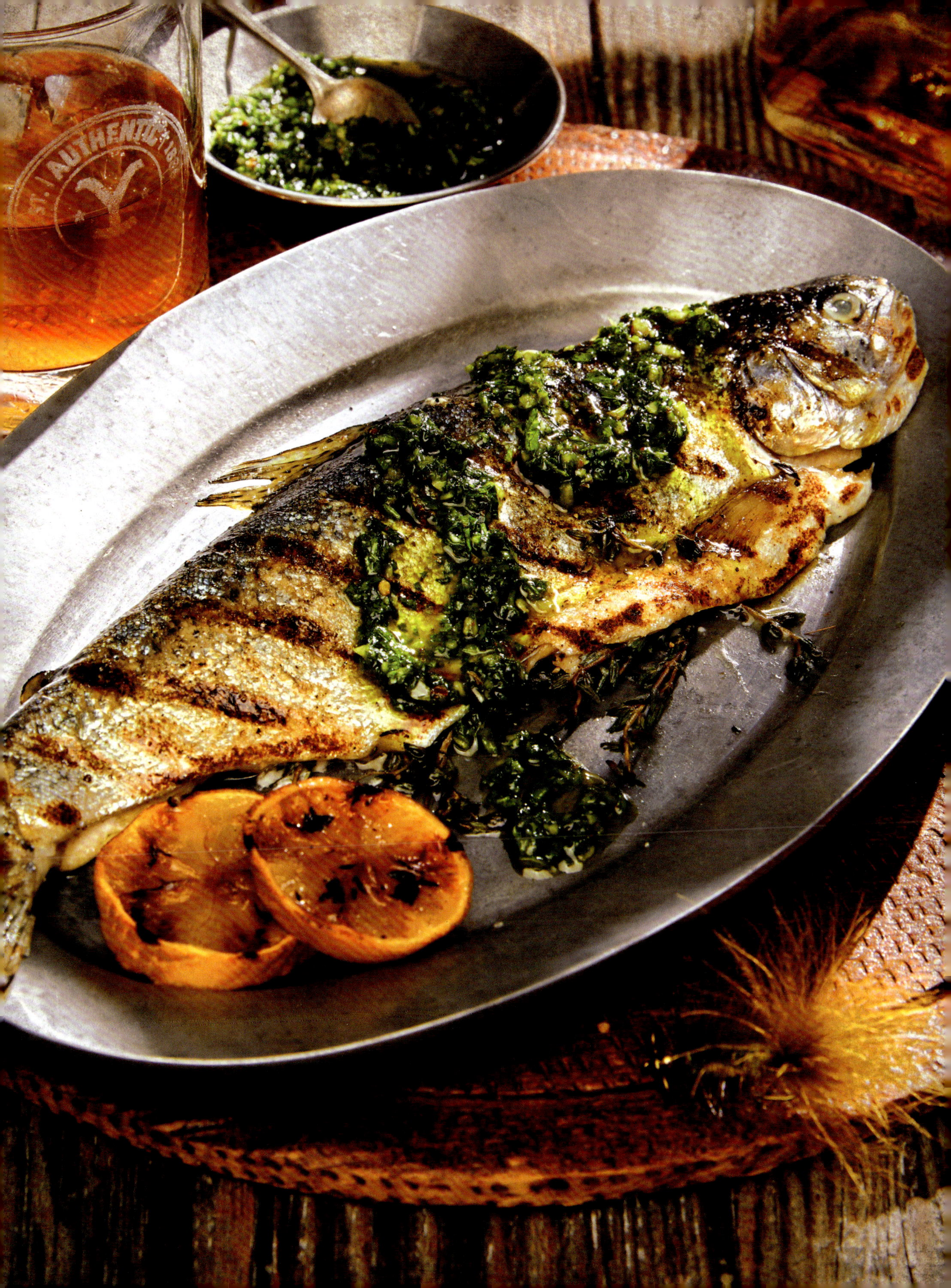

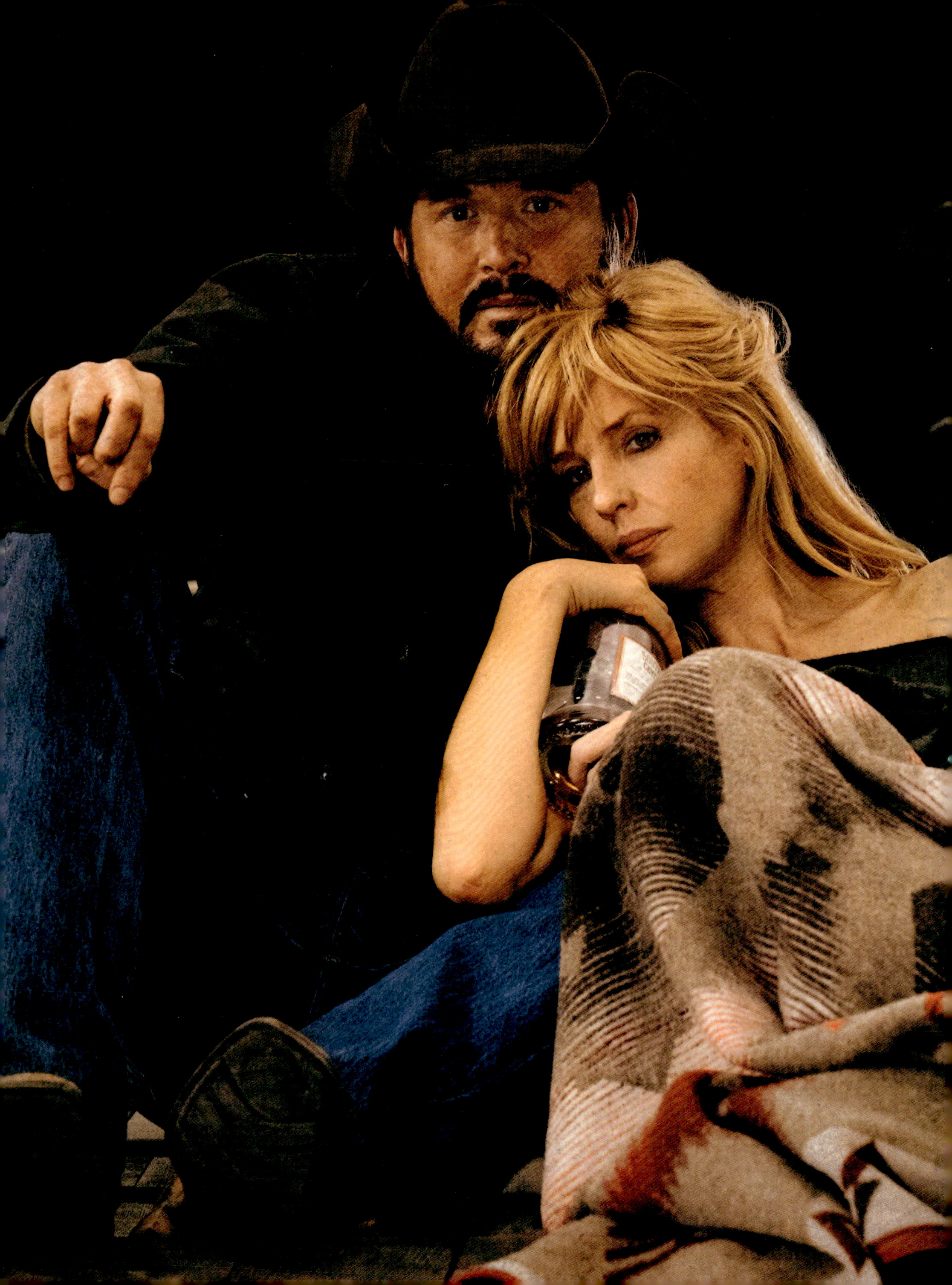

continued from page 94

For the Trout

4 small whole rainbow trout (about 12 oz / 340 g each), cleaned, or 4 large rainbow trout fillets (6–8 oz / 170–225 g each)

Olive oil for coating

Kosher salt and freshly ground black pepper

8 sprigs fresh thyme, or 1 teaspoon minced fresh thyme leaves

2 lemons, sliced into ¼-inch- (6-mm-) thick rounds

MAKES 4 SERVINGS

Grill the lemon slices over the hottest part of the fire, turning once until lightly browned, 1–2 minutes per side.

Transfer the fish to individual plates, or a serving platter, and garnish with the grilled lemon slices.

Stir the vinegar into the chimichurri and serve the fish at once with the chimichurri alongside.

YELLOWSTONE
PROTECT THE FAMILY!
Protect the land
DUTTON RANCH
MONTANA

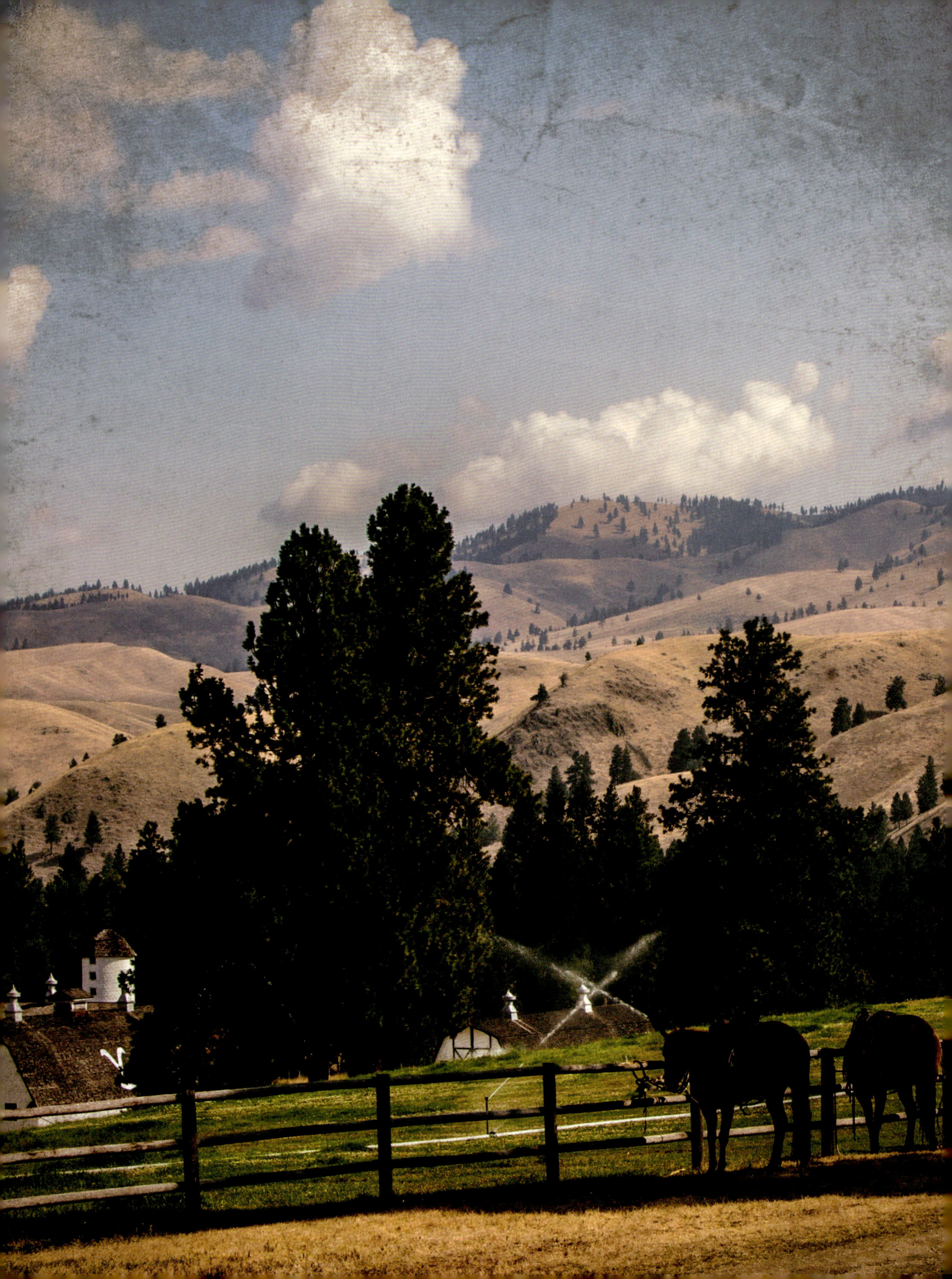

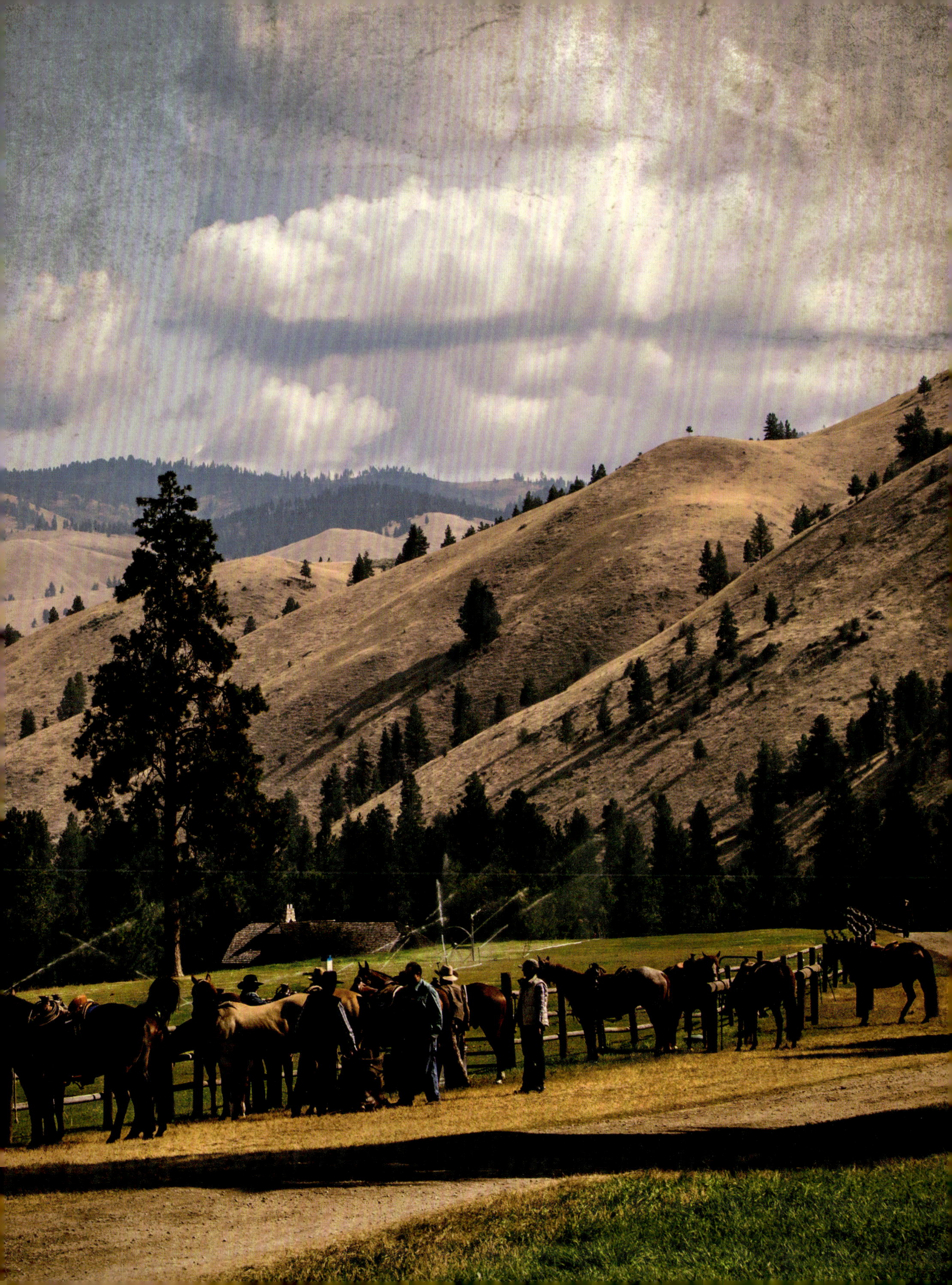

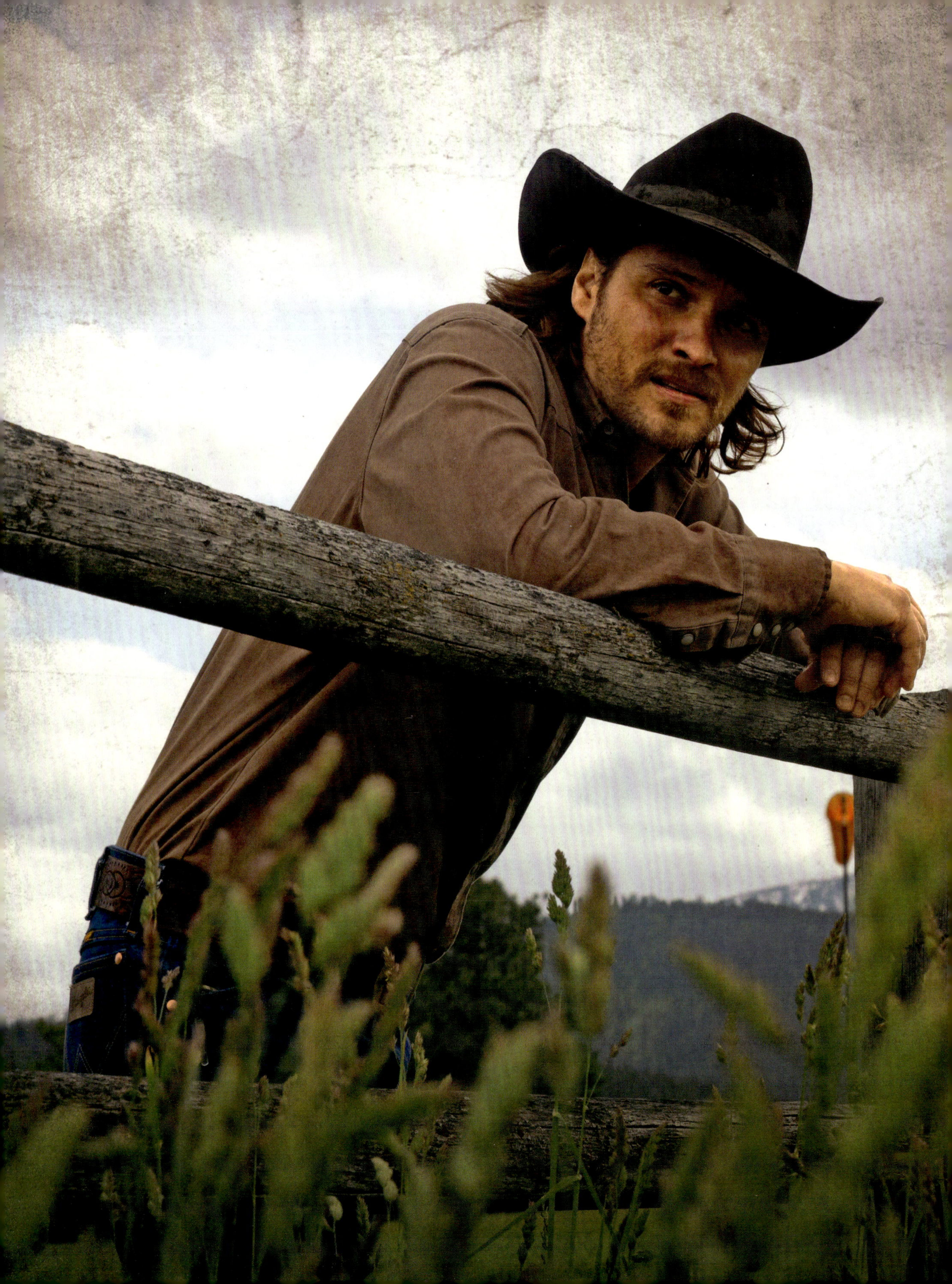

SIDE DISHES

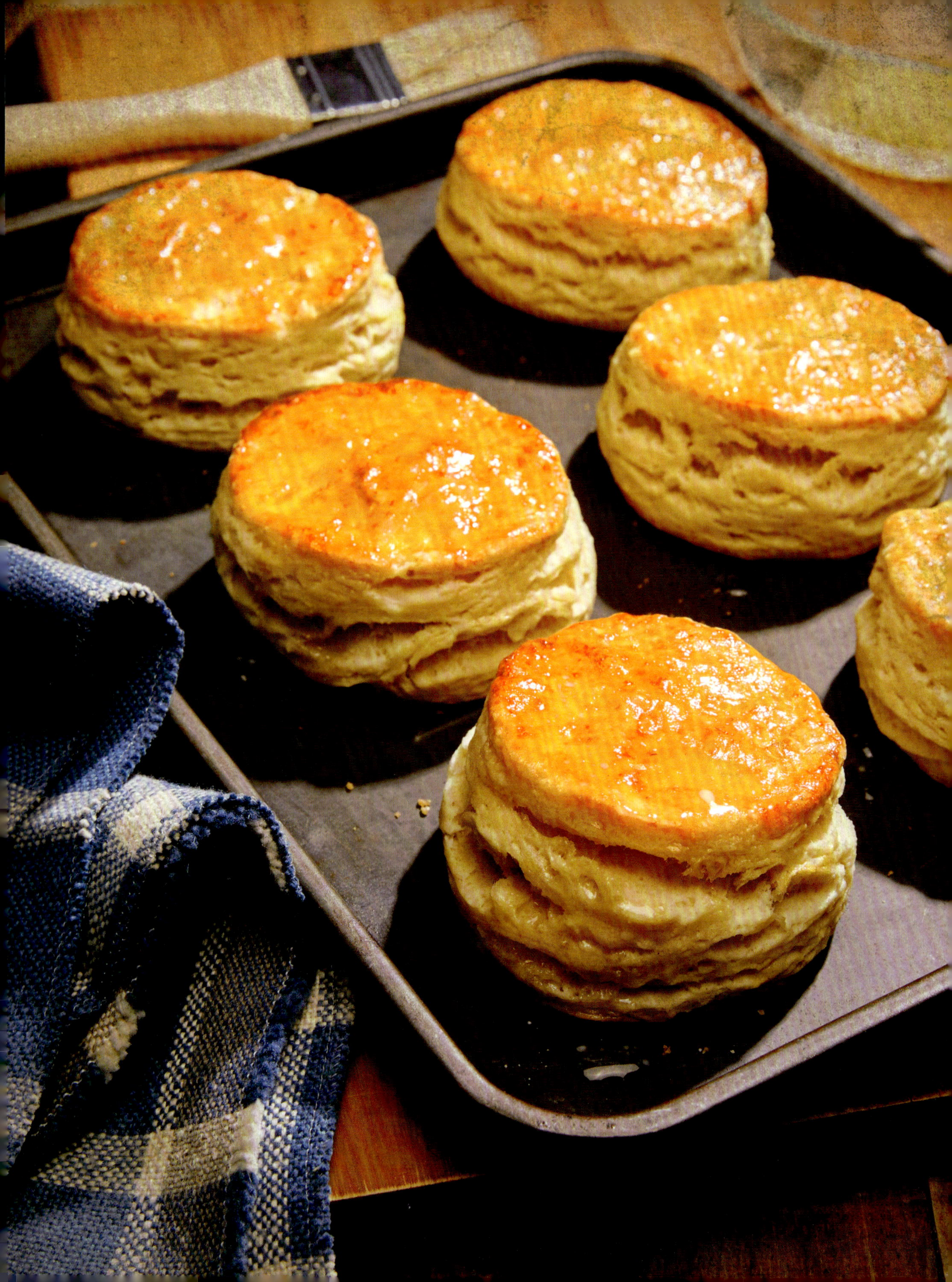

This Is How You Make a F$%ing* BISCUIT

Biscuits play a big role in the show. On one of our last days of Season 3, we shot a scene where I was in the kitchen making a hearty breakfast that included a giant tray of biscuits—and that's how these biscuits received their name. In another scene, while camping, Tate asks for three biscuits, and John tells him that he is just like his father, Kayce. "My wife used to make two Dutch ovens full of biscuits, one for your father, and one for the rest of us. He'd stand right by the fire and ask his mother 'how long?' When they were finally ready, he'd take a plate of biscuits, nothing else, and just go sit at the edge of the firelight with his back to us and he'd go at it with both hands." "They were really good," says Kayce. John asked his wife why she took so long to make them when Kayce would eat anything she put in front of him, and she replied, "Yes, but if I don't make 'em, I can't watch him eat 'em." You'll feel that same satisfaction when you watch these biscuits disappear.

INGREDIENTS

2 cups (250 g) all-purpose flour, plus flour for dusting

2 tablespoons baking powder

¼ teaspoon baking soda

1 teaspoon kosher salt

½ cup (115 g) very cold unsalted butter, diced, plus 1 tablespoon, melted

1 cup (240 ml) buttermilk

MAKES ABOUT 8 BISCUITS

INSTRUCTIONS

Preheat the oven to 450°F (230°C).

Sift the flour, baking powder, baking soda, and salt into the bowl of a food processor. Add ½ cup (115 g) of the cold diced butter and pulse just until the butter is the size of peas. Pour in the buttermilk and pulse just until the dough starts to come together.

Dust a work surface with flour and turn the dough onto it. Press the dough together, pat it out into a disk about ½ inch (12 mm) thick, and then give it about 5 folds. Press it out again into a ½-inch- (12-mm-) thick disk. Using a 3-inch (7.5-cm) round biscuit cutter or an empty tin can, cut out as many biscuits as you can. Press the scraps together gently and cut out as many more biscuits as you can. Arrange the biscuits on a baking sheet, spaced slightly apart.

Bake until golden brown, 10–13 minutes; do not overbake. Brush the biscuits with the melted butter and enjoy!

Monica's
JALAPEÑO-CHEDDAR CORNBREAD

Late in Season 2, the Dutton family—John, Kayce, Monica, and Tate—gather around the table for a big ranch meal—cornbread, bacon, eggs, fruit, toast, the works. Monica reprimands Tate for reaching for a cornbread muffin and tells him to wait until everyone sits. "If you wait for everyone to sit at this table, you'll never eat," says John. Cornbread is a cowboy staple, and on any respectable ranch you'll likely see cornbread every day—for breakfast, lunch, dinner, and snacks. I make it often for the cast and crew, and Taylor Sheridan is a big fan. I remember one day when Taylor told his kid, "When someone from the South offers you cornbread, you take the cornbread."

INGREDIENTS

- ½ cup (120 ml) vegetable oil, plus oil for greasing
- 1 cup (130 g) fine cornmeal
- 1 cup (120 g) all-purpose flour
- 2 teaspoons baking powder
- ½ teaspoon baking soda
- 1 teaspoon kosher salt
- 2 large eggs
- 1 can (15 oz / 425 g) creamed corn
- 1½ cups (350 ml) buttermilk
- 1 small yellow onion, finely chopped
- 1 can (4 oz / 115 g) diced jalapeño chiles, drained
- 1½ cups (6 oz / 175 g) grated sharp Cheddar cheese

MAKES 6–8 SERVINGS

INSTRUCTIONS

Preheat the oven to 375°F (190°C). Grease a 10-inch (25-cm) cast-iron frying pan, or baking pan, with oil; then place it in the oven to preheat.

In a small bowl, whisk together the cornmeal, flour, baking powder, baking soda, and salt until combined. In a large bowl, whisk together the eggs, creamed corn, buttermilk, ½ cup oil, onion, and jalapeños. Add the dry ingredients to the wet ingredients and stir until just combined. Stir in the Cheddar.

Spread the batter into the warm frying pan, return to the oven, and bake until golden brown and a toothpick inserted into the center comes out clean, 30–45 minutes. Let cool slightly on a wire rack, and then cut into wedges and serve warm.

Variation: For plain cornbread, omit the jalapeños and Cheddar cheese.

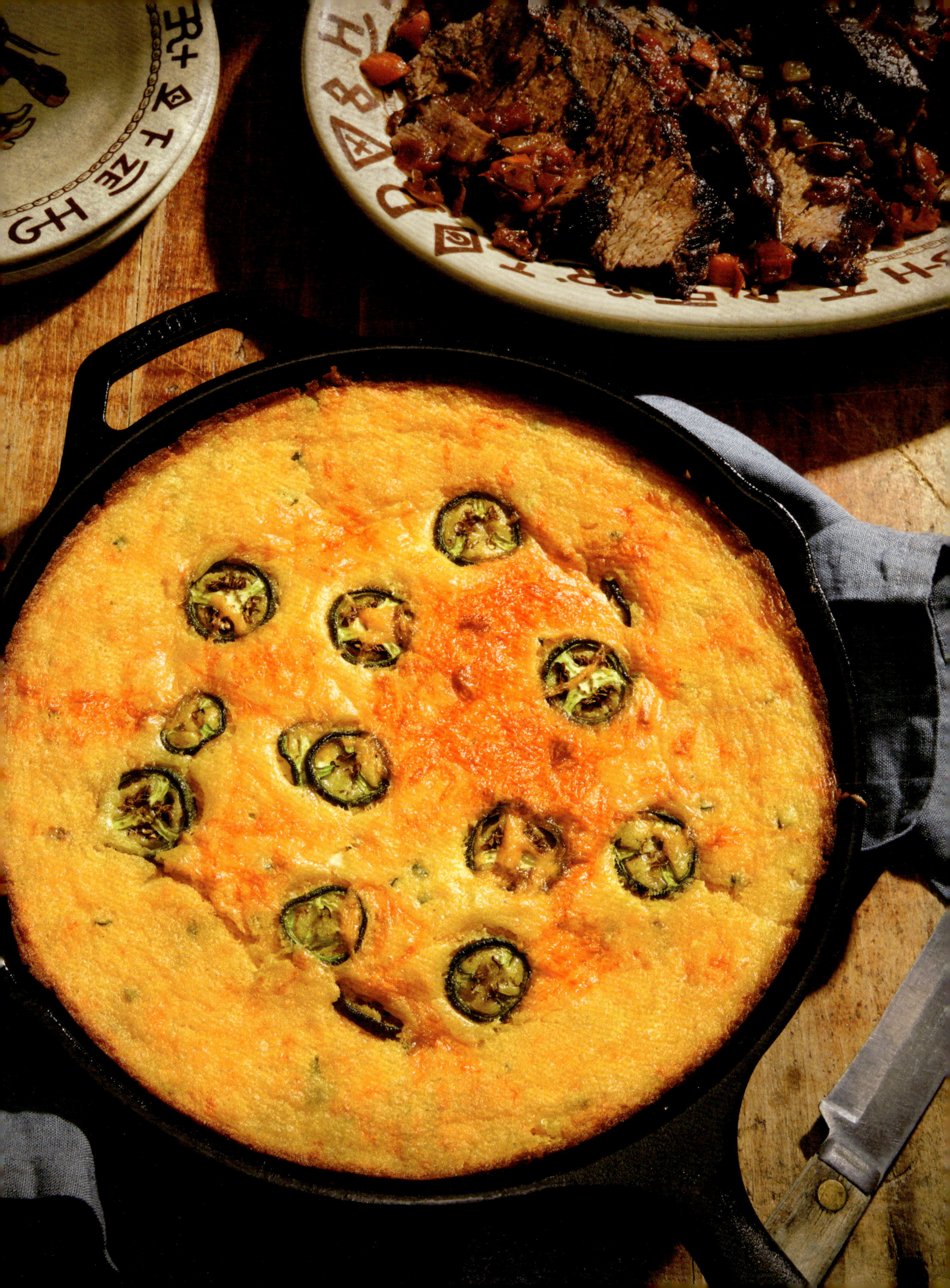

GOLDEN SQUASH CASSEROLE

This summer casserole was always on the dinner table at family dinners when I was growing up. It's a great way to cook up a lot of squash. Everyone on or around the Yellowstone Ranch—heck, all over Montana and probably the rest of the country too—grows summer squash because it's such an easy crop to grow. In fact, people are always showing up on set with bushels of squash in the summertime, and I have to find a way to use it all—I hate to waste any food. Not only is this casserole easy to make and delicious, but it's also hearty enough to eat as a main dish. And, if you leave out the bacon, it becomes a good vegetarian dish—perfect for summer!

INGREDIENTS

Kosher salt and freshly ground pepper

8 yellow crookneck squash (about 3 lb / 1.4 kg), trimmed and cut into ½-inch (13 mm) slices

4 slices thick-cut bacon

1 small yellow onion, chopped

2 large eggs, beaten

1 cup (4 ½ oz / 115 g) shredded sharp Cheddar cheese

1 tablespoon Worcestershire sauce

MAKES 4–6 SERVINGS

INSTRUCTIONS

Preheat the oven to 350°F (180°C). Grease a 1-qt (1 l) baking dish.

Fill a large saucepan half full of salted water and bring to a boil over high heat. Add the squash and boil until tender, about 5 minutes. Drain in a fine-mesh sieve, and then transfer to a large bowl. Using a fork or potato masher, mash the squash slightly. Set aside.

In a frying pan over medium heat, cook the bacon, turning, as needed, until crisp, about 6 minutes. Transfer the bacon to paper towels to drain, and then crumble once cooled.

Pour off all but 3 tablespoons of the bacon fat in the pan. Return the pan to medium heat, add the onion, and cook, stirring occasionally until tender, about 5 minutes.

Transfer the onion and crumbled bacon to the bowl with the mashed squash, along with the eggs, Cheddar, and Worcestershire sauce. Season with salt and pepper. Stir until well combined. Spoon the squash mixture into the prepared baking dish.

Bake until golden brown and bubbly, about 30 minutes. Serve at once.

CORNBREAD DRESSING

Even though cornbread dressing is usually reserved for the holidays or Thanksgiving and served with turkey, it's truly a wonderful dish and a great way to use up leftover cornbread. In my mind, there are only two uses for leftover cornbread: in this dressing, or in a dish I used to eat as a child called "coush coush," which is an old Cajun breakfast cereal recipe. My family would make it with cold, leftover cornbread crumbled into a bowl and then top it with some milk and a slice of sharp Cheddar cheese. I remember so many mornings eating it for breakfast with my grandfather.

INGREDIENTS

- 4 tablespoons (60 g) unsalted butter, plus butter for greasing
- 1 cup (140 g) finely chopped celery
- ½ cup (70 g) finely chopped white onion
- ½ cup (45 g) chopped scallions, white and green parts
- 1 recipe plain cornbread (see Monica's Jalapeño-Cheddar Cornbread variation, page 104) or store-bought (10-inch / 25-cm pan) plain cornbread, cut into largish cubes
- ¼ cup (15 g) minced fresh flat-leaf parsley
- 1½ cups (350 ml) chicken stock, preferably homemade
- Kosher salt and freshly ground black pepper

MAKES 6–8 SERVINGS

INSTRUCTIONS

Preheat the oven to 350°F (180°C). Grease a 9 x 13 inch (23 x 33 cm) baking dish generously with butter.

In a large frying pan over medium heat, melt the butter. Add the celery, onion, and scallions and cook, stirring until softened, about 5 minutes. Transfer to a large bowl.

Add the cornbread to the bowl with the vegetables, along with the parsley, and stir gently; then pour in the stock and stir gently again until evenly moistened. Transfer to the prepared baking dish and cover with aluminum foil.

Bake for 30 minutes; then remove the foil and continue to bake until nicely browned and heated through, about 20 minutes longer. Serve at once.

GATOR'S TIP

If you like, top the cornbread dressing with crumbled hard-boiled eggs—it's optional, but traditional in the South.

Yeasted Bunkhouse BEER ROLLS

Nearly anytime you see anyone at the Dutton Ranch gathered around the table for a meal, you can be assured there will be a basket of fluffy dinner rolls. I made these a little more *Yellowstone* by adding beer to them, since beer seems to flow through the Bunkhouse like the river that runs through the ranch. Don't be put off because of the yeast; the rolls are simple to make and are great with just about everything, particularly the Bunkhouse Beer-Braised Beef Stew with Root Vegetables (page 49).

INGREDIENTS

- 7 tablespoons (105 g) unsalted butter
- 1 tablespoon honey
- 1 cup (240 ml) lager-style amber beer
- 1 package (2¼ teaspoons) instant dry yeast
- 3 cups (365 g) all-purpose flour, plus flour for dusting
- 1 large egg, lightly beaten
- 1½ teaspoons kosher salt
- Salted butter for serving

MAKES 14 ROLLS

INSTRUCTIONS

In a saucepan over low heat, melt 6 tablespoons (90 g) of the butter with the honey. Pour in the beer and stir to combine. Check the temperature with an instant-read thermometer. It should be 100°–115°F (38°–46°C). If the temperature is too high, set aside to cool slightly; if too low, warm gently over low heat.

Pour the beer mixture into the bowl of a stand mixer, or a large bowl, add the yeast, and stir until it dissolves. Let stand for 5 minutes; then add the flour, egg, and salt.

Attach the dough hook to the mixer and knead the dough on medium speed for about 5 minutes, or for 10 minutes by hand. The dough will be soft and sticky. Form the dough into a ball in the bowl, cover the bowl with plastic wrap, and let rise in a warm, draft-free spot until doubled in size, about 1 hour.

Line a baking sheet with parchment paper.

Dust a work surface with flour and place the dough onto it. Divide the dough into 14 equal pieces, each about 2 ounces (60 g) each. (A scale is handy for this!) Roll each piece into a ball and place all the balls on the prepared baking sheet, spacing them just next to each other but not touching. Cover the dough balls loosely with plastic wrap and let stand until puffy, about 1 hour.

Preheat the oven to 375°F (190°C).

Bake the rolls until they are golden, about 18 minutes. Melt the remaining 1 tablespoon butter; then brush the rolls with melted butter as soon as they come out of the oven.

Serve warm with salted butter.

BUNKHOUSE - OR - BUST

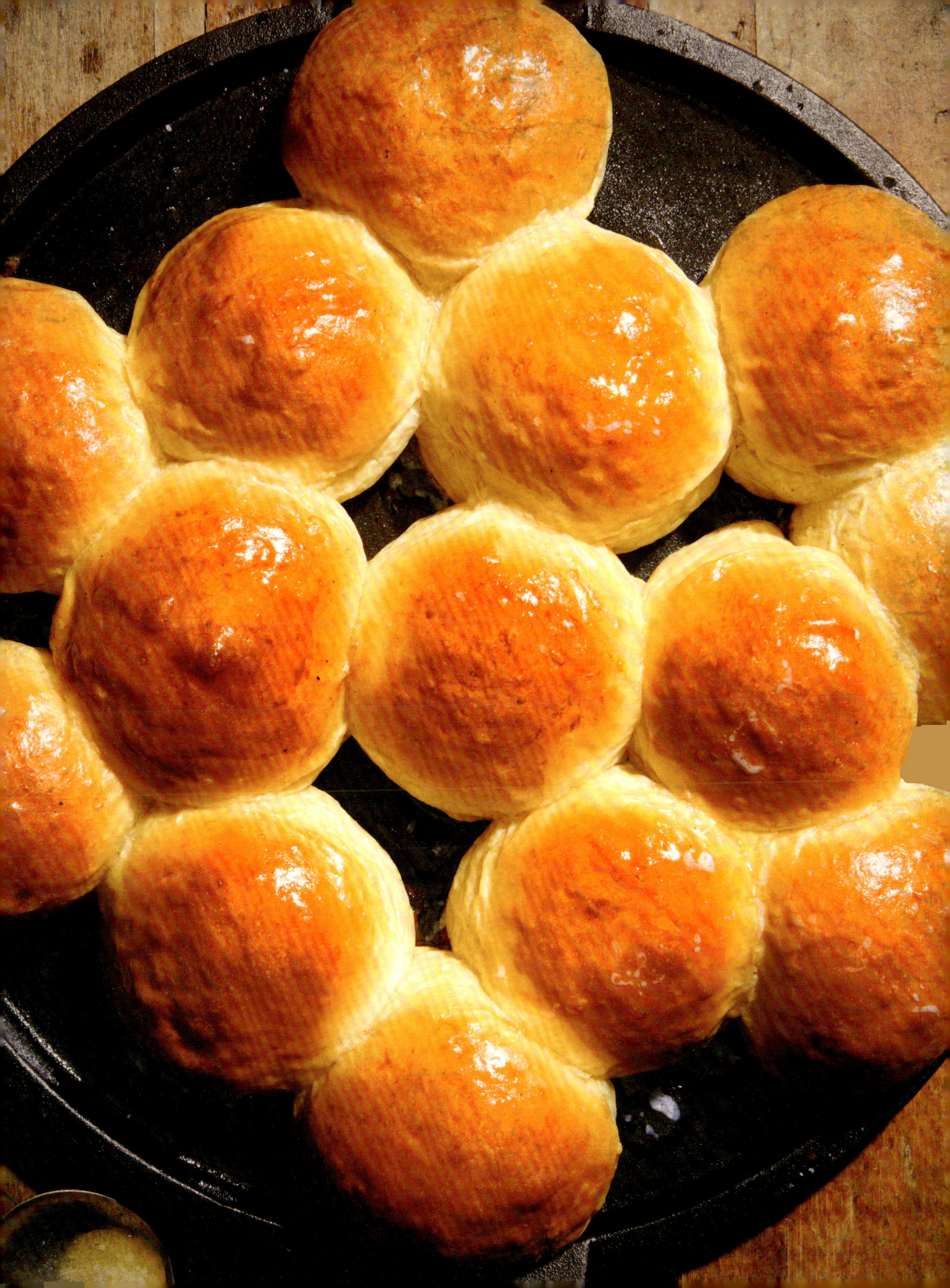

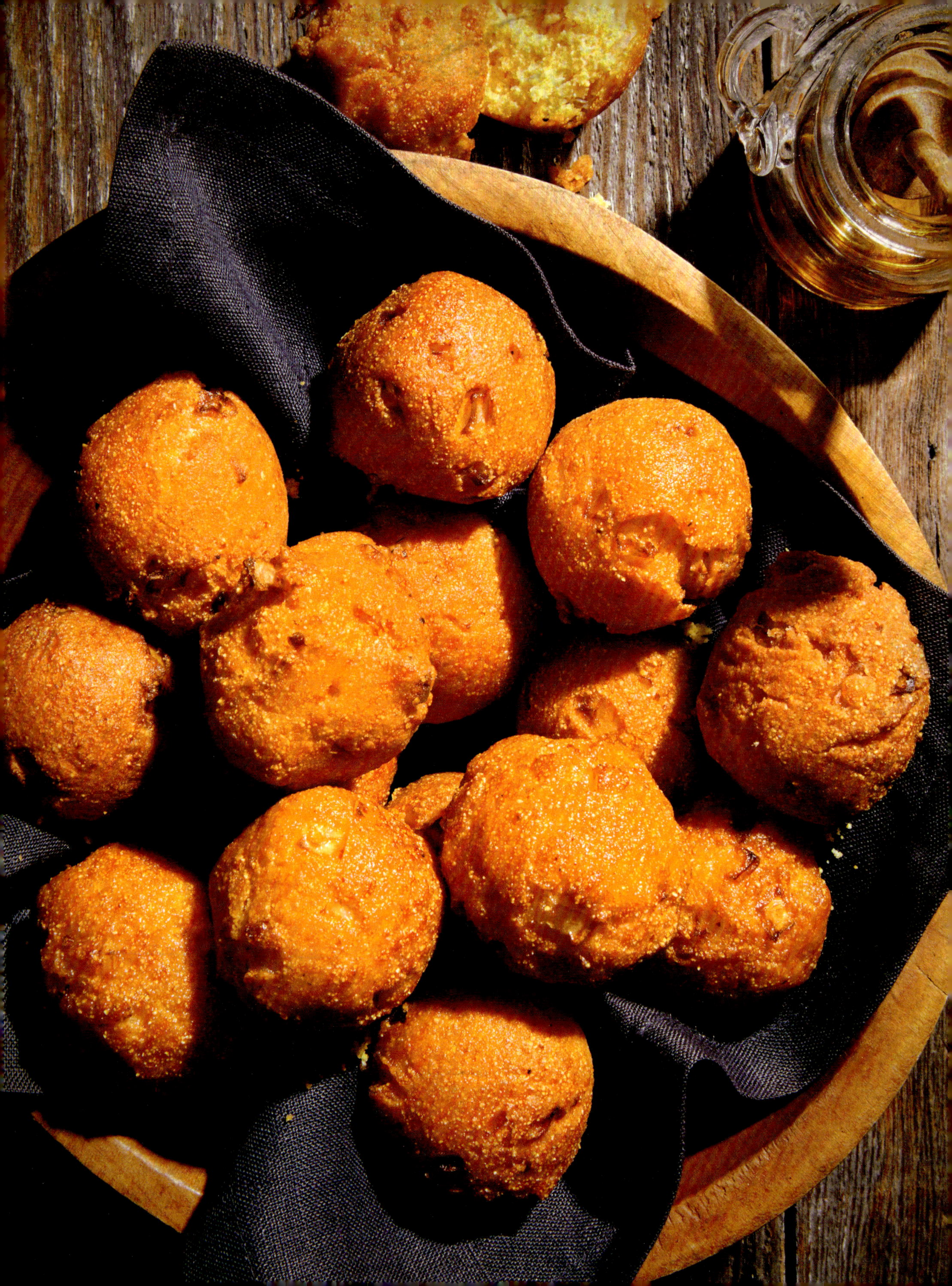

HUSH PUPPIES

Hush puppies are a real Southern treat, and pretty much anytime you eat fried seafood in the South, you can be sure it will be served with hush puppies. If you've never had them, hush puppies are like deep-fried, golden-brown nuggets of cornbread. They are unbelievably delicious when you make them right, and this recipe is pretty straightforward. The only word of caution is that they can become like lead weights or overly greasy if not made properly—so make sure not to overmix the batter and fry them at the correct temperature. Serve these hush puppies with my Gator's Louisiana Fried Shrimp (page 23). Remoulade, tartar sauce, and even just ketchup are all great sauces for dipping. Keep the hush puppies warm in a low oven (200°F/95°C) while you fry the remaining hush puppies in batches.

INGREDIENTS

1½ cups (195 g) fine cornmeal

½ cup (60 g) all-purpose flour

2 tablespoons sugar

2 teaspoons baking powder

1 teaspoon kosher salt

½ teaspoon freshly ground black pepper

1 large egg

⅔ cup (160 ml) whole milk

½ cup (70 g) finely chopped yellow onion (½ small onion)

Canola or peanut oil for frying

Remoulade, tartar sauce, or your favorite dipping sauce

MAKES ABOUT 2 DOZEN HUSH PUPPIES

INSTRUCTIONS

In a bowl, whisk together the cornmeal, flour, sugar, baking powder, salt, and pepper until blended. In another bowl, whisk together the egg, milk, and onion. Add the wet ingredients to the dry ingredients and stir until just combined; do not overmix. The batter will be thick.

Fill a wide saucepan or pot with 2 inches (5 cm) of the oil, but no more than halfway full, and heat over medium-high heat until the oil reaches 365°F (185°C) on a deep-frying thermometer. Adjust the heat, as needed, to maintain the temperature.

Place a wire rack next to the stovetop and line it with paper towels.

Working in batches to avoid overcrowding the pan, scoop about 1½ tablespoons of the batter (a small cookie scoop works well for this) and carefully add it to the hot oil, adding 5–6 hush puppies per batch. Fry the hush puppies, turning once or twice with tongs until deep golden brown and cooked through, about 4 minutes. Using tongs or a slotted spoon, transfer to the paper towel–lined rack to drain. Repeat to fry all the hush puppies, letting the oil come back to temperature between batches.

Serve at once, with the dipping sauce alongside.

COWBOY UP

Ranch Hand
BAKED BEANS

After a hard day's work running cattle on the ranch, there's honestly nothing better than sitting down to a big barbecued meal. Whenever I fire up the smoker, the entire cast and crew get excited. They know that if I'm gonna make barbecue, I'm gonna fill up that smoker with all kinds of good things: pulled pork, ribs, brisket, and maybe even smoked turkey. Baked beans—and Monica's Jalapeño-Cheddar Cornbread (see page 104)—are a mainstay and required eating with any form of barbecue. As far as I'm concerned, if you don't serve baked beans with your barbecue, you didn't have a barbecue. The only place beans don't belong is in your chili (just ask any of the cowboys)!

INGREDIENTS

½ lb (225 g) thick-cut bacon slices, chopped

1 large yellow onion, finely chopped

3 cloves garlic, minced

1 lb (450 g) dried pinto beans, picked over, soaked overnight in water to cover, and drained

2 cups (475 ml) chicken stock, preferably homemade

2 cups (475 ml) water

1 cup (240 ml) favorite barbecue sauce

½ cup (120 ml) ketchup

¼ cup (60 g) firmly packed light brown sugar

¼ cup (60 ml) dark molasses (not blackstrap)

2 tablespoons apple cider vinegar

2 tablespoons country-style Dijon mustard

1 tablespoon chili powder

Kosher salt and freshly ground black pepper

MAKES 6–8 SERVINGS

INSTRUCTIONS

In a large Dutch oven or heavy pot over medium heat, cook the bacon, stirring occasionally until crispy, 6–8 minutes. Using a slotted spoon, transfer the bacon to paper towels to drain. Pour off all but 2–3 tablespoons of the bacon fat in the pot.

Add the onion to the pot and cook, stirring until softened, 5–7 minutes. Add the garlic and cook, stirring until fragrant, about 1 minute. Add the beans and pour in the stock and water. Raise the heat to high and bring to a boil. Reduce the heat to low, cover the pot, and simmer, stirring every so often until the beans are tender but not falling apart, 45 minutes–1 hour (depending on the age of the beans). Drain the beans and return them to the pot.

Preheat the oven to 350°F (180°C).

Stir the barbecue sauce, ketchup, brown sugar, molasses, vinegar, mustard, chili powder, 1 teaspoon salt, and ½ teaspoon pepper into the beans. Transfer the pot to the oven, and bake, stirring occasionally until the mixture is deep dark brown and thickened, about 1 hour. Taste and adjust the seasoning with salt and pepper.

Serve at once.

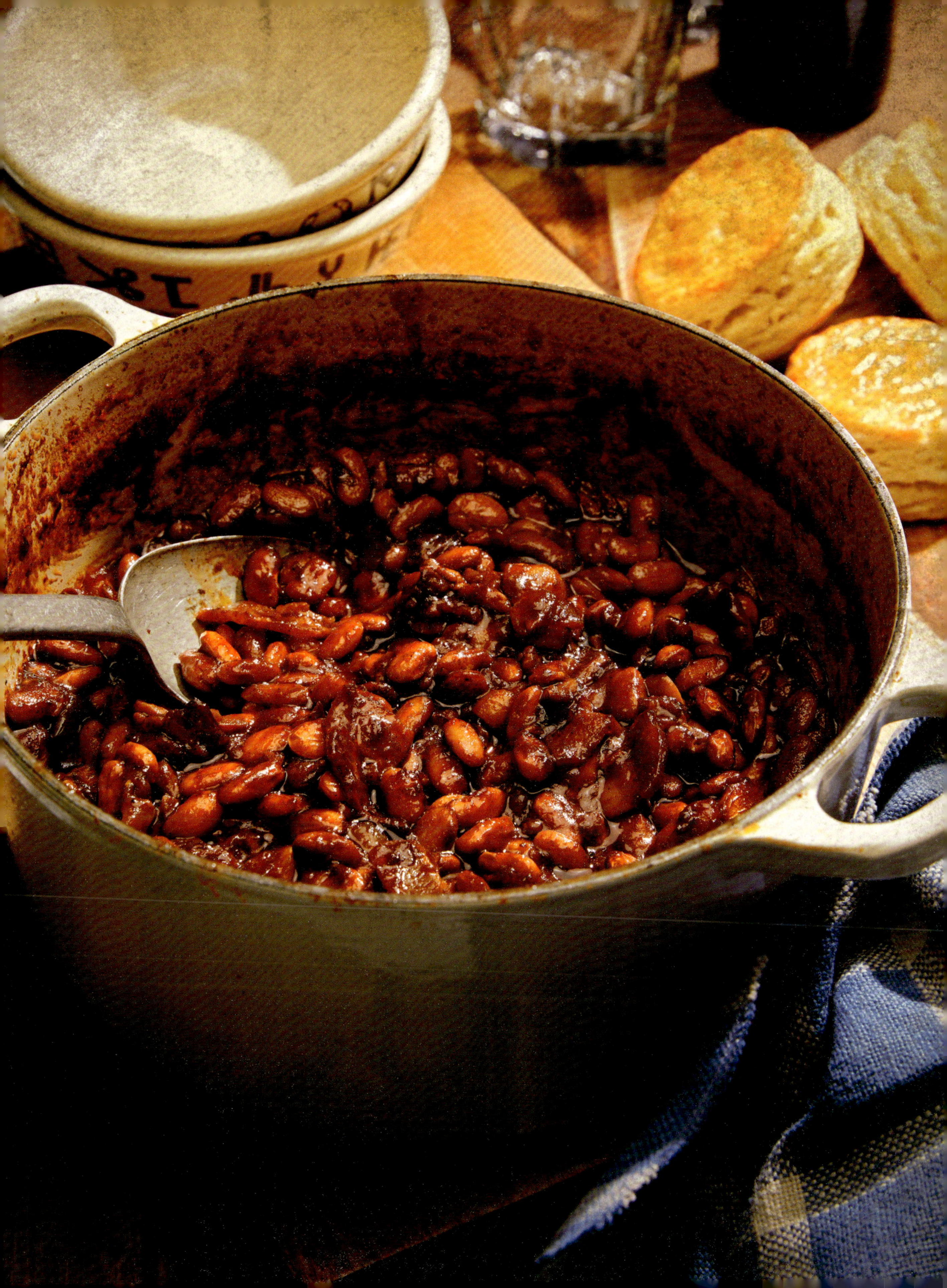

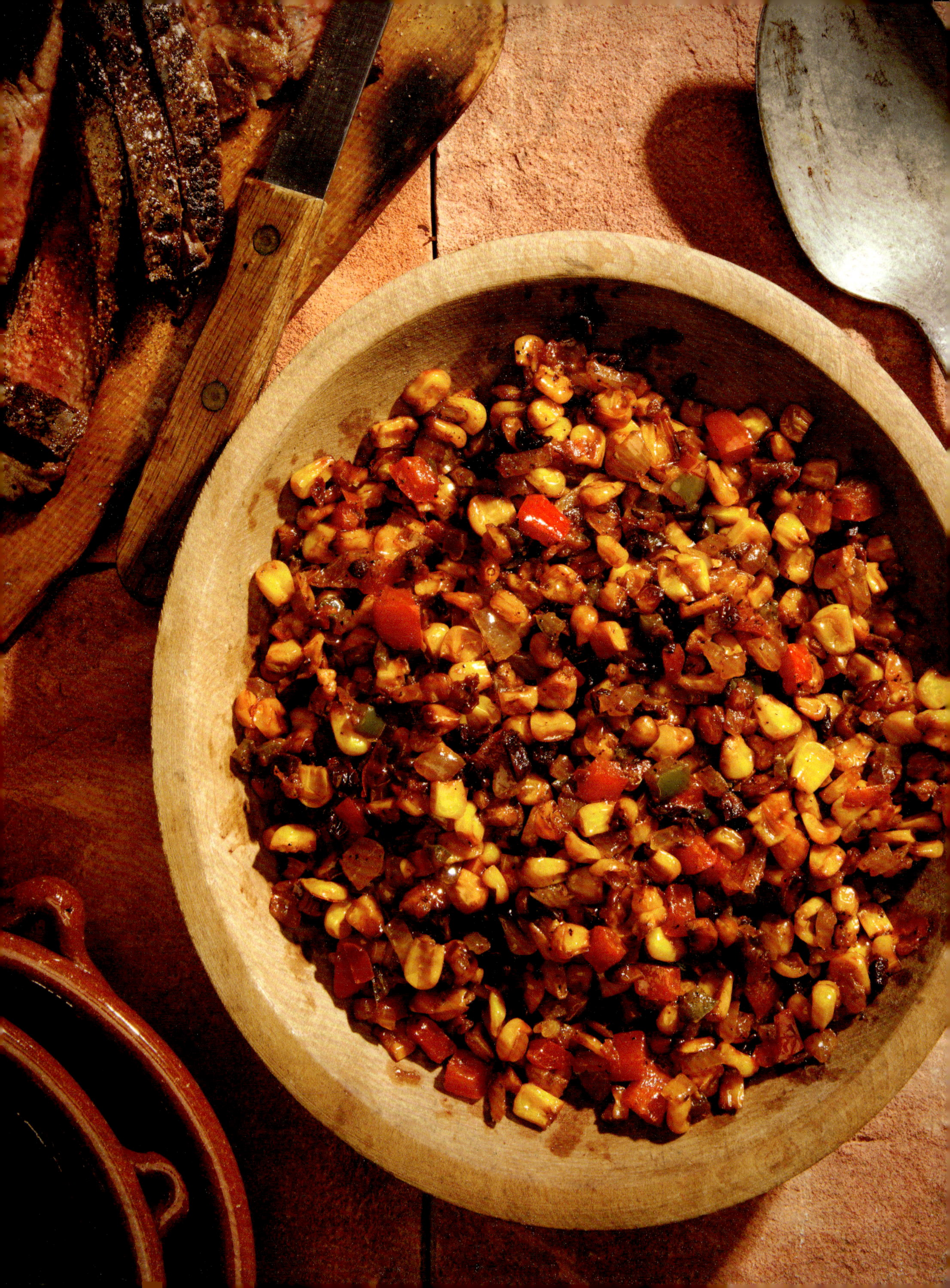

CORN MAQUE CHOUX

Corn maque choux—pronounced "mawk shoo"—is a very old Cajun recipe that is most often served as a side dish. It's essentially a mixture of corn, peppers, tomatoes, and plenty of Cajun seasoning. If you love fresh corn like I do, it's a spectacular dish, and vegetarian friendly. The most important thing about making this recipe is to use fresh corn, ideally at its summer peak; otherwise, it simply won't be as tasty. I make a ton of corn maque choux during peak corn season. One of the crew members absolutely loves this dish, so I always make sure he gets a hearty serving before anyone else on set.

INGREDIENTS

6 ears fresh corn, shucked

¼ cup (60 ml) vegetable oil

1 white onion, finely chopped

1 red bell pepper, stemmed, seeded, and diced

1 or 2 jalapeño chiles, seeded and finely chopped, or to taste

½ cup (100 g) diced seeded ripe tomato

2 tablespoons finely chopped sun-dried tomato

Kosher salt and freshly ground black pepper

3 tablespoons unsalted butter

1 teaspoon Cajun seasoning, plus seasoning as needed

MAKES ABOUT 6 SERVINGS

INSTRUCTIONS

Cut the corn kernels off the cob into a large bowl. Using the back of the knife, scrape the corncobs over the bowl to collect the remaining flesh and milk of the corn.

In a large Dutch oven over medium-high heat, warm the oil. Add the corn and cook, stirring often with a wooden spoon until it browns and gets a bit of color, 15–20 minutes. Add the onion, bell pepper, jalapeño, fresh tomato, sun-dried tomato, ½ teaspoon salt, and 1½ teaspoons pepper. Reduce the heat to medium and cook, stirring often until the vegetables are tender-crisp, about 10 minutes.

Add the butter and Cajun seasoning to the corn and stir until the butter melts and the mixture is well combined. Taste and adjust the seasoning with more salt, pepper, and Cajun seasoning.

Serve at once.

RODEO COWBOY CAVIAR

In Season 2, Jimmy finds out he might not be the most capable ranch hand, but he does have a real penchant for bronc riding in the rodeo. This bean and vegetable salsa "salad" is world-class, and a delicious snack for any cowboy—rodeo star or not. It can be eaten straight from the bowl with a bunch of tortilla chips, or used to top a steak or pulled pork tacos.

INGREDIENTS

For the Vinaigrette

- ⅓ cup (80 ml) olive oil
- ¼ cup (60 ml) red wine vinegar
- 2 cloves garlic, minced
- 1 teaspoon sugar
- Kosher salt and freshly ground black pepper

For the "Caviar"

- 1 can (15 oz / 425 g) black-eyed peas, drained and rinsed
- 1 can (15 oz / 425 g) black beans, drained and rinsed
- 1 cup (170 g) fresh corn kernels (from 2 ears) or frozen, thawed
- 2 large plum tomatoes, cored, seeded, and diced
- ½ small red onion, finely chopped
- 1 red bell pepper, seeded and finely chopped
- 1 jalapeño chile, seeded and finely chopped
- ½ cup (30 g) chopped fresh cilantro, plus cilantro for garnish
- 2 scallions, sliced, white and green parts
- Kosher salt and freshly ground black pepper
- Tortilla chips for serving

MAKES 6–8 SERVINGS

INSTRUCTIONS

To prepare the vinaigrette, in a jar with a tight-fitting lid combine the oil, vinegar, garlic, sugar, ½ teaspoon salt, and ½ teaspoon pepper. Cover and shake vigorously until emulsified.

To prepare the "caviar," in a large bowl toss together the black-eyed peas, black beans, corn, tomatoes, red onion, bell pepper, and jalapeño. Cover and refrigerate for at least 2 hours, or up to overnight.

When ready to serve, add the cilantro and scallions and toss with the vinaigrette to combine. Taste and season with salt and pepper.

Serve with tortilla chips for scooping.

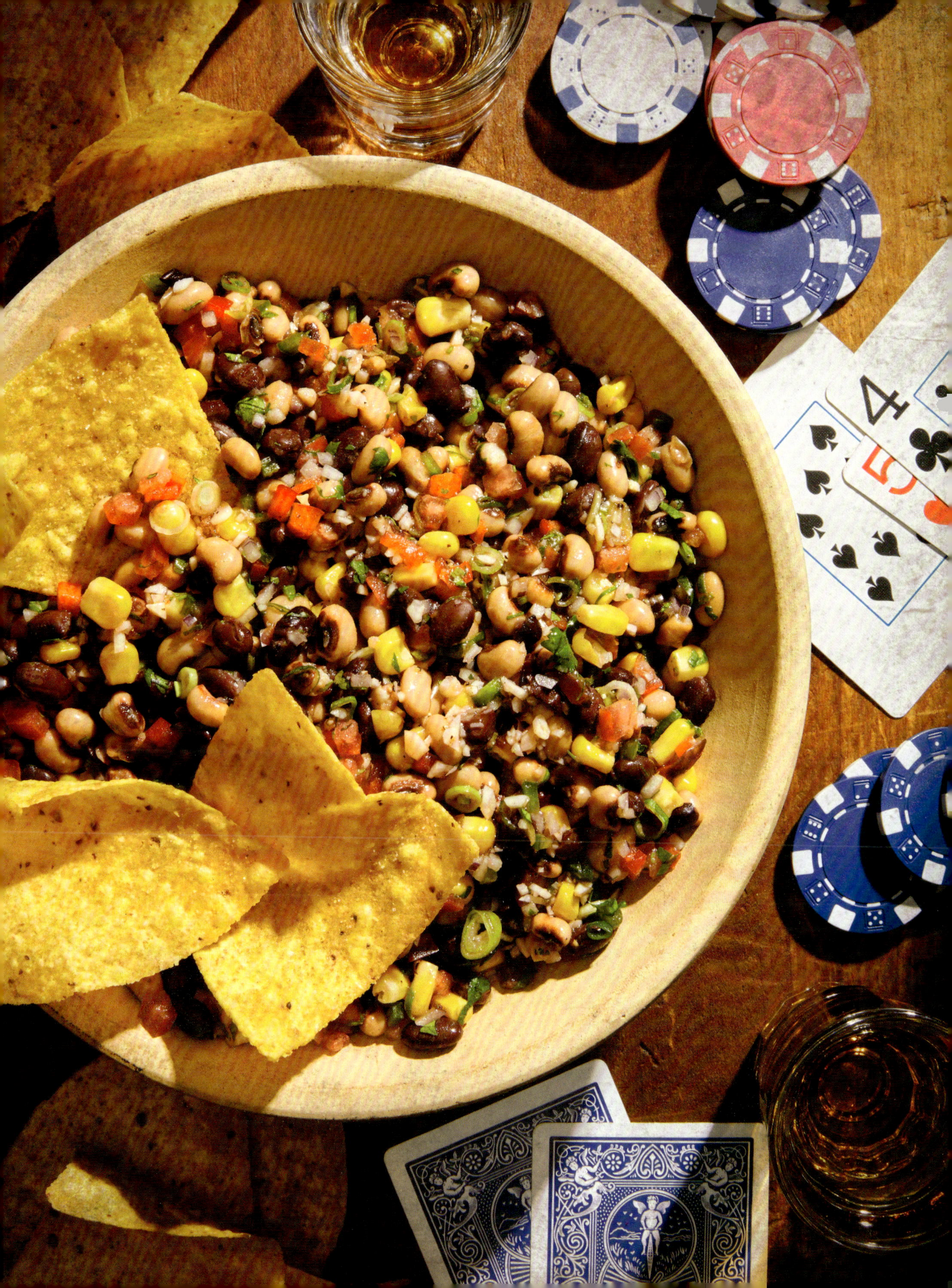

PICKLED ONIONS

When John walks into Ruby's Café, it's clear he's well-known among the cowboys filling it. The waitress walks up with a smile to ask, " Doc letting you eat steak again?" "I got a clean bill of health, Maggie. I can eat whatever the hell I want," answers John. "You still like it rare?" she asks. "Just pull it out of the cooler, whisper of fire, and put it on the plate," he responds. However you like John's Perfect Rib Eye Steak (page 46) cooked, it will always be enhanced by serving these lightly pickled onions alongside. They're a simple, quick embellishment that seems plain but really elevates grilled or smoked dishes, like Smoked Pulled Pork (page 67).

INGREDIENTS

2 sweet white or red onions

Boiling water for soaking

1 cup (240 ml) water

½ cup (100 g) sugar

¼ cup (60 ml) distilled white vinegar

1 teaspoon celery salt

MAKES ABOUT 2 CUPS (250 G)

INSTRUCTIONS

Peel the onions, and then slice crosswise into ⅛–¼-inch- (3–6-cm-) thick rings. Transfer to a large bowl. Pour enough boiling water over the onions to cover them. Let stand for 5 minutes, and then drain in a fine-mesh sieve. Transfer the soaked onions back to the bowl.

In a saucepan over medium-high heat, combine the water, sugar, vinegar, and celery salt. Simmer, stirring, just until the sugar dissolves. Pour the brine over the onions and let cool. Cover and refrigerate for at least 3 hours before serving. The onions can be stored in an airtight container in the refrigerator for up to 2 weeks.

CRUNCHY COLESLAW

Anytime I barbecue or grill for the cast and crew I *always* serve this dish on the side. The secret is crumbling up ramen noodles and mixing them with the shredded cabbage—hence, the name—and then using the seasoning packets to make a vinaigrette. My mom gets 100 percent credit for this dish, though, as it was the only way my siblings and I would eat cabbage. And while growing up, we ate it with every meal outdoors. I cannot think of anything that reminds me more of summer than crunchy coleslaw. It's a perfect side dish—as long as you don't burn the almonds.

INGREDIENTS

½ cup (60 g) slivered almonds

2 teaspoons white sesame seeds

½ cup (120 ml) unseasoned rice vinegar

2 packages (3 oz / 90 g each) chicken-flavored instant ramen

2 tablespoons sugar

¼ cup (60 ml) vegetable oil

4 scallions, finely chopped, white and green parts

½ teaspoon freshly ground black pepper

½ head green cabbage, cored and finely shredded

MAKES ABOUT 6 SERVINGS

INSTRUCTIONS

In a frying pan over medium heat, toast the almonds, stirring occasionally until the edges of the almonds are nearly burnt, about 5 minutes. Add the sesame seeds and cook, stirring until slightly toasted, 30–60 seconds. Set aside to cool.

In a jar with a tight-fitting lid, combine the vinegar, ramen seasoning packets, and sugar. Cover and shake until the sugar dissolves. Add the oil, scallions, and pepper. Re-cover and shake vigorously until the dressing is emulsified. Set aside.

Place the cabbage in a large bowl. Crush the ramen noodles into the bowl. Add the toasted almonds and sesame seeds. Pour in the dressing and toss to mix well. Refrigerate for at least 15 minutes before serving.

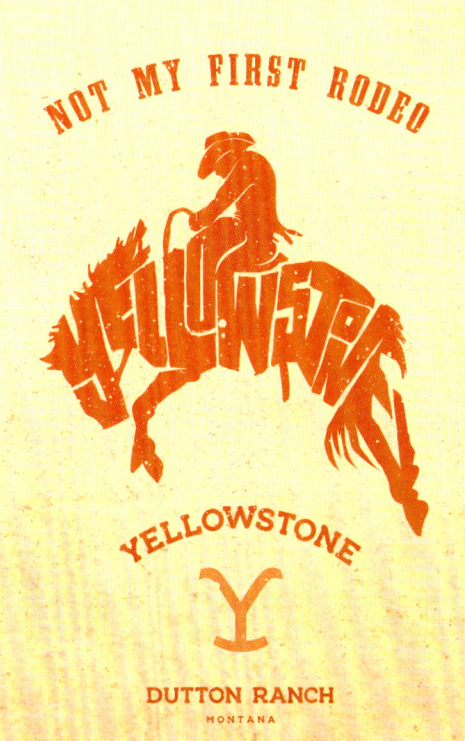

Tator's Mustard POTATO SALAD

This potato salad has a huge kick of mustard—and I mean *a lot* of it. But it is, hands down, the most delicious potato salad—and unlike any other version out there. My dad gets all the credit for this recipe. He always taught me that it's important to take your time and not rush when making anything. I make 200 pounds (90 kg) of this recipe regularly, and it can take up to 6 hours! (Don't worry, this won't take you that long to make.) Like a lot of my side dishes, I serve this one to the cast and crew often, since it goes with just about everything. In my opinion, potato salad is one of the best and most important side dishes on any table.

INGREDIENTS

2½ lb (1.1 kg) small red or Yukon gold potatoes, unpeeled, cut into 1-inch (2.5-cm) chunks

Kosher salt

6 hard-boiled eggs, peeled and halved

¾ cup (175 ml) yellow mustard, preferably French's

⅓ cup (80 ml) mayonnaise

1½ teaspoons sugar

1 teaspoon freshly ground black pepper

1 teaspoon Cajun seasoning, plus seasoning for garnish

Chopped fresh chives for garnish

MAKES 6 SERVINGS

INSTRUCTIONS

Fill a large pot half full of water and add the potatoes and 2 tablespoons salt. Bring to a boil over high heat; then reduce the heat to medium-low and boil gently, stirring occasionally until the potatoes are tender but not falling apart, 15–20 minutes. Drain well in a fine-mesh sieve, and then transfer to a large bowl and let cool.

Separate the egg yolks from the egg whites. Transfer the egg whites to a cutting board, roughly chop them, and add to the potatoes.

Put the egg yolks into a small bowl and crush them with the back of a fork or with your hands. Add the mustard, mayonnaise, sugar, pepper, and Cajun seasonings to the egg yolks and mix with a fork to combine well. The mixture should have a very strong flavor, as it will season the whole dish. Add the egg yolk mixture to the bowl of potatoes and egg whites and stir well to combine, breaking up the potatoes as you go, but leaving some a bit chunky.

Refrigerate for at least 1 hour or up to overnight before serving. Sprinkle the potato salad with a bit of Cajun seasoning to serve.

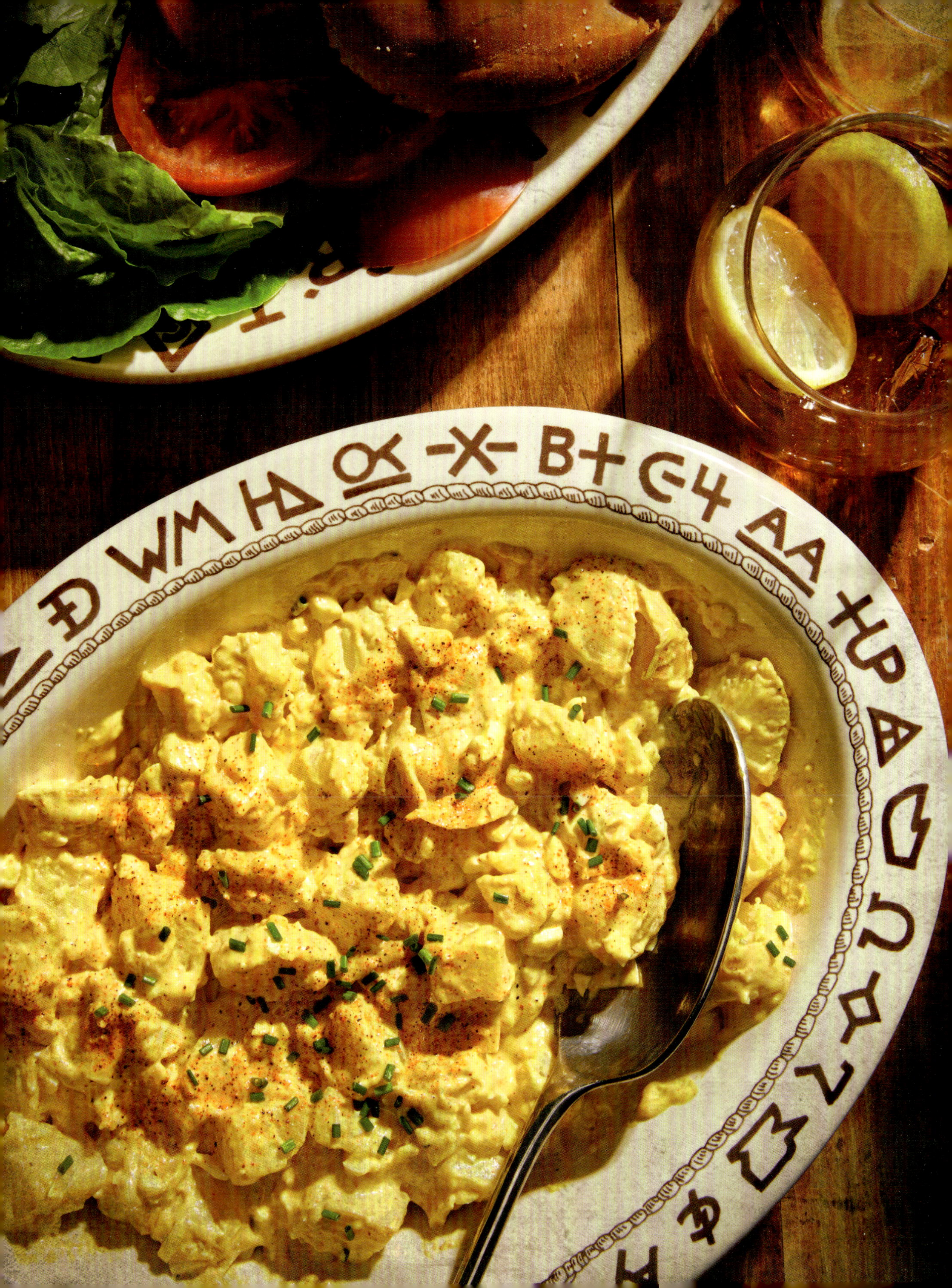

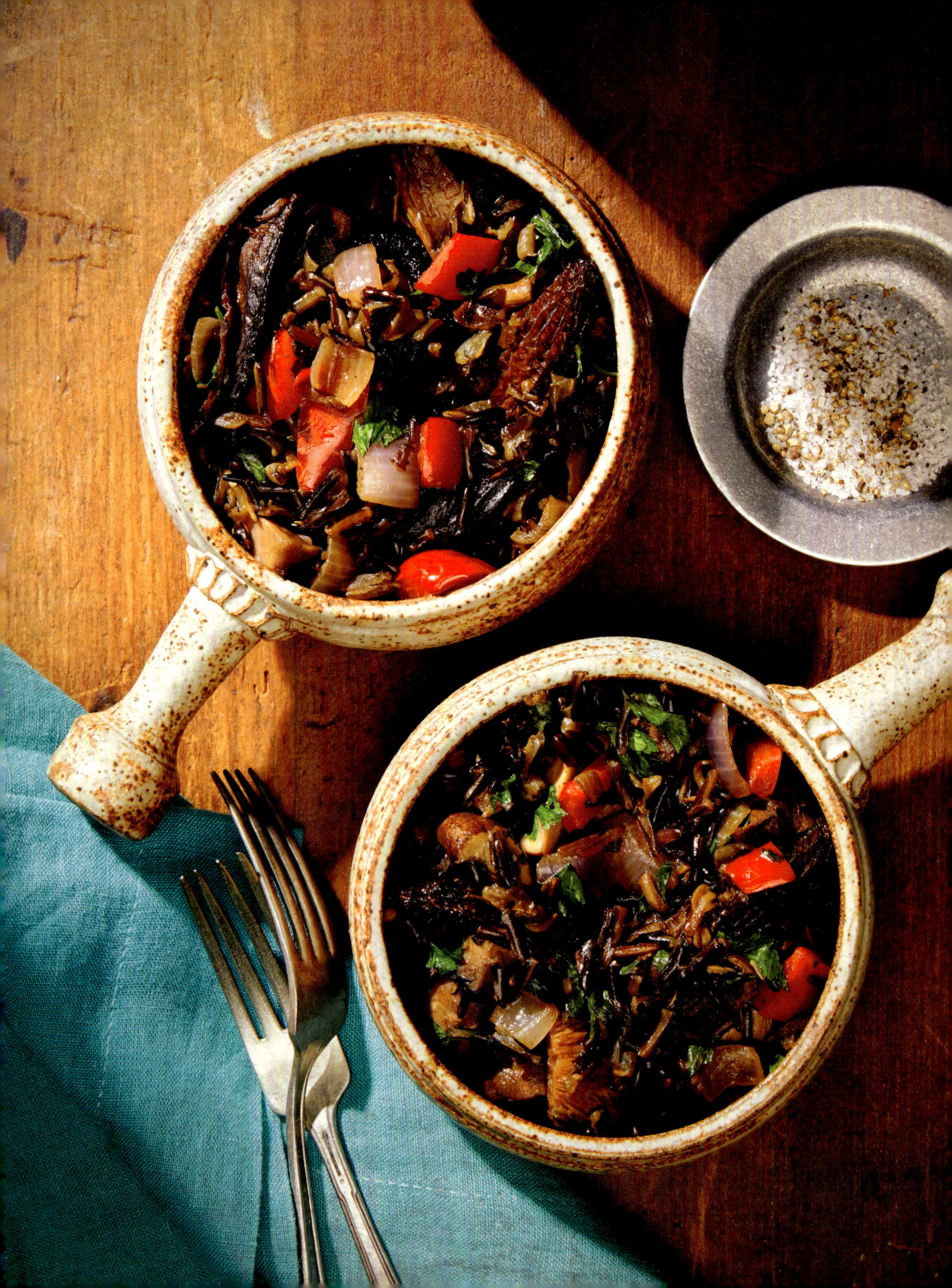

WILD RICE PILAF

Wild rice isn't actually rice at all—even though it cooks similarly to rice—but the seed of a semi-aquatic grass that is native to North America (and Montana). It grows in bays, tidal rivers, and lakes and thrives in northwestern Montana. It is an important ingredient in Indigenous cultures and has many health benefits. I serve so much rice on the film set that sometimes I like to mix it up and do something different, and this pilaf is just the ticket. I add a bunch of mushrooms, but feel free to leave them out if you like.

INGREDIENTS

1¼ cups (200 g) wild rice

4 cups (1 l) chicken stock or vegetable stock, preferably homemade

Kosher salt and freshly ground black pepper

3 tablespoons unsalted butter

1 small yellow onion, finely chopped

1 small red bell pepper, seeded and chopped

½ lb (225 g) mixed wild mushrooms, or cremini or button mushrooms, brushed clean and chopped

¼ cup (15 g) minced fresh flat-leaf parsley

MAKES 6–8 SERVINGS

INSTRUCTIONS

Rinse the wild rice in a fine-mesh sieve and drain well.

In a saucepan over high heat, bring the stock to a boil. Add the wild rice and 1 teaspoon salt. Return to a boil and then reduce the heat to low, cover the pan, and simmer the wild rice for 45 minutes.

Remove from the heat and let stand, covered, for 10 minutes. The wild rice should be tender and the grains puffed up with the inner part visible; if not, continue to cook for 10 minutes longer, covered. Drain the rice of any excess liquid, reserving ¼ cup (60 ml) of the cooking liquid.

While the wild rice cooks, in a large frying pan over medium heat, melt the butter. Add the onion, bell pepper, and mushrooms and cook, stirring until the vegetables are tender and starting to brown, about 8 minutes.

Add the cooked wild rice to the pan. Cook over medium heat until heated through, about 4 minutes, adding a little of the reserved cooking liquid to moisten the rice, if you like. Stir in the parsley and season to taste with salt and pepper. Transfer to a serving bowl and serve at once.

Beth and Jamie's
TWICE-BAKED POTATOES
with Bacon and Cheese

In Season 2, John encourages rodeo queen Cassidy Reid to run for Montana's attorney general against his son, Jamie, because John is furious with Jamie for prioritizing his campaign ahead of his family. The family insists on Cassidy staying for a rare family dinner one evening. Beth's hatred for Jamie is palpable, and she puts both Jamie and Cassidy in their places, creating a hostile environment that seems to surprise even John. The table is laden with food—fluffy dinner rolls, twice-baked potatoes, salad, and steak—but despite the bounty, Beth drives Jamie from the table by stabbing his leg with a butter knife. Still, those twice-baked potatoes were delicious—and yours will be too.

INGREDIENTS

4 large russet potatoes, scrubbed and patted dry

Olive oil for coating

Kosher salt and freshly ground black pepper

4 slices thick-cut bacon, chopped (optional)

4 tablespoons (60 g) unsalted butter, at room temperature, cut into pieces

¼ cup (60 ml) whole milk, warmed

¼ cup (60 g) sour cream

4 oz (115 g) Cheddar cheese, shredded (about 1 cup)

1 tablespoon chopped fresh chives, plus chives for garnish

MAKES 4–6 SERVINGS

INSTRUCTIONS

Position a rack in the upper third of the oven and preheat the oven to 400°F (200°C).

Pierce the potatoes all over with a paring knife. Rub the potatoes lightly with oil and season all over with salt. Place the potatoes directly on the oven rack. Bake until tender when pierced with the knife, about 1 hour.

While the potatoes bake, in a frying pan over medium-low heat, cook the bacon, if using, stirring occasionally until crisp, about 6 minutes. Using a slotted spoon, transfer the bacon to paper towels to drain.

Reduce the oven temperature to 350°F (180°C).

Remove the potatoes from the oven and cut them in half lengthwise. Scoop the potato flesh into a bowl, leaving a ¼-inch- (6-mm-) thick shell for each.

Add the butter, 1 teaspoon salt, and ½ teaspoon pepper to the bowl and, using a potato masher or a fork, mash the potatoes well. Add the milk, sour cream, half of the cheese, the reserved bacon, if using, and the chives. Beat with a fork until well mixed and fluffy. Spoon the potato mixture back into the potato shells, mounding it evenly. Press the remaining cheese on top of the filling, dividing it equally. Transfer the potatoes to a baking dish.

Bake until the cheese is melted and the filling is heated through, 25–30 minutes.

Garnish with a sprinkle of chives and serve at once.

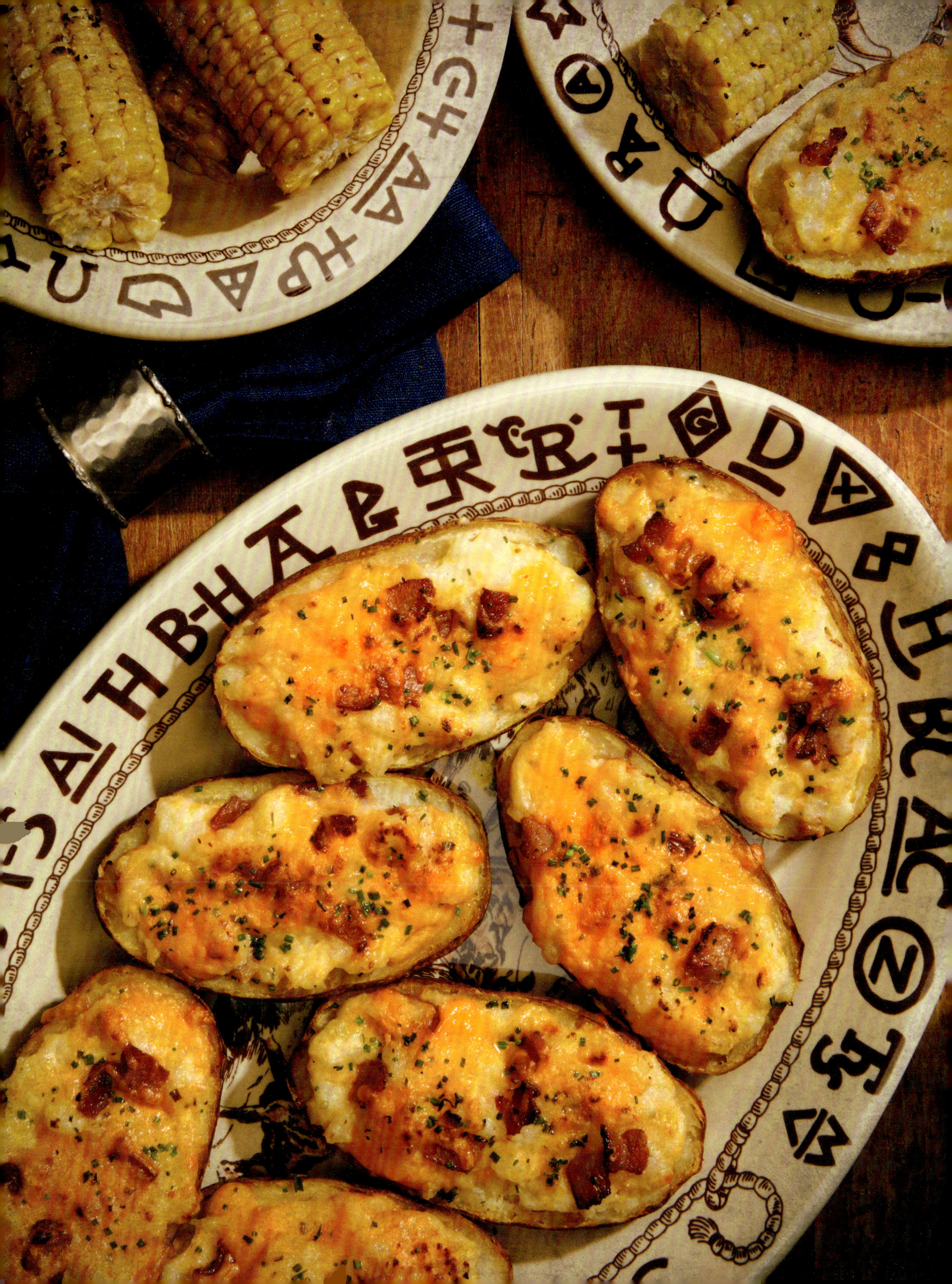

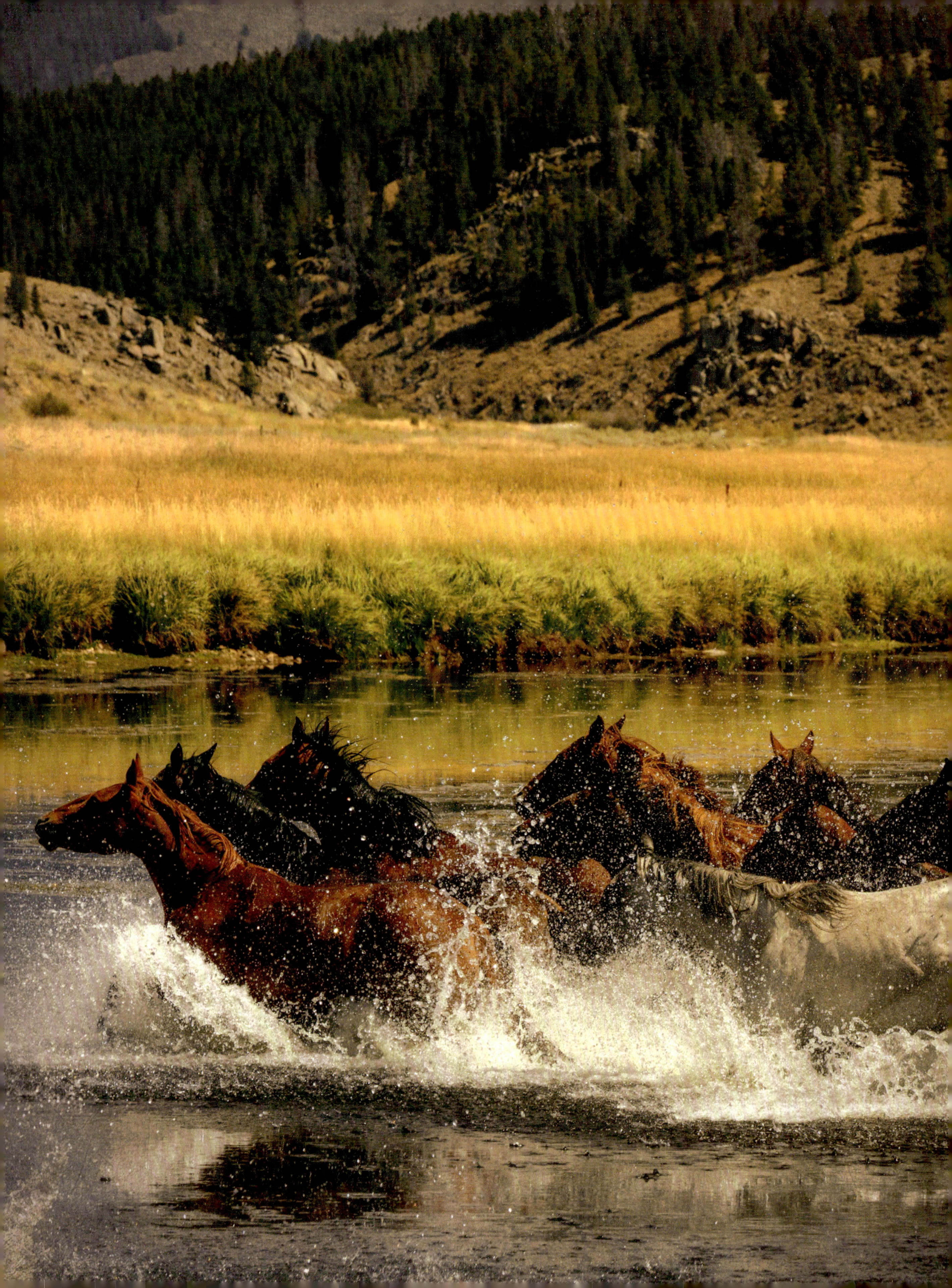

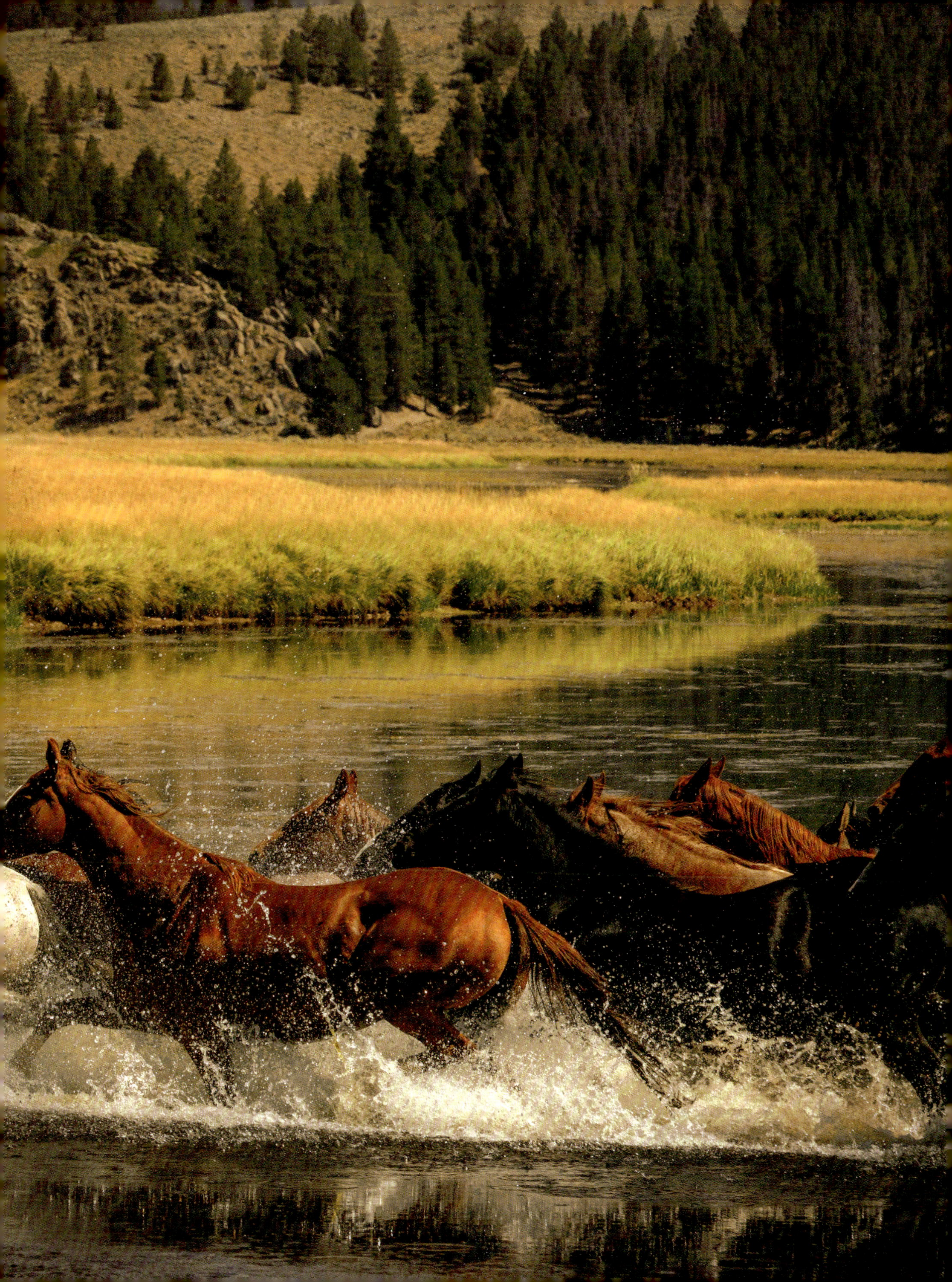

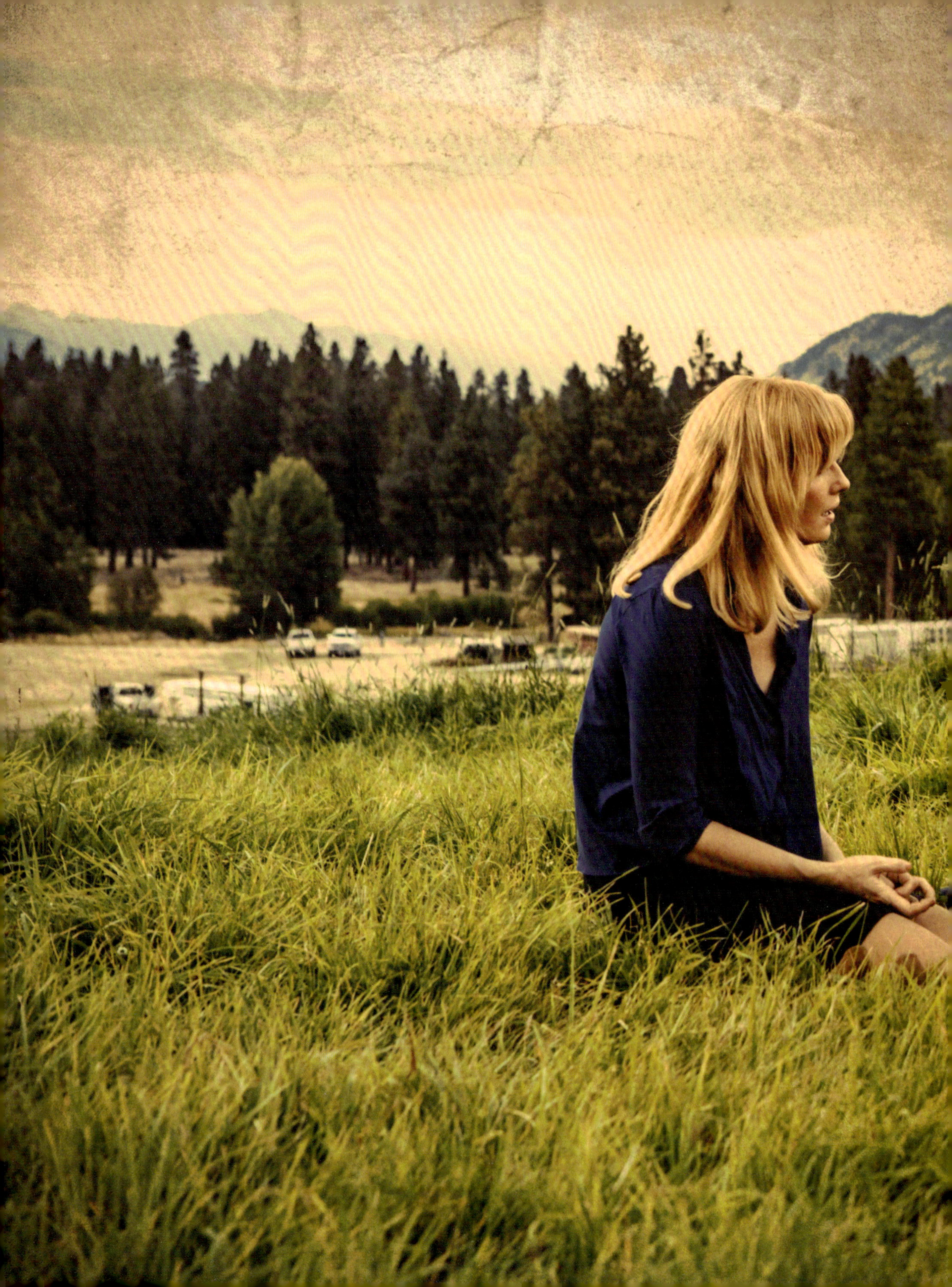

DESSERTS

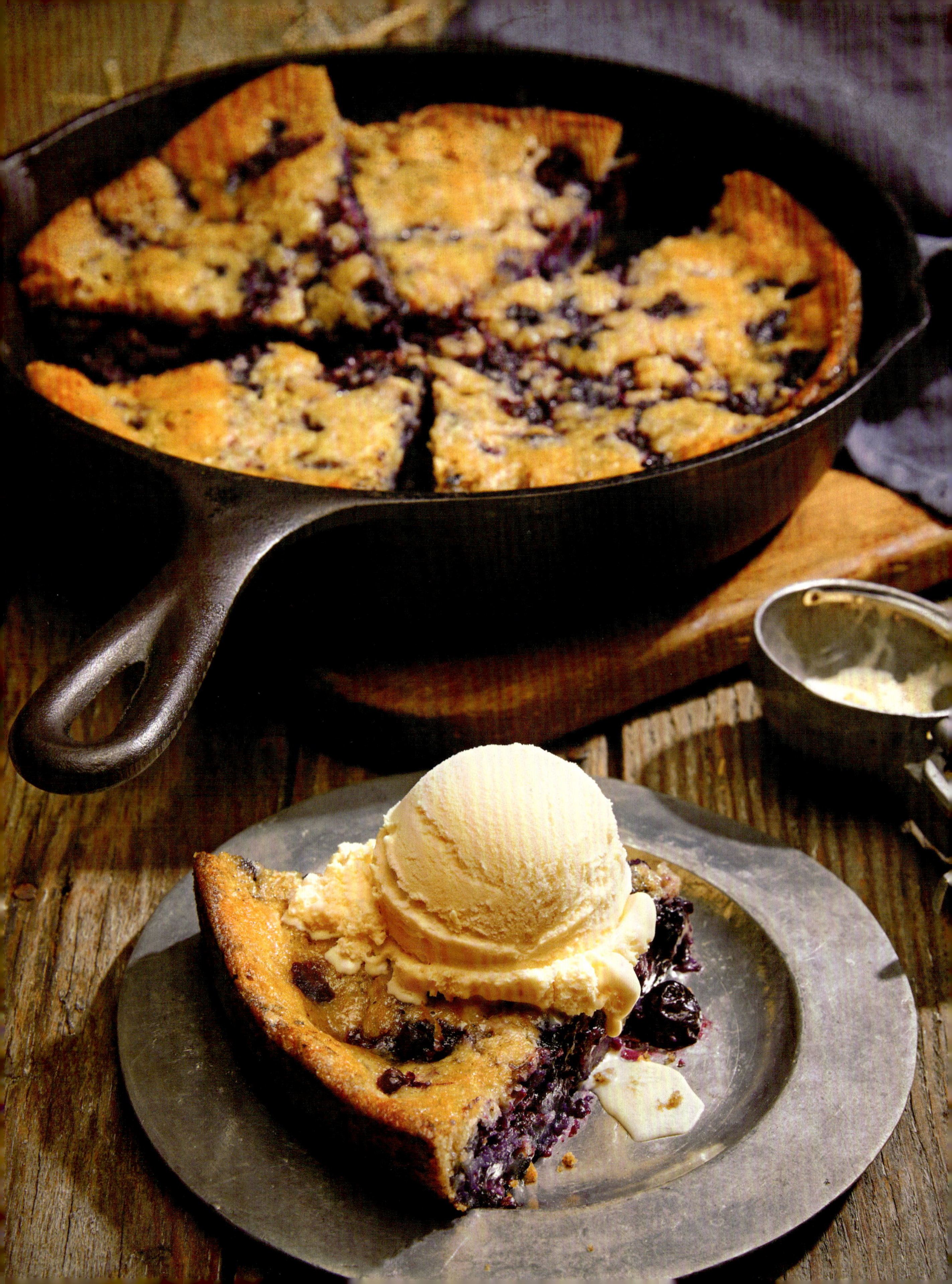

Beth and Rip's
SWEET BLUEBERRY COBBLER

In the first two seasons of *Yellowstone*, we see Beth and Rip both come together and push each other away, but in Season 3, their relationship becomes sweet and easy (well, as sweet and easy as Beth can be). In episode 7, Beth has a heart-to-heart with her father, and John asks Beth, "Do you love him?" Beth nods. "He makes you happy?" he asks. "Since the moment I met him," she replies. "Well, happy is all I've ever wanted for you, sweetheart. You give him your hand, if he gives you that," advises John and gives his blessing for Beth to ask Rip to marry her. This dessert is as sweet and easy as Beth and Rip's relationship. I've made this cobbler a zillion times with a million different types of fruits and berries, and people just love it. It's critical to my ranch repertoire and can be made in large quantities. Serve it warm with scoops of vanilla ice cream.

INGREDIENTS

- 1 cup (120 g) all-purpose flour
- 2 teaspoons baking powder
- ⅓ cup (70 g) granulated sugar, plus 2 tablespoons, plus granulated sugar for sprinkling
- ¼ cup (60 g) firmly packed light brown sugar
- ¼ teaspoon fine sea salt
- Pinch of ground cinnamon
- Pinch of ground nutmeg
- 1 cup (240 ml) whole milk
- 1 large egg, beaten
- 1 teaspoon vanilla extract
- 1 lb (450 g) fresh blueberries (2½ cups)
- 1 teaspoon finely grated lemon zest
- 1 tablespoon fresh lemon juice
- ½ cup (115 g) unsalted butter
- Vanilla ice cream for serving

MAKES ABOUT 6 SERVINGS

INSTRUCTIONS

Preheat the oven to 350°F (180°C).

In a bowl, whisk together the flour, baking powder, ⅓ cup (70 g) of the granulated sugar, brown sugar, salt, cinnamon, and nutmeg to combine. In another bowl, whisk together the milk, egg, and vanilla until blended.

In a third bowl, toss together the blueberries, lemon zest, lemon juice, and remaining 2 tablespoons granulated sugar.

Place the butter in a 10-inch cast-iron pan and place the pan in the oven. When the butter is melted, whisk together the flour mixture and the milk mixture until just combined; there will be a few lumps remaining, which is okay. Pour the batter evenly over the melted butter, and then spoon the blueberry mixture evenly over the batter.

Bake until the juices are bubbling and the cobbler is cooked through and golden brown, 45–50 minutes.

Let cool slightly before serving with scoops of vanilla ice cream.

GATOR'S TIP

Feel free to substitute any fruit you like for the blueberries. Pitted and chopped peaches, nectarines, and cherries, or a mixture of raspberries and blackberries are all terrific.

Classic SOUTHERN PECAN PIE

Pecan pie is the flavor of my childhood. It's my favorite pie, by far. In the South, there are pecan trees everywhere, and everyone makes this pie. When my father was a child, he would earn some extra spending money by picking pecans and then selling them to the local hardware store. This version is about as classic as it gets—gooey, nutty, and sweet. If you can be bothered to make your own piecrust, more power to you, but store-bought crust is just fine too. I usually pull this recipe out for holidays and special occasions, but sometimes I make it just because I miss that Southern taste. Be sure to toast your pecans to bring out their flavor and add some texture.

INGREDIENTS

For the Pecan Pie

- 1½ cups (170 g) roughly chopped pecan halves (about 6 oz / 170 g), plus 8–10 pecan halves
- 1 unbaked piecrust (for 9-inch / 23-cm) pie pan, thawed, if frozen
- 3 large eggs, beaten
- 1 cup (240 ml) dark corn syrup
- ½ cup (100 g) firmly packed light brown sugar
- 1 teaspoon vanilla extract
- ¼ teaspoon fine sea salt
- 4 tablespoons (60 g) unsalted butter, melted

For the Whipped Cream

- 1 cup (240 ml) heavy cream
- 2 tablespoons granulated or confectioners' sugar
- ½ teaspoon vanilla extract

MAKES 6–8 SERVINGS

INSTRUCTIONS

Preheat the oven to 350°F (180°C).

To prepare the pie, spread the chopped pecans on a baking sheet and place the pecan halves next to them. Toast in the oven until fragrant, stirring once or twice, about 10 minutes. Set aside to cool.

Roll out the piecrust, if necessary, and fit it in a 9-inch (23-cm) pie pan.

In a large bowl, whisk together the eggs, corn syrup, brown sugar, vanilla, and salt until well combined. Stir in the melted butter. Stir in the chopped pecans and mix until evenly coated. Pour the mixture into the piecrust. Arrange the pecan halves in the center on top.

Bake until the filling is puffed and set (the center might jiggle just slightly) and the crust is golden, 45–50 minutes. Let cool completely on a wire rack.

To prepare the whipped cream, in a bowl combine the cream, sugar, and vanilla. Using a handheld electric mixer, beat the cream mixture on medium-high speed until soft peaks form. Do not overbeat. Use immediately or cover and refrigerate until ready to serve. If there is any separation, briefly beat with a whisk until the whipped cream comes back together.

Serve big wedges of the pie with plenty of whipped cream on top.

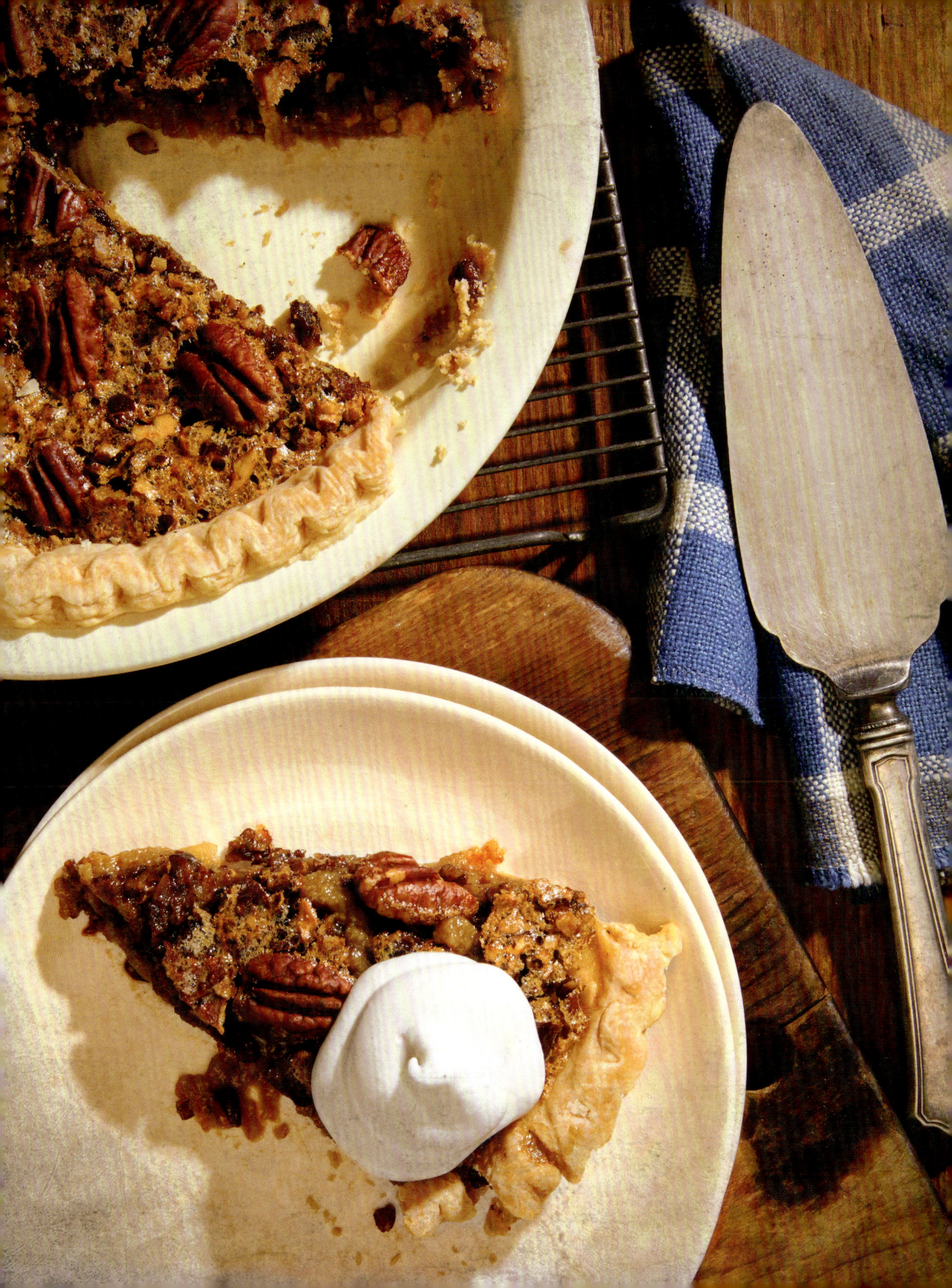

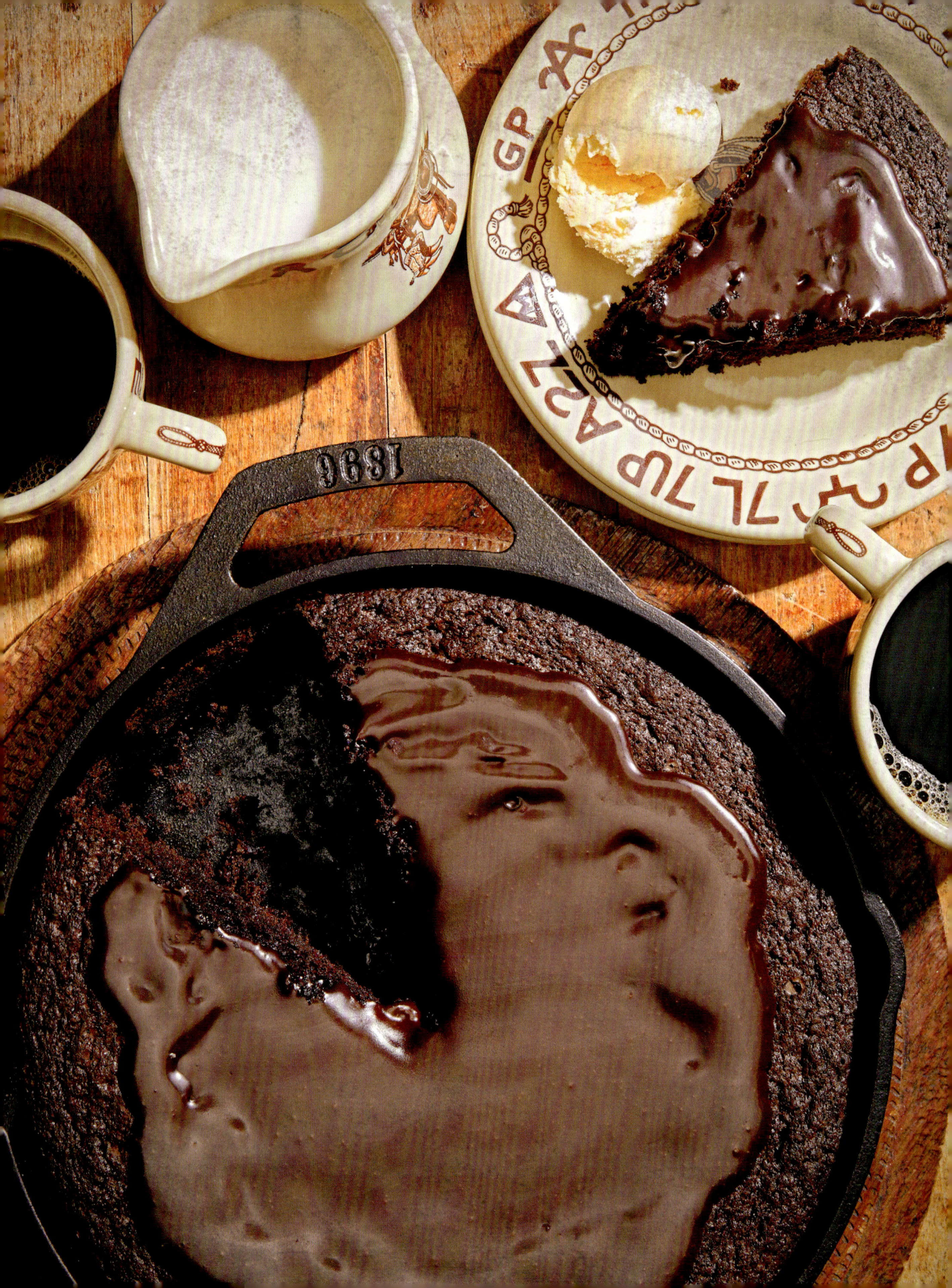

Carter's Cast-Iron
COFFEE-CHOCOLATE CAKE

In Season 4, episode 8, John, Beth, Rip, and Carter are having dinner together in the lodge dining room when Beth and John argue, and she storms away, with Rip close at her heels. John takes the opportunity to scrape the salad back in the bowl and take a big piece of steak for himself. Carter takes a massive scoop of the cake right out of the center and plops it onto his plate and on top of the steak. The nice thing about this cake is that you can mix the entire batter in the skillet that you bake it in. If you find yourself grilling outside for ranch hands, simply place the whole pan on the grill over indirect heat.

INGREDIENTS

For the Coffee-Chocolate Cake

1 cup (120 g) all-purpose flour

½ cup (40 g) natural cocoa powder

1 teaspoon baking soda

½ teaspoon kosher salt

½ cup (115 g) unsalted butter

¼ cup (60 ml) vegetable oil

¾ cup (4 oz / 115 g) semisweet chocolate chips

1 cup (200 g) granulated sugar

⅔ cup (160 ml) freshly brewed coffee

4 large eggs

2 teaspoons vanilla extract

For the Glaze

3 tablespoons unsalted butter

¼ cup (20 g) natural cocoa powder, sifted

2 tablespoons freshly brewed coffee, plus coffee as needed

Pinch of kosher salt

1 cup (115 g) confectioners' sugar, sifted

Vanilla ice cream for serving

MAKES 8 SERVINGS

INSTRUCTIONS

Preheat the oven to 350°F (180°C).

To prepare the cake, in a bowl, whisk together the flour, cocoa powder, baking soda, and salt to blend. In a 10-inch (25-cm) cast-iron frying pan with 2-inch- (5-cm-) high sides over low heat, melt the butter with the oil. Remove from the heat and stir in the chocolate chips until they are just melted. Whisk in the granulated sugar, coffee, eggs, and vanilla. Add the flour mixture to the chocolate mixture in the pan and stir gently to combine.

Transfer the frying pan to the oven and bake until a toothpick inserted into the center of the cake comes out clean, about 30 minutes. Transfer the frying pan to a wire rack and let the cake cool.

To prepare the glaze, in a small saucepan over low heat, melt the butter. Remove from the heat and whisk in the cocoa powder, coffee, and salt. Add the confectioners' sugar and whisk until smooth. The glaze should be thick but spreadable; if it is too thick, add a little more coffee, ¼ teaspoon at a time, to reach the desired consistency.

Pour the glaze over the cake and spread it evenly, using a small spatula. Let stand until the glaze is set, about 1 hour.

Serve wedges straight from the pan, ideally with a big scoop of vanilla ice cream.

SWEET POTATO BOURBON PIE

This may be the most Gator recipe in my dessert repertoire. I've made this with all types of yams, sweet potatoes, and even pumpkin. However, orange-fleshed garnet yams (technically sweet potatoes) are my favorite. I used to make the pie with sherry, but it's not 1965 anymore, so now I use bourbon—which is fitting, because on *Yellowstone*, and in Montana, we drink bourbon. I promise if you show up to Thanksgiving dinner with this pie, you'll get invited back. Choose small- to medium-size sweet potatoes so they cook a bit more quickly. You can peel, chop, and boil the sweet potatoes, but it can change the amount of liquid in the puree. So, I find it is better to bake them, which also caramelizes and condenses the sugars in the sweet potatoes.

INGREDIENTS

- 1 unbaked piecrust (for 9-inch/23-cm pie pan), thawed, if frozen
- 2 lb (1 kg) orange-fleshed sweet potatoes
- ½ cup (100 g) firmly packed light brown sugar
- ⅓ cup (70 g) granulated sugar
- 2 large eggs, beaten
- ½ cup (120 ml) half-and-half
- 4 tablespoons (60 g) unsalted butter, melted
- ¼ cup (60 ml) bourbon
- 1 teaspoon vanilla extract
- ½ teaspoon ground cinnamon
- ½ teaspoon ground nutmeg
- ½ teaspoon ground ginger
- ½ teaspoon baking powder
- ½ teaspoon kosher salt
- Whipped cream (see Classic Southern Pecan Pie, page 132) for serving

MAKES 6–8 SERVINGS

INSTRUCTIONS

Roll out the piecrust, if necessary, and fit it in a 9-inch (23-cm) pie pan. Line the crust with parchment paper and fill it with pie weights (dried beans or uncooked rice work well). Freeze the crust for at least 30 minutes, or up to 1 month in advance, wrapped well.

Preheat the oven to 375°F (190°C). Line a baking sheet with aluminum foil.

Once the piecrust has been frozen for 30 minutes, scrub the sweet potatoes and pierce them all over with a fork or small knife and place them on the prepared baking sheet. Bake until very tender, about 45 minutes. Set aside until cool enough to handle.

While the sweet potatoes bake, place the piecrust in the oven alongside them and bake until the crust looks dry and just starts to brown, about 15 minutes. Carefully remove the parchment and pie weights. If the crust still looks raw, return it to the oven for about 5 minutes longer. Set aside to cool.

Remove and discard the sweet potato skins and place the flesh in a large bowl. Using a potato masher or a fork, mash the sweet potatoes into a slightly chunky puree. You should have 2 cups (650 g).

Position a rack in the lower third of the oven and reduce the oven temperature to 350°F (180°C).

continued on page 139

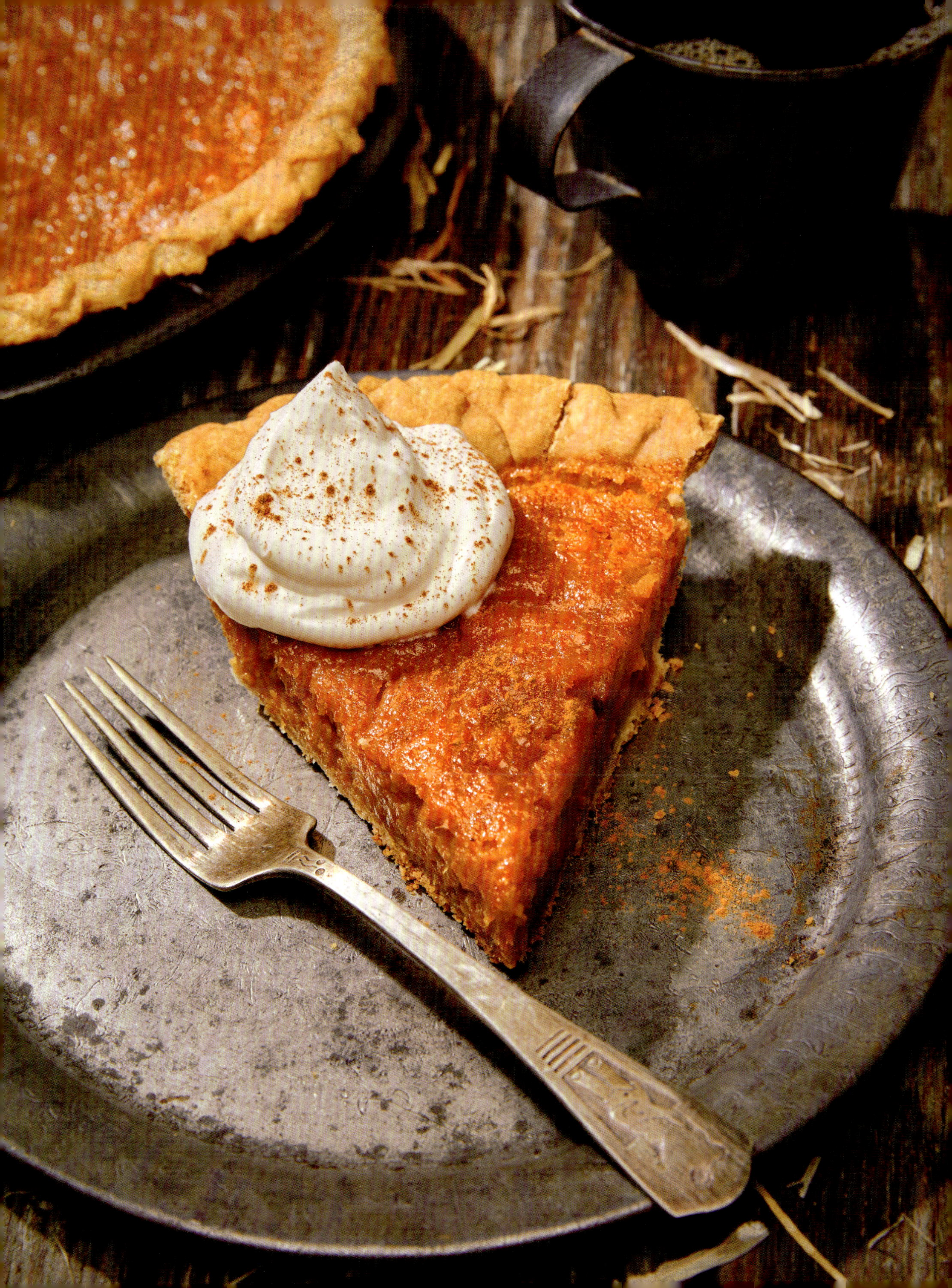

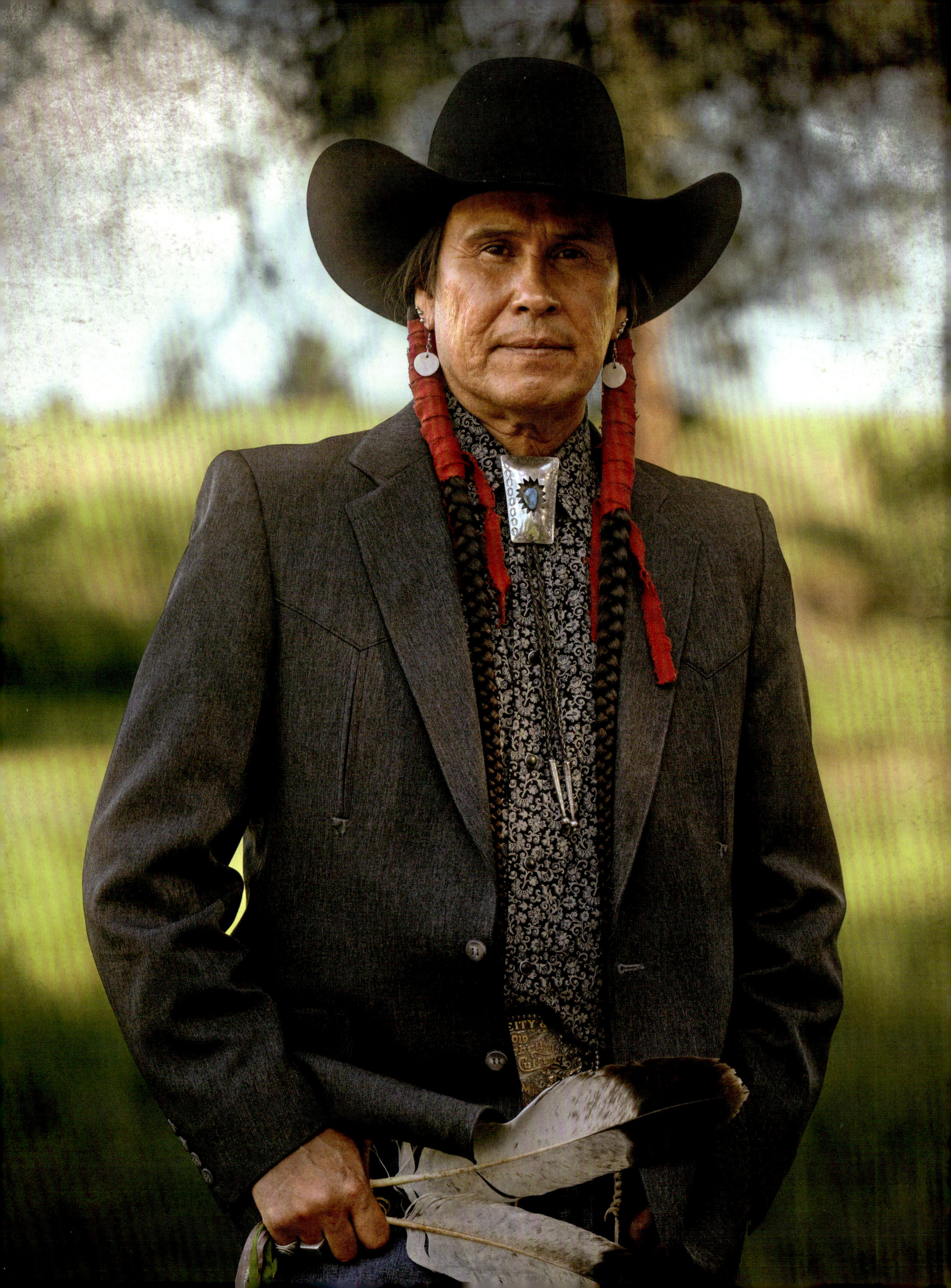

continued from page 136

Add the sugars, eggs, half-and-half, melted butter, bourbon, vanilla, spices, baking powder, and salt to the bowl with the sweet potato. Using a whisk or a handheld electric mixer, beat the ingredients on medium speed until well combined and smooth. Pour the sweet potato mixture into the prepared piecrust.

Bake on the lower rack until the filling is set and the crust is golden, 1 hour–1 hour 15 minutes. Transfer to a wire rack to cool.

Serve at room temperature or chilled, dolloped with whipped cream.

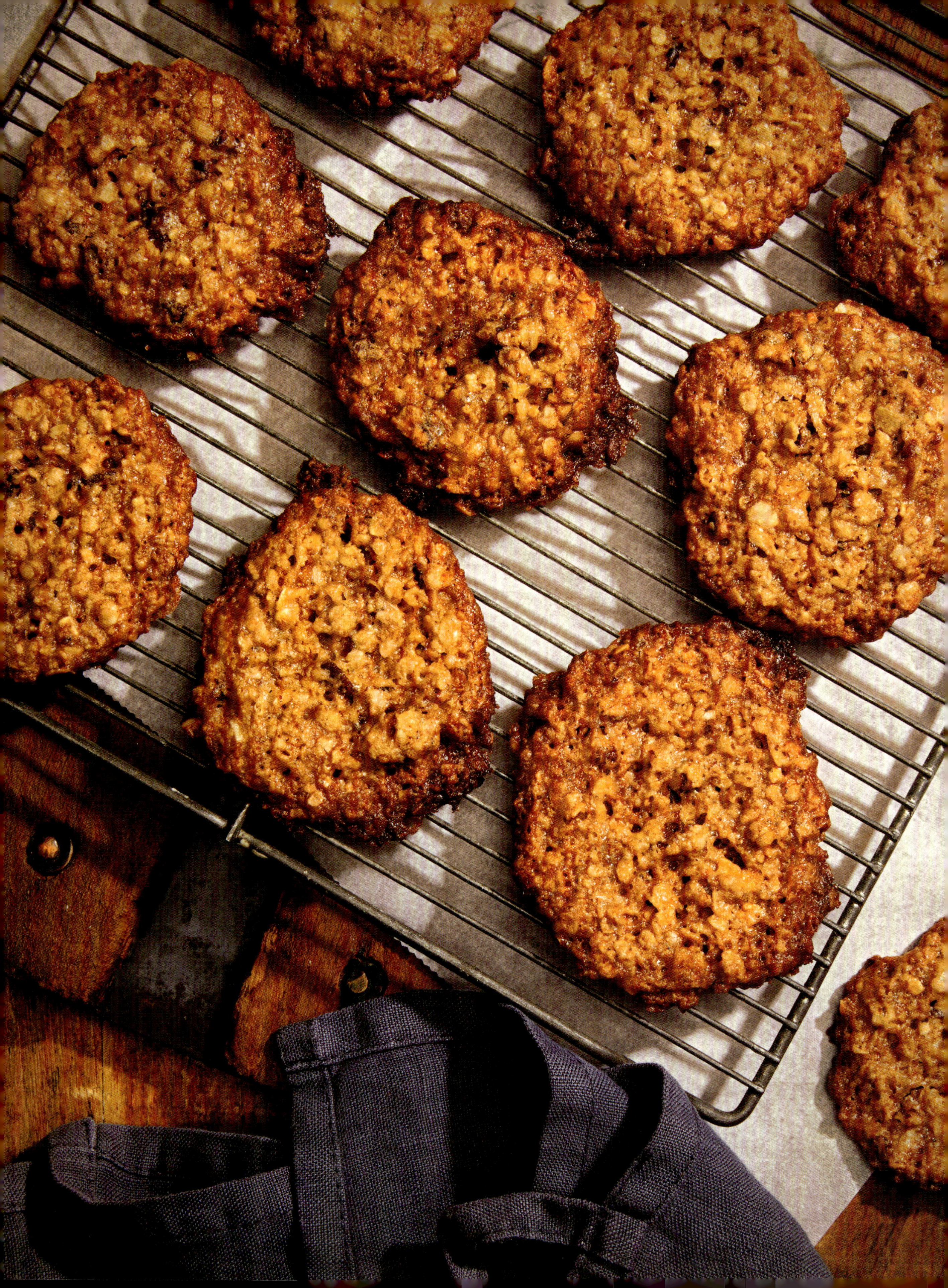

Evadelle's LACE COOKIES

Evadelle, also known as "Maw Maw," was my grandmother. Every Christmas, she would send us a box of her Chocolate-Pecan Fudge (page 145) and these lace cookies. They're like a thin, crisp, caramelized oatmeal and pecan cookie. My dad would immediately consume the entire tin of fudge—so I rarely ever got to try it—and consequently I always ended up with these cookies. Good thing they're delicious. I must have eaten a million of them growing up. (Once you start eating, it's hard to stop.) The cast and crew love when I make cookies, so I always bake a ton, especially around the holidays. Over the years, I've reached out to crew members to give me their family cookie recipes and then I add them to my assortment, which means a lot to them. However, I always include my Maw Maw's lace cookies.

INGREDIENTS

- ½ cup (115 g) unsalted butter
- 1 cup (210 g) firmly packed light brown sugar
- ½ cup (60 g) finely chopped toasted pecans
- 1 large egg, lightly beaten
- 1 teaspoon vanilla extract
- ½ teaspoon kosher salt
- 1 cup (100 g) quick-cooking rolled oats
- 2 tablespoons all-purpose flour
- 1 teaspoon baking powder

MAKES ABOUT 2 DOZEN COOKIES

INSTRUCTIONS

Position 2 racks in the upper third and lower third of the oven and preheat the oven to 350°F (180°C). Line 2 baking sheets with aluminum foil, dull side up.

In a small saucepan over medium-low heat, melt the butter. Add the brown sugar and stir until it dissolves, about 2 minutes. Transfer to a bowl and whisk in the pecans, egg, vanilla, and salt, and then stir in the oats. Sift the flour and baking powder over the oat mixture and stir gently to combine. Let the batter stand for 15 minutes.

For each cookie, spoon about 1 tablespoon of the cookie batter onto the prepared baking sheets, spacing about 2 inches (5 cm) apart, and only putting 6 cookies on each sheet.

Bake until golden brown and spread out, 9–11 minutes. Let cool on the pans until set, about 15 minutes, and then transfer to a wire rack to cool completely.

Bourbon Pineapple BREAD PUDDING

I've easily made a hundred different bread puddings in my life. Although French bread is best, any kind of sturdy white bread will do (challah and brioche make great bread pudding). I developed this version because I'm a big pineapple guy. Some people might like to put rum in the sauce, but I've gotta add bourbon to mine, of course.

INGREDIENTS

For the Bread Pudding

- 4 tablespoons (60 g) unsalted butter, melted, plus butter for greasing
- 1½ lb (680 g) stale French bread, brioche, or challah, cut into 1½-inch (4-cm) cubes
- 4 large eggs
- 4 large egg yolks
- 1 cup (240 ml) half-and-half
- 1 cup (240 ml) whole milk
- ⅔ cup (140 g) granulated sugar
- 2 teaspoons vanilla extract
- ½ teaspoon kosher salt
- ¼ teaspoon ground cinnamon
- ¼ teaspoon ground nutmeg

For the Bourbon-Pineapple Sauce

- 2 cups (12 oz / 340 g) diced fresh pineapple
- 1 cup (240 ml) bourbon
- ½ cup (100 g) firmly packed light brown sugar
- ½ teaspoon ground cinnamon
- ¼ teaspoon kosher salt
- 1 teaspoon vanilla extract
- Whipped cream (see Classic Southern Pecan Pie, page 132) for serving

MAKES 8 SERVINGS

INSTRUCTIONS

To prepare the bread pudding, preheat the oven to 350°F (180°C). Grease a 9 x 13 inch (23 x 33 cm) baking dish generously with butter.

Spread the bread cubes on a large, rimmed baking sheet and bake, stirring occasionally until toasted, 10–15 minutes (depending on the type of bread). Transfer to the prepared baking dish, spreading into an even layer.

While the bread toasts, in a large bowl whisk together the eggs, egg yolks, half-and-half, milk, granulated sugar, vanilla, salt, cinnamon, and nutmeg until blended. Pour the egg mixture evenly over the bread cubes. Press the bread down into the egg mixture so it will evenly absorb the liquid. Let stand for about 30 minutes so the bread soaks up the egg mixture.

Drizzle the melted butter over the bread mixture.

Bake the pudding until puffed and golden brown, about 45 minutes.

While the pudding bakes, prepare the sauce. In a saucepan over medium heat, combine the pineapple, bourbon, brown sugar, cinnamon, and salt. Bring to a gentle boil; then reduce the heat to medium-low and simmer, stirring occasionally until the pineapple is soft and brown, about 20 minutes. Stir in the vanilla. Set aside and cover to keep warm.

Serve big scoops of the pudding topped with plenty of sauce and whipped cream.

GATOR'S TIP

I've also used donuts, hot dog buns, sweet rolls, croissants, and even leftover biscuits for this recipe.

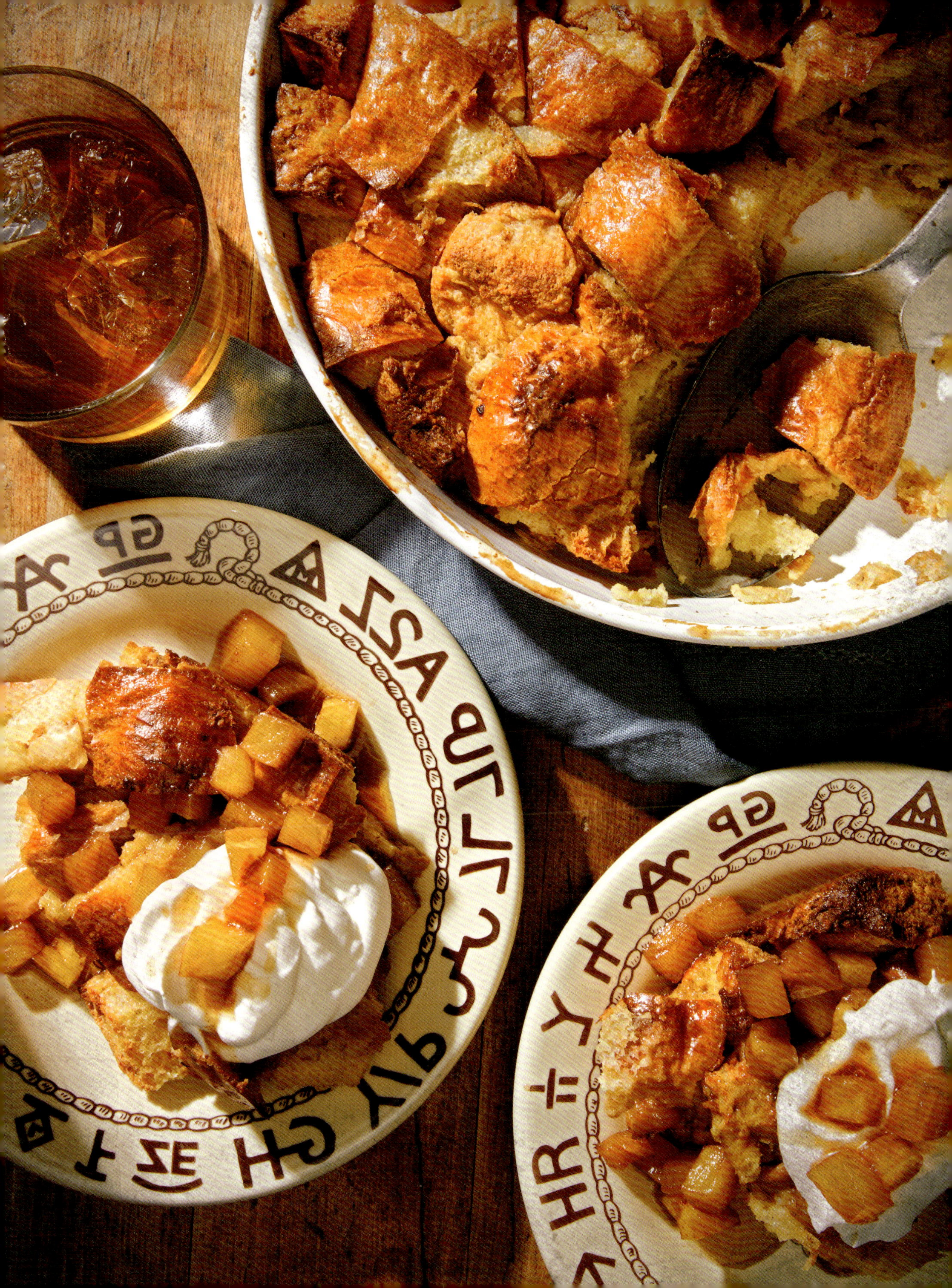

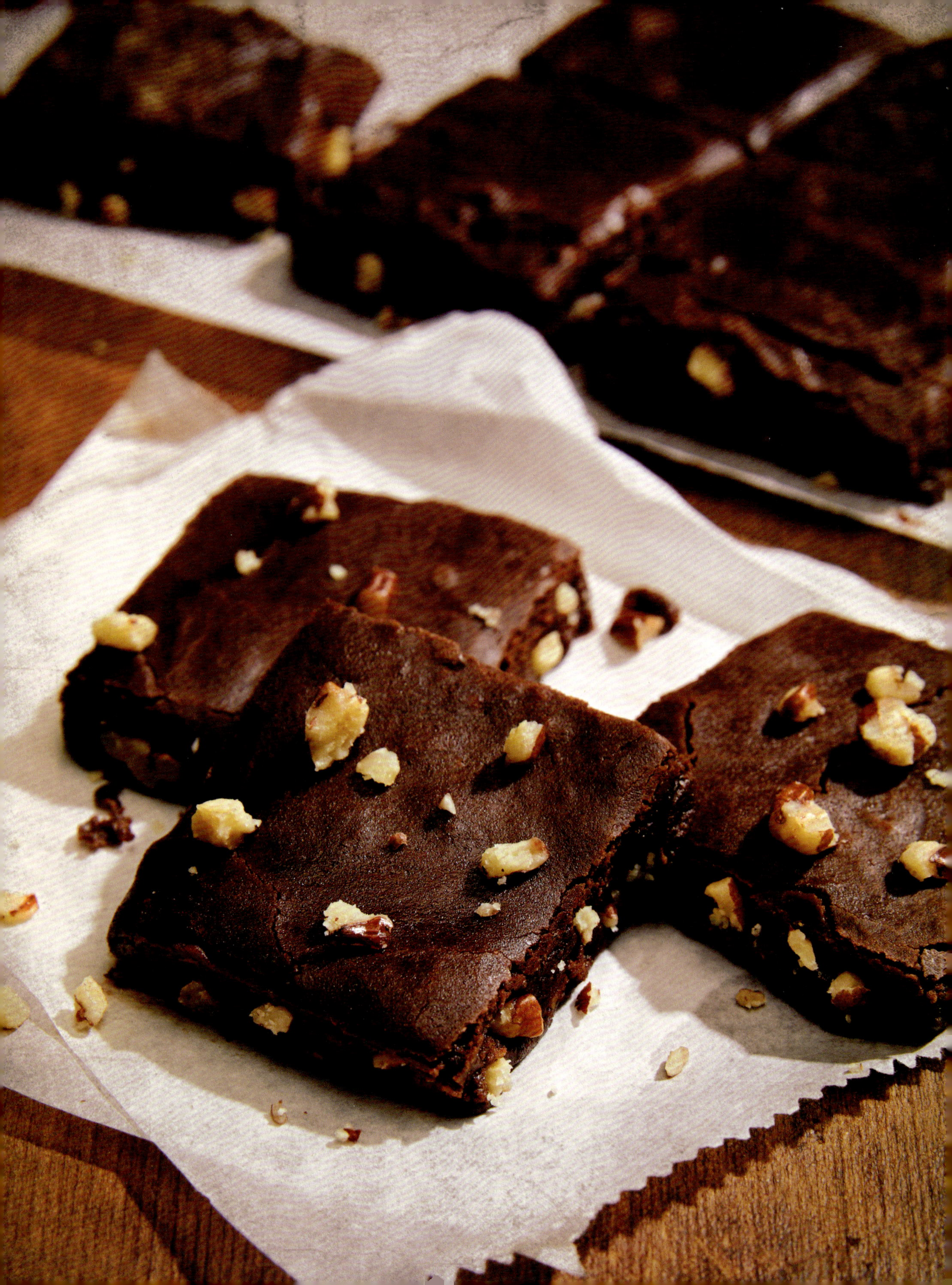

Maw Maw's
CHOCOLATE-PECAN FUDGE

Maw Maw was famous for her fudge. And fudge is not an easy thing to make; in fact, it's notoriously difficult, especially if you make it the authentic old-fashioned way like Maw Maw did, without the shortcut of using marshmallow. The key to making fudge is to be really accurate with the temperatures, so you need a candy thermometer to make this. But if you follow these directions carefully, you are assured of a great result—and one that, hopefully, you will get a piece of after serving!

INGREDIENTS

2 tablespoons unsalted butter, melted, plus butter for greasing

3 cups (600 g) sugar

⅔ cup (60 g) natural cocoa powder

¼ teaspoon kosher salt

1½ cups (350 ml) whole milk

2 tablespoons light corn syrup

1 teaspoon vanilla extract

1 cup (4 oz / 115 g) chopped toasted pecans, plus more pecans for garnish (optional)

MAKES SIXTEEN 2-INCH (5-CM) FUDGE SQUARES

INSTRUCTIONS

Line an 8-inch (20-cm)-square baking pan with parchment paper so the two sides go up and over the edges. Grease the parchment with butter. Set aside.

In a large deep saucepan, whisk together the sugar, cocoa powder, and salt. Add the milk and corn syrup and whisk to combine. Bring to a boil over medium heat, stirring constantly until the sugar dissolves; this should take about 5 minutes. As soon as the mixture boils, stop stirring and insert a candy thermometer or deep-frying thermometer. Continue to cook until the temperature on the thermometer reaches 235°–240°F (113°–116°C), about 15 minutes. Watch carefully, as you may need to adjust the heat so the mixture continues to boil but doesn't boil over. As soon as the mixture reaches the correct temperature, remove the pan from the heat.

Add the melted butter and vanilla, but do not stir. Set aside and let the mixture cool to 110°–122°F (43°–50°C); this should take about 30 minutes.

Transfer the cooled fudge to the bowl of a stand mixer fitted with the paddle attachment, or to a large bowl, and using a handheld electric mixer, beat on medium-high speed until the fudge loses its gloss, 5–8 minutes. Beat in the pecans on low speed until distributed.

Quickly spoon the mixture into the prepared baking pan and press into an even layer with your hands. Garnish the top with more pecans, if desired. Set aside to cool completely.

When cool and set, carefully remove the fudge from the pan, using the parchment as handles. Cut into sixteen 2-inch (5-cm) squares. To store, layer the fudge with parchment paper in an airtight container and store at room temperature for up to 1 week.

Big-Ass CHOCOLATE CHIP COOKIES

In Season 1, after Kayce gets picked up by the police, Monica and Tate head to the ranch where John offers them breakfast. Monica is too upset to eat, but John asks Tate if he wants to just "skip straight to dessert." "What kinda dessert?" Tate asks with a grin. "There's some cookies in there the size of pie plates," says John. Tate runs inside and returns with a *big-ass* chocolate chip cookie. "Boy, you weren't kidding!" I remember when we shot this scene; it was one of my first weeks on set. I have photos of me holding these cookies, and I swear they were as big as my head.

INGREDIENTS

- ½ cup plus 2 tablespoons (145 g) unsalted butter, at room temperature
- ¾ cup (155 g) firmly packed light brown sugar
- ⅔ cup (140 g) granulated sugar
- 1 large egg
- 1 large egg yolk
- 1½ teaspoons vanilla extract
- 2¼ cups (280 g) all-purpose flour
- 1 teaspoon baking soda
- ½ teaspoon baking powder
- ½ teaspoon kosher salt
- 2 cups (12 oz / 340 g) semisweet chocolate chips

MAKES A BAKER'S DOZEN (ABOUT 13 COOKIES)

INSTRUCTIONS

Position 2 racks in the upper third and lower third of the oven and preheat the oven to 375°F (190°C). Line 2 large, rimmed baking sheets with parchment paper.

In a large bowl, using a handheld electric mixer, beat the butter and sugars on medium-high speed until creamy. Add the egg, egg yolk, and vanilla and beat until combined. Using a rubber spatula, scrape down the sides of the bowl.

In a small bowl, whisk together the flour, baking soda, baking powder, and salt until combined. Add the flour mixture to the butter mixture and beat on low speed just until blended. Add the chocolate chips and beat just until combined.

Divide the dough into 13 balls, each about 3 ounces (90 g). Roll each into a loose ball and arrange 4 dough balls on each baking sheet, spacing them apart and pressing them lightly into disks about ½ inch (12 mm) thick.

Bake until golden and just set in the middle, rotating the pans between the racks halfway through baking, about 14 minutes total. Remove the cookies from the oven and use a spatula to flatten them gently.

Let cool on the pan for 5 minutes, and then transfer the cookies to a wire rack to cool completely. Repeat with the remaining dough balls. Store in an airtight container at room temperature for up to 5 days.

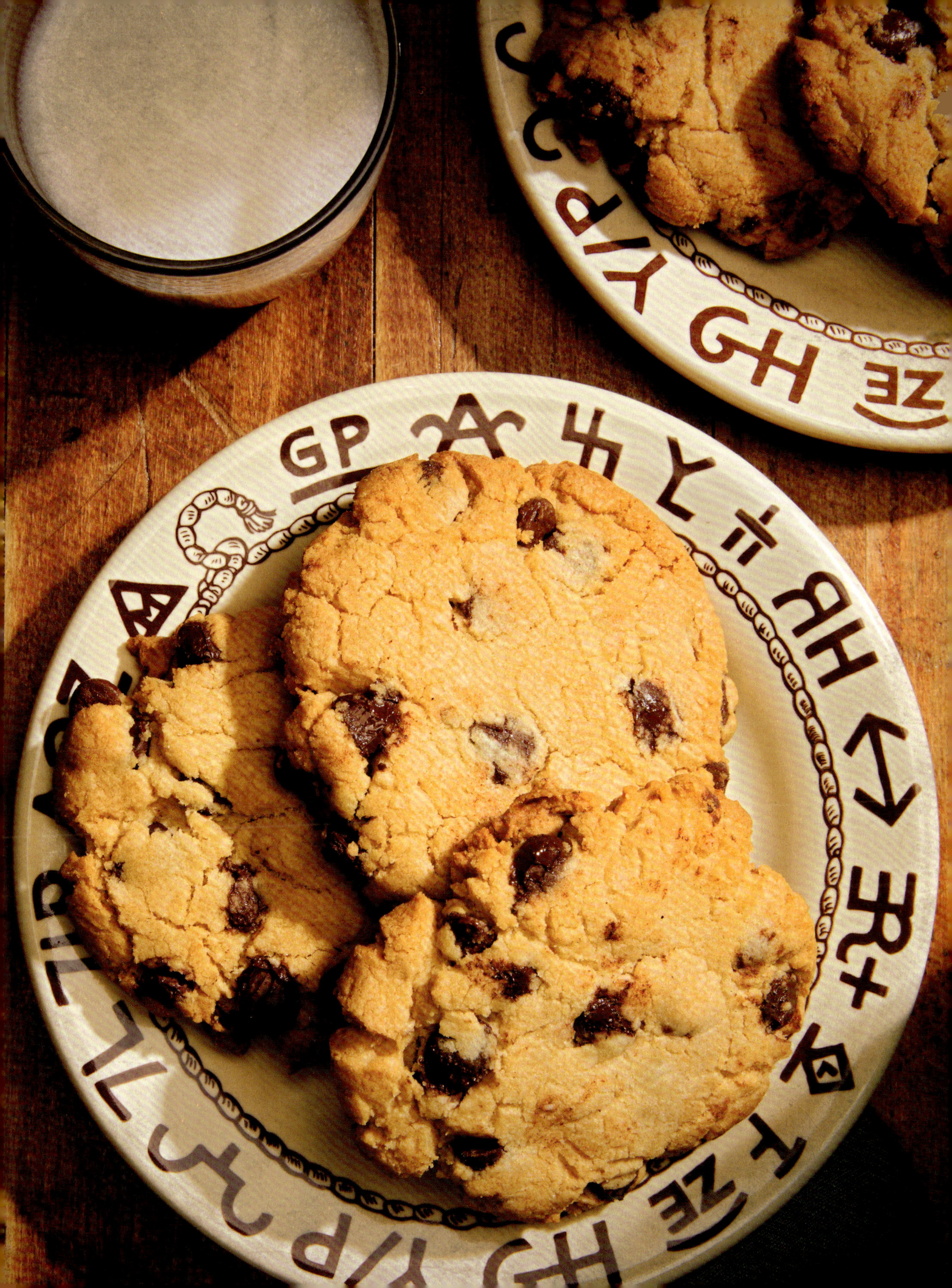

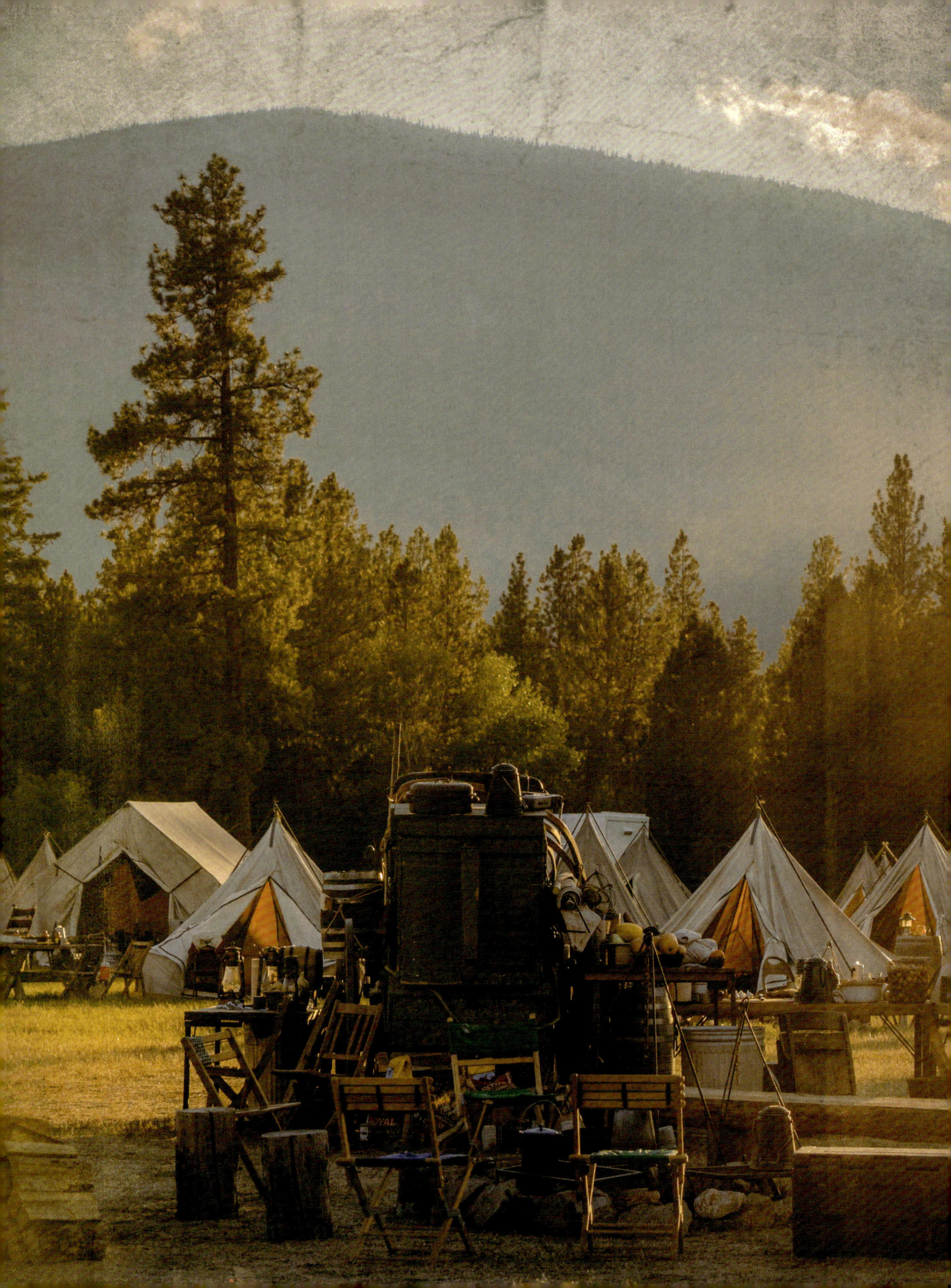
ROYAL

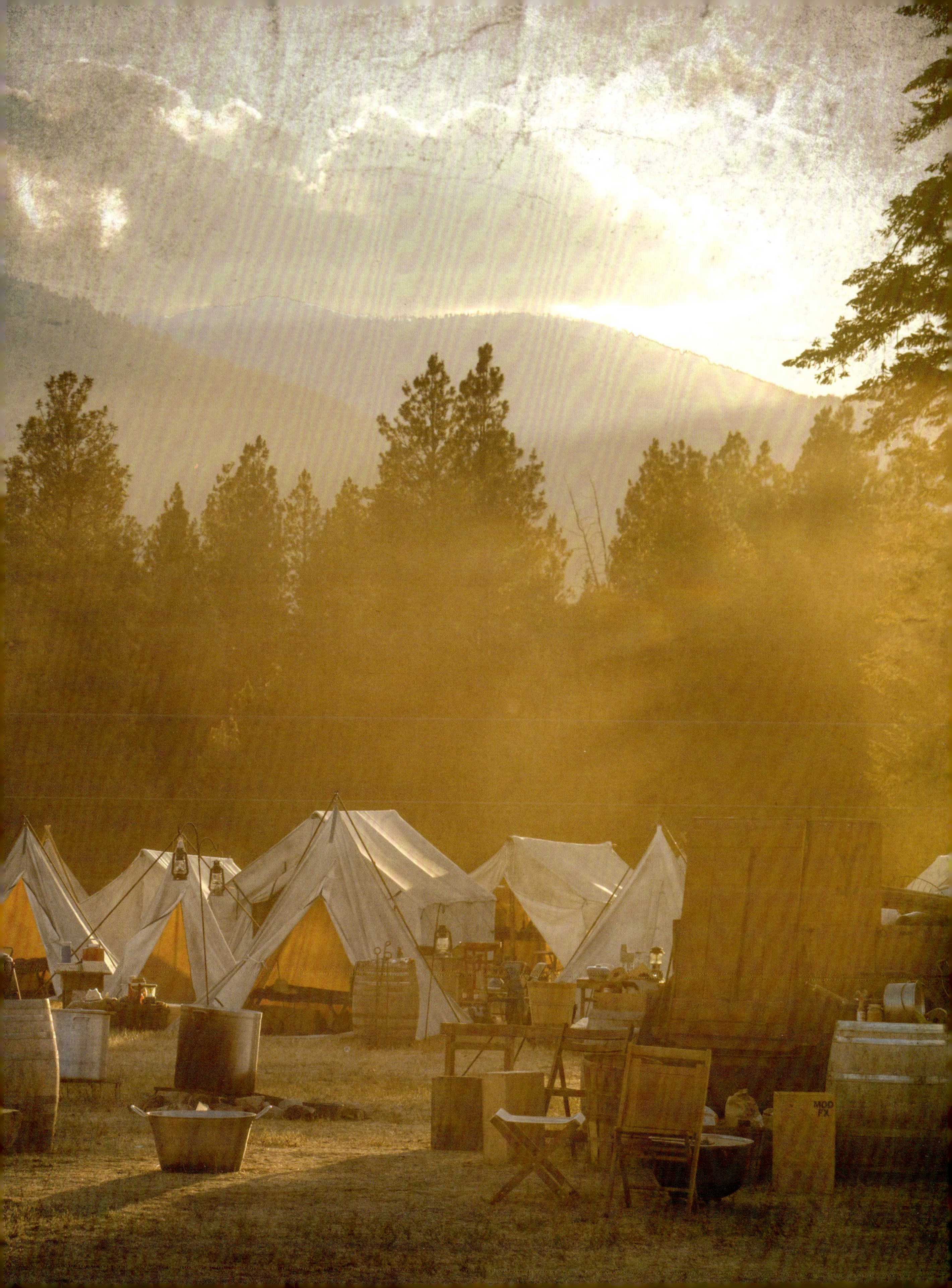
MOD
FX

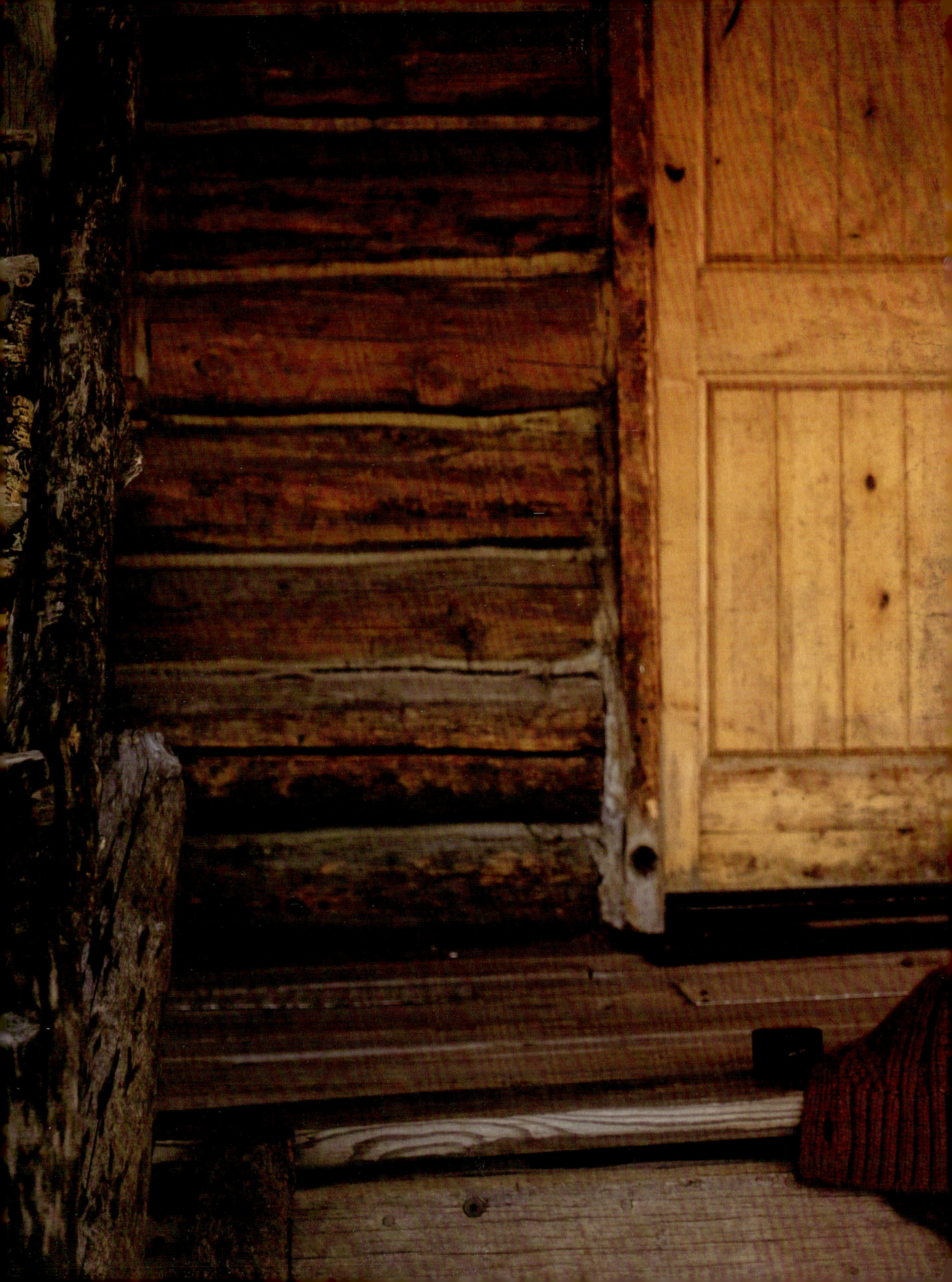

DRINKS

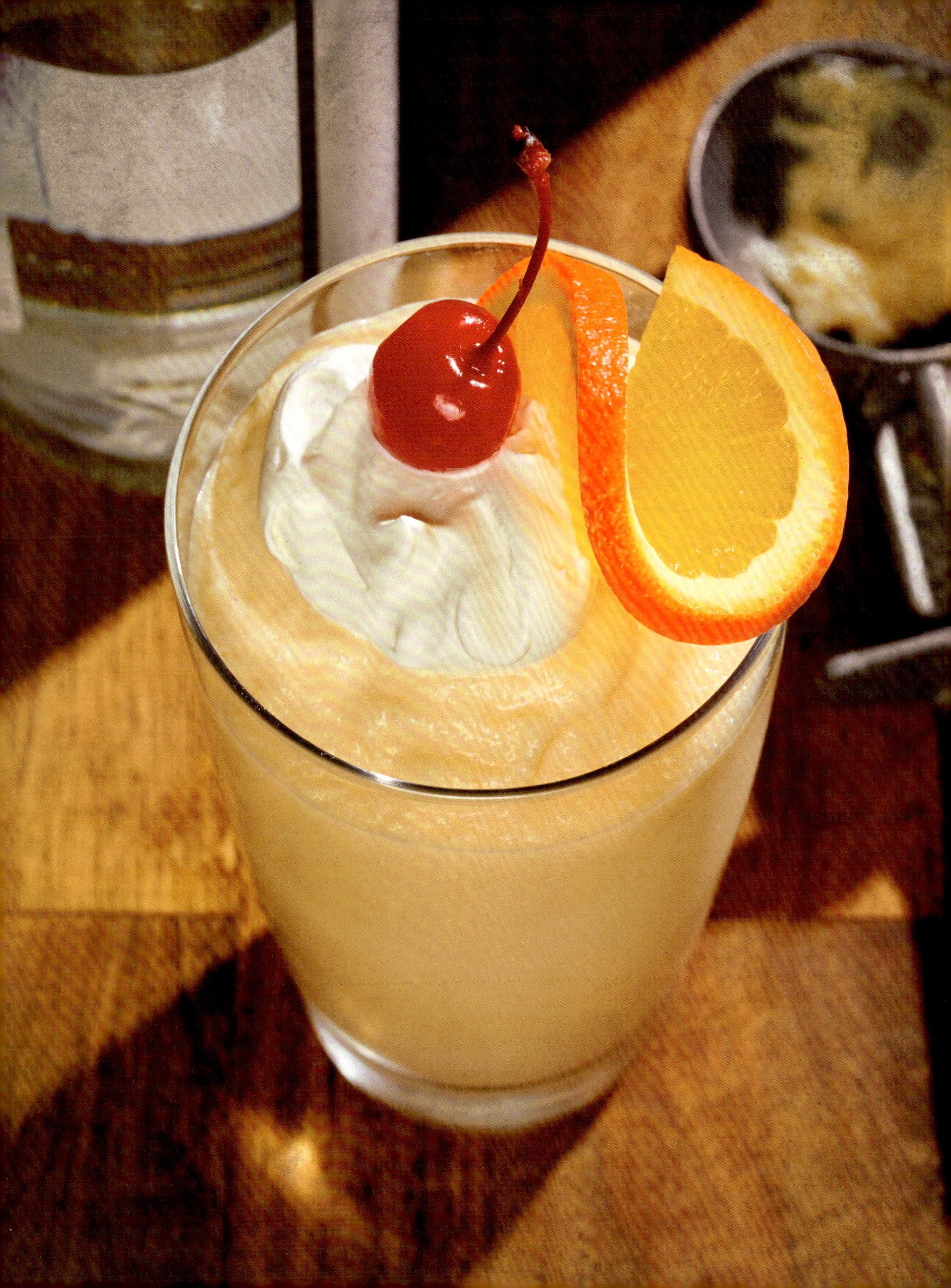

Beth's "Two Scoops of Ice Cream, Three Shots of Vodka" SMOOTHIE

The morning after being beaten up by the Beck brothers' henchmen in Season 2, Beth slowly and painfully wanders into the lodge dining room where the family is having breakfast. "How ya feeling, honey?" asks John. "Like I just left the f*cking spa, Dad," replies Beth. Her face is so badly bruised that she cannot even eat a piece of melon, so she asks for a smoothie. "Hey, Gator, would you mind making me a smoothie, please?" she asks. "Sure, what kind of smoothie?" I respond. "Two scoops of ice cream, three shots of vodka." When I bring it to her on the porch, she pulls out and tosses the orange and cherry garnishes and says, "Bless you." You might be surprised, but this smoothie is damned good, kind of like a Creamsicle with the kick of vodka. Needless to say, when we filmed this scene, we never imagined it would go viral!

INGREDIENTS

2 large scoops vanilla ice cream

3 shots vodka (3 oz / 90 ml)

¼ cup (60 ml) fresh orange juice

¼ teaspoon vanilla extract

Dollop of whipped cream (see Classic Southern Pecan Pie, page 132)

1 slice orange

1 Maraschino cherry

MAKES 1 SMOOTHIE

INSTRUCTIONS

In a high-speed blender, combine the ice cream, vodka, orange juice, and vanilla and blend until smooth. Transfer to a pint-size (475-ml) glass. Top with the whipped cream. Garnish with an orange slice and cherry and serve.

Summer's WHEATGRASS SMOOTHIE

After John meets vegan animal activist Summer in Season 4, she ends up at the breakfast table where Beth rakes her over the coals (in typical Beth fashion). In the scene, I offer Summer some eggs and she gives me a lecture about GMO orange juice. "Do you like wheatgrass?" sneers Beth. "I do," replies Summer. "We have a whole field of it," says Beth and then looks at me to say, "Hey, Gator, would you go out back, pick some wheatgrass, throw it in a blender . . . she's gonna love it." The scene takes a comical turn as Summer explains what she will and will not eat. In the end, I just make her a smoothie. Unfortunately, Beth drives her away before she can even taste it. Vegan or not, this is a great smoothie made with wheatgrass, spinach, avocado, banana, almond butter, and almond milk. It'll carry you through the day, whether you're working the ranch—or arguing with Beth.

INGREDIENTS

1 large frozen banana, cut into chunks

1 cup (40 g) packed baby spinach

¼ ripe avocado, pitted, peeled, and cubed

1 shot wheatgrass juice (1 oz / 30 ml)

½ cup (120 ml) almond milk

¼ cup (70 g) almond butter

1 large squishy date, pitted and chopped

2 teaspoons flax meal (optional)

MAKES 1 LARGE OR 2 SMALL SMOOTHIES

INSTRUCTIONS

In a high-speed blender, combine the banana, spinach, avocado, wheatgrass juice, almond milk, almond butter, date, and flax meal, if using, and blend until smooth. Transfer to a glass, or glasses, and serve.

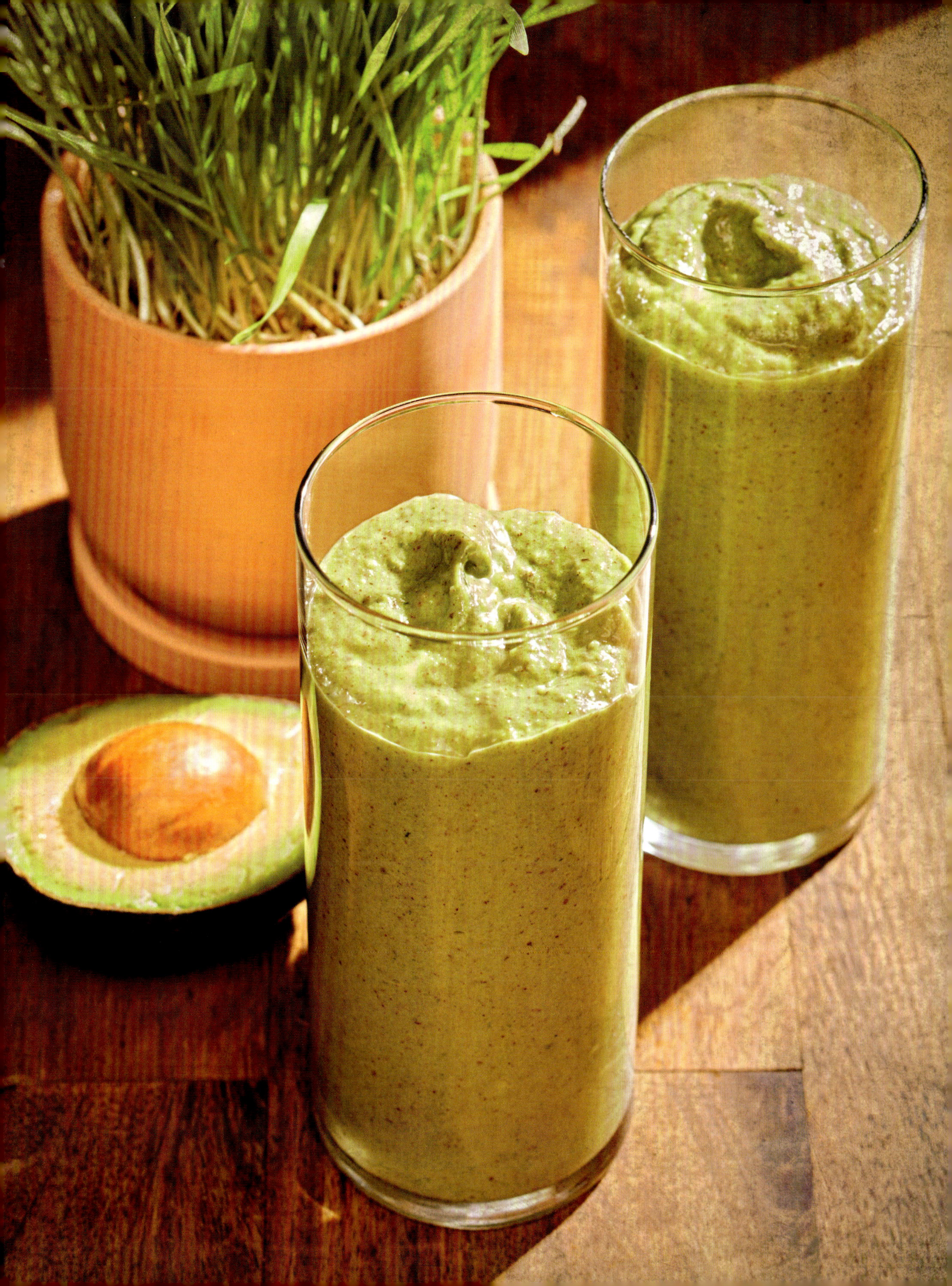

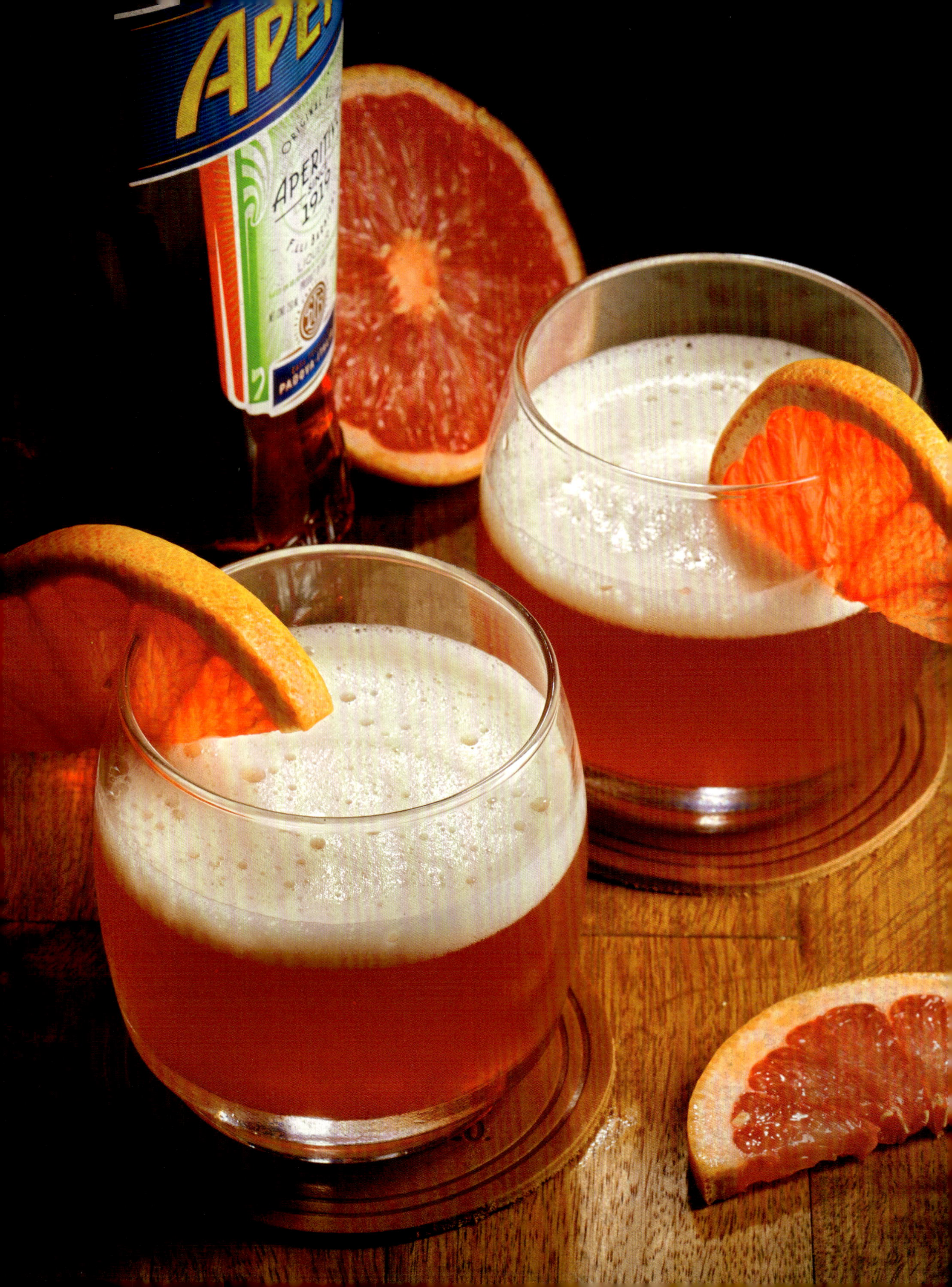
PADOVA

Bunkhouse BITTER BEER-BOURBON COCKTAIL

When Jimmy finally returns home to the Bunkhouse after his rodeo accident in Season 3, he finds the Bunkhouse parties are still happening—including with his new girlfriend, Mia. When Rip comes to shut down the party, he realizes Beth is already there, dancing. The music can be heard all over the ranch, and Kayce asks John, "Are they havin' a barn dance or something?" John answers, "They're cutting loose. Had one helluva day. Now it sounds like they're gonna have one helluva night." A mix of bourbon, grapefruit juice, bitters, Aperol, and a hoppy-style beer makes this one helluva beer "cocktail," perfect for any party—whether it's a rowdy one at the Bunkhouse or a swanky one at the lodge.

INGREDIENTS

3 oz (90 ml) bourbon

3 oz (90 ml) fresh grapefruit juice, chilled

1 oz (30 ml) Aperol

6 dashes grapefruit or lemon bitters

1 bottle (12 oz / 350 ml) IPA beer

2 slices grapefruit

MAKES 2–4 COCKTAILS

INSTRUCTIONS

In a cocktail shaker, combine the bourbon, grapefruit juice, Aperol, and bitters. Fill the shaker with ice, and then cover and shake for 10 seconds.

Strain the bourbon mixture into two 1-pint glasses (or 4 rocks glasses), dividing evenly. If using pint glasses, top each with 6 oz (175 ml) of the beer. For rocks glasses, add 3 oz (87.5 ml) of the beer to each glass. Garnish each with a grapefruit slice and serve.

Beth and Rip's
BOURBON APPLE CIDER OLD-FASHIONED

After a frustrating day, Rip comes home to the cabin and finds Beth sitting on the stoop, sipping a bourbon. After he downs three beers (and calms down), she asks him to come sit with her, and then hands him a box with a ring. "I didn't think you were a diamonds and gold kind of girl," she says. "I don't need presents, Beth. Just you," he replies. "Well, that's what it means. It means that you have me, that I'm yours. It means come live your life with me. It's settled, we'll get married," says Beth. "Married, huh?" asks Rip. "Yes, baby. I'm asking you to marry me. Will you do that?" she responds. "Well, I would have to ask your father . . ." he hesitates. "It's okay, I spared you the indignity. So what do you say?" Beth asks. "Well, I would've liked some diamonds, actually," jokes Rip. This updated cocktail is a bit of a twist on an "old-fashioned" classic, much like the modern marriage proposal between Beth and Rip. It gets its twist from the apple cider syrup, which makes this bourbon drink worthy of a celebration.

INGREDIENTS

1½ cups (350 ml) apple cider

2 tablespoons firmly packed dark brown sugar

4 oz (120 ml) bourbon

4 dashes Angostura bitters

1 tablespoon water

4 very thin apple slices

2 orange twists

MAKES 2 COCKTAILS

INSTRUCTIONS

Fill a bowl with water and ice. Have ready a smaller bowl that will fit into the ice bath.

In a small saucepan over medium-low heat, simmer the apple cider until reduced to ¼ cup (60 ml), about 20 minutes. Add the brown sugar and stir until it dissolves. Pour the syrup into the small bowl and place it into the ice bath. Set aside to cool completely. Transfer to a jar with a tight-fitting lid and refrigerate until ready to use, or up to 1 week.

In a cocktail shaker, combine the bourbon, bitters, 2 tablespoons of the apple cider syrup, and water. Fill the shaker with ice and stir gently until combined.

Add a few ice cubes to each of 2 rocks glasses. Strain the bourbon mixture into the glasses, dividing evenly. Garnish each with 2 apple slices and an orange twist and serve.

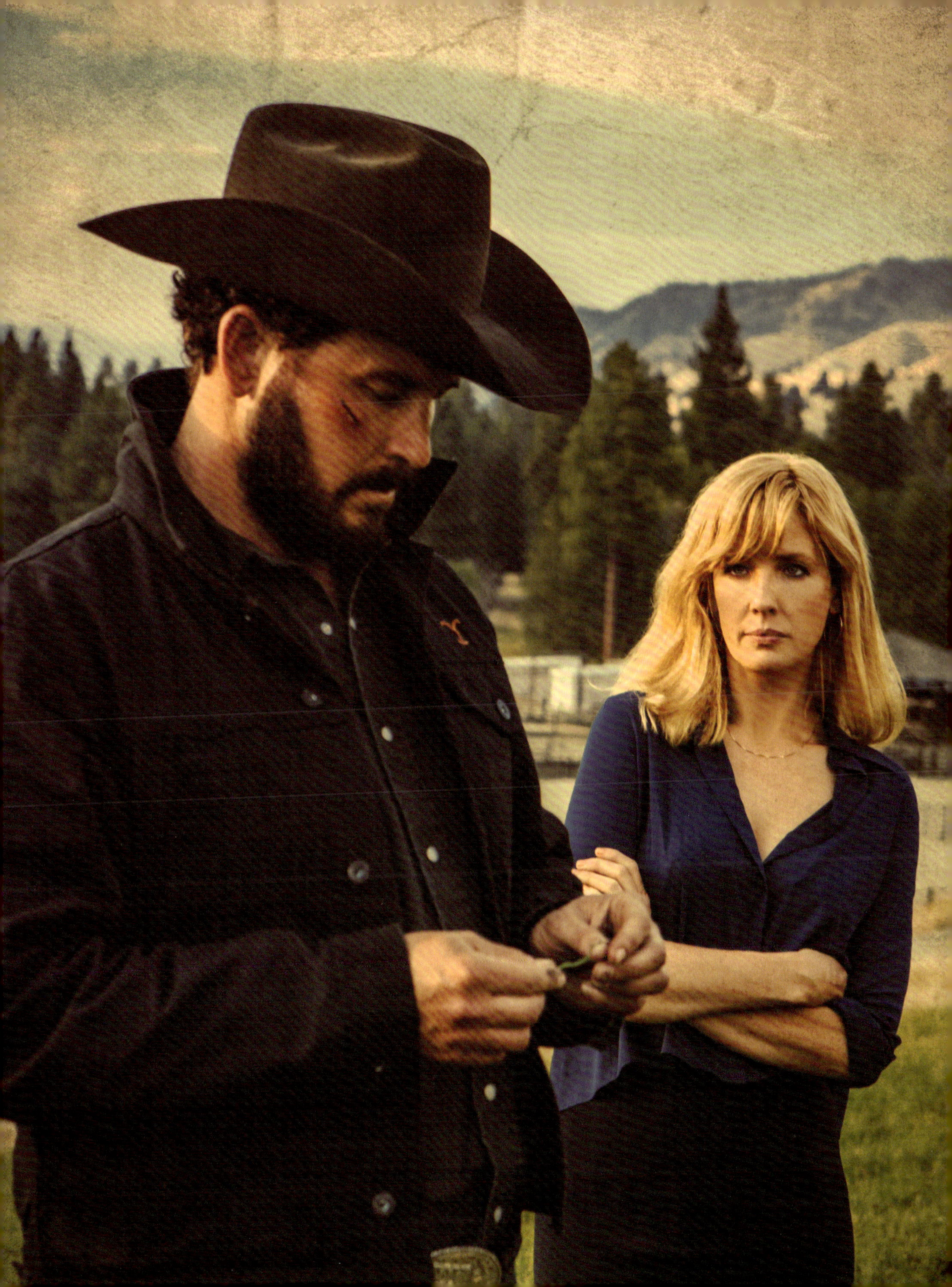

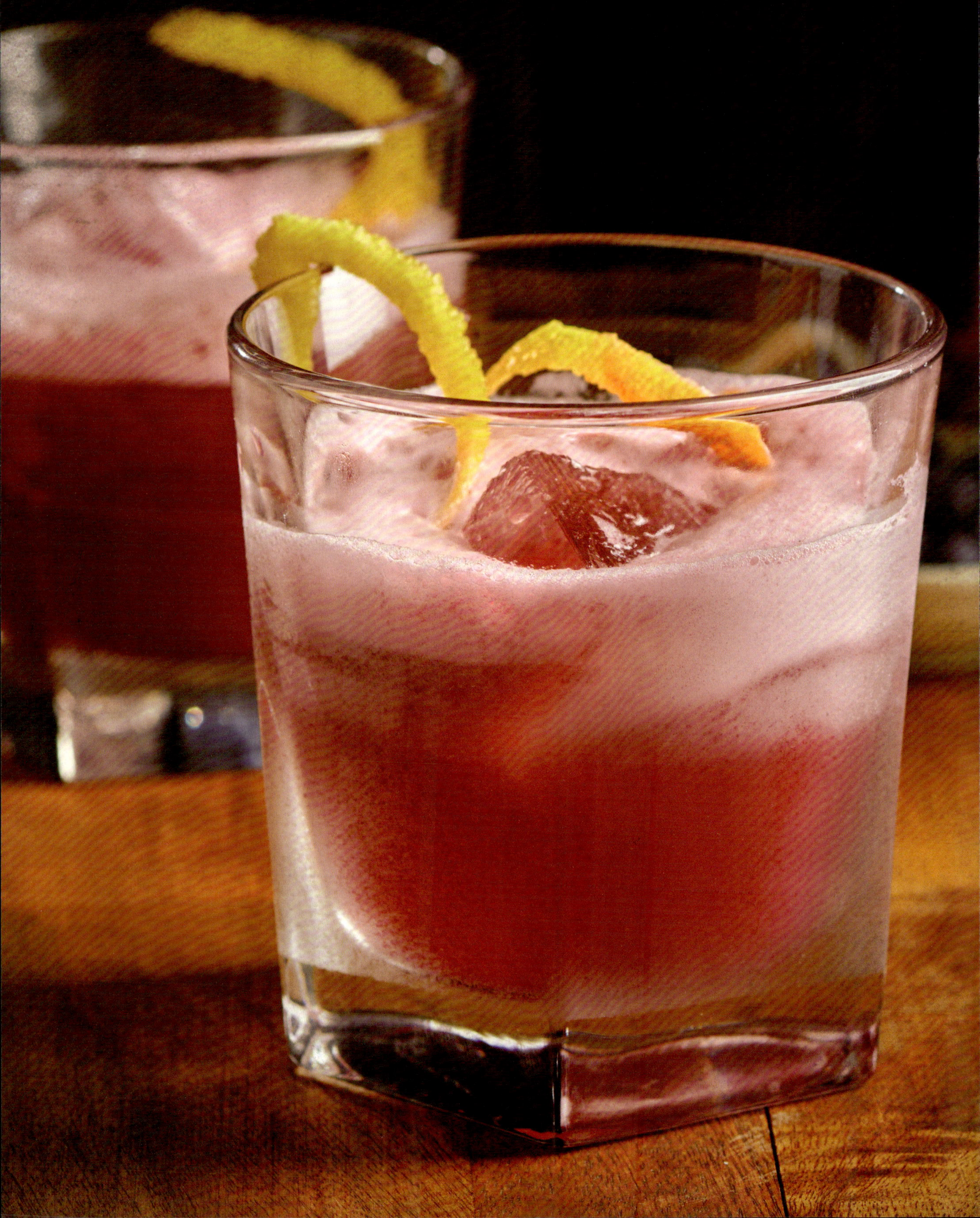

John and Jamie's HUCKLEBERRY WHISKEY SOUR

One night, John is sitting in the lodge in front of a large crackling fire, looking at photos of his wife, when Jamie storms in, filled with anger. "You always preached the truth; you said it's all a man has. Judge him by nothing else," says Jamie. "Are there different rules for judging you? I know the lie you told me every day of my life." "And what lie is that, son?" asks John. "That's the lie. You called me 'son' and you made me call you 'father.'" Although John and Jamie's relationship continues to sour throughout *Yellowstone*, this huckleberry variation on a whiskey sour can help to mend any rift.

INGREDIENTS

- 4 oz (120 ml) sweet whiskey (not smoky) or bourbon
- 3 tablespoons fresh lemon juice
- 3 tablespoons huckleberry syrup, or to taste
- 1 tablespoon egg white
- 2 lemon twists
- About 6 fresh or frozen huckleberries (optional)

MAKES 2 COCKTAILS

INSTRUCTIONS

In a cocktail shaker, combine the whiskey, lemon juice, huckleberry syrup, and egg white. Cover and shake for 10 seconds. Fill the shaker with ice, re-cover, and shake vigorously for at least 30 seconds until frothy.

Add a few ice cubes to each of 2 rocks glasses. Strain the cocktail into the glasses, dividing evenly. Garnish each with a lemon twist and a few huckleberries, if using, and serve.

GATOR'S TIP

Huckleberries are big in Montana, but if you cannot find the syrup locally, check online for distributors.

Beth's Coffee
VODKA MARTINI

Beth's fierceness—and love of martinis—is fully on display from the very first episode of *Yellowstone*. When a married man from out of town tries to pick up Beth in a hotel bar, she quickly puts him in his place, verbally twisting the knife in deep. "Let's be honest, Ted, you didn't come here to fish. You're hunting. That's why you are sitting in a bar instead of standing in a river." And then she calmly struts off with her vodka martini. Here, I added some coffee to spice it up for a perfect after-dinner cocktail.

INGREDIENTS

- 4 oz (120 ml) vodka
- 2 oz (60 ml) very strong coffee or espresso, chilled
- 2 oz (60 ml) coffee liqueur, such as Kahlúa
- Simple syrup, (see Note) to sweeten (optional)
- 2 lemon twists

MAKES 2 COCKTAILS

INSTRUCTIONS

In a cocktail shaker, combine the vodka, coffee, and coffee liqueur. Fill the shaker with ice. Cover and shake gently until combined. Taste and sweeten to taste with simple syrup, if desired.

Strain the cocktail into 2 martini glasses, dividing evenly. Garnish each with a lemon twist and serve.

NOTE: To make simple syrup, add equal parts water and sugar to a small saucepan, bring to a boil, and stir until the sugar dissolves. Let cool completely, and then transfer to a jar and refrigerate until chilled. The simple syrup can be refrigerated for up to 1 week.

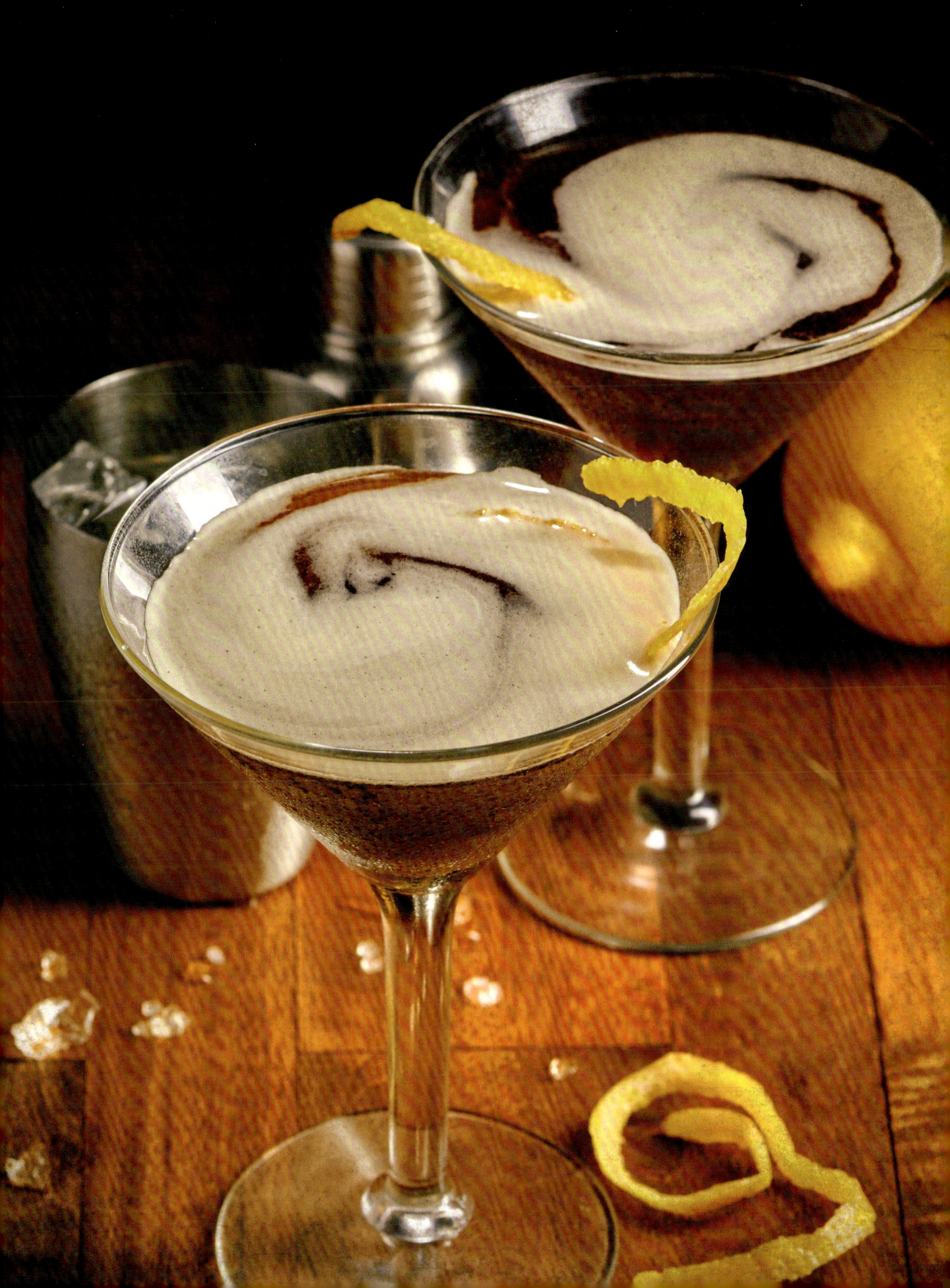

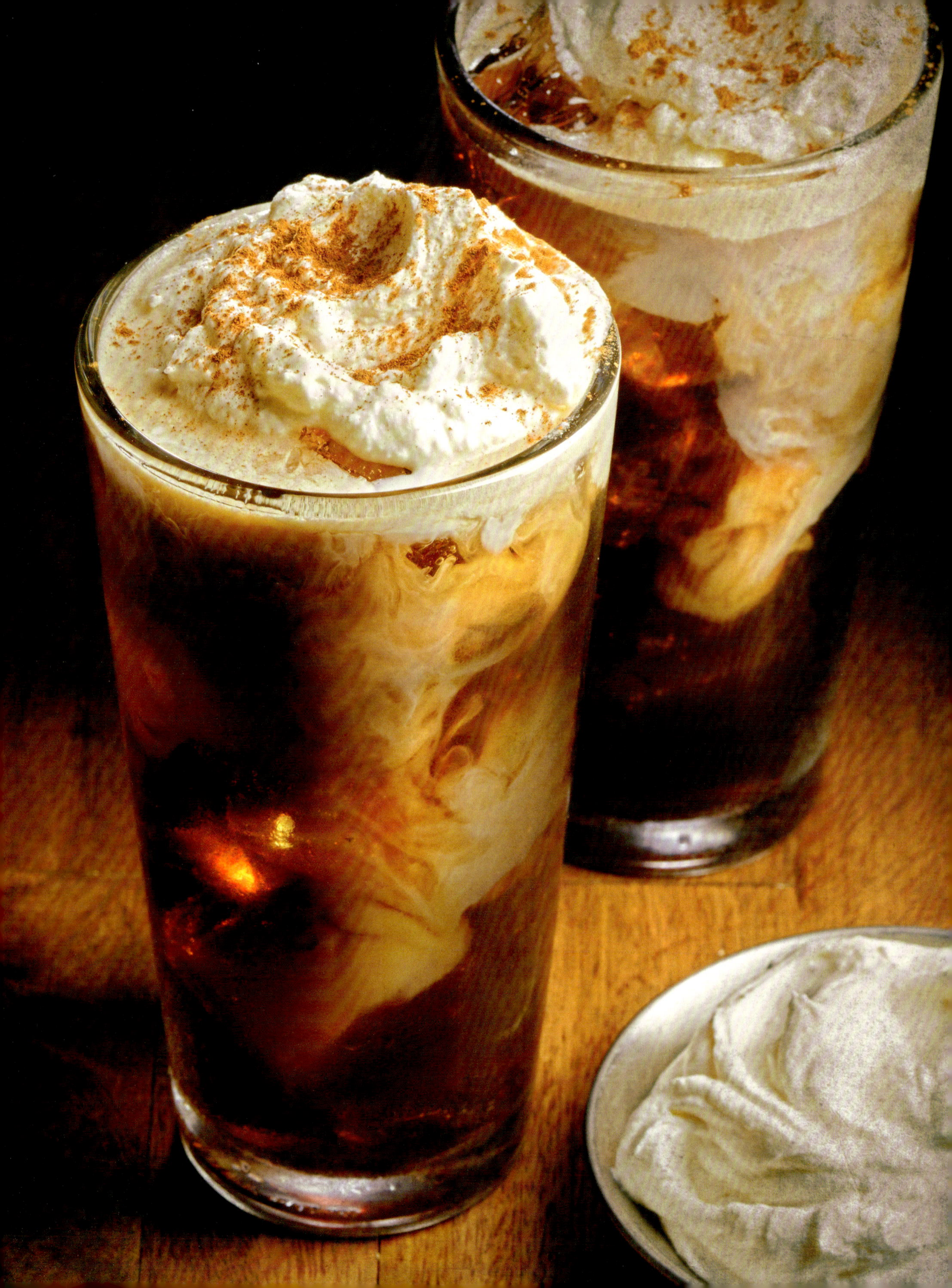

Great Aunt Cara's
ICED IRISH WHISKEY COFFEE

If one of the *Yellowstone* characters isn't drinking whiskey or a beer, then they are usually drinking coffee. It's amazing how much coffee I go through on set, and this recipe merges my two loves: whiskey and coffee, which Great Aunt Cara from *1923* would surely be proud of. This recipe contains a double dose of whiskey, because you make a whiskey syrup with brown sugar and then add a shot of whiskey on top, making it a great nightcap and perfect to sip in front of a big fire in the ranch lodge. I probably wouldn't recommend this drink at breakfast.

INGREDIENTS

- 4 oz (120 ml) Irish whiskey or bourbon
- ¼ cup (60 g) firmly packed light brown sugar
- 2 tablespoons water
- 16 oz (475 ml) strong coffee, chilled
- ¼ teaspoon vanilla extract
- 2 tablespoons heavy cream
- Whipped cream (see Classic Southern Pecan Pie, page 132) for serving
- Ground cinnamon for dusting

MAKES 2 COCKTAILS

INSTRUCTIONS

Fill a bowl with water and ice. Have ready a smaller bowl that will fit into the ice bath.

In a small saucepan over medium-low heat, combine 2 ounces (30 ml) of the whiskey, the brown sugar, and water. Simmer, stirring, until the sugar dissolves. Pour the syrup into the small bowl and place it into the ice bath. Set aside to cool completely. Transfer to a jar with a tight-fitting lid and refrigerate until ready to use, or up to 1 week.

In a cocktail shaker, combine the remaining 2 ounces (30 ml) whiskey, the coffee, vanilla, and whiskey syrup. Fill the shaker with ice and stir gently until combined.

Add ice cubes to each of 2 pint-size (475-ml) glasses. Strain the coffee mixture into the glasses, dividing evenly. Drizzle the cream into each glass, dividing evenly. Garnish each with dollops of whipped cream and a dusting of cinnamon and serve.

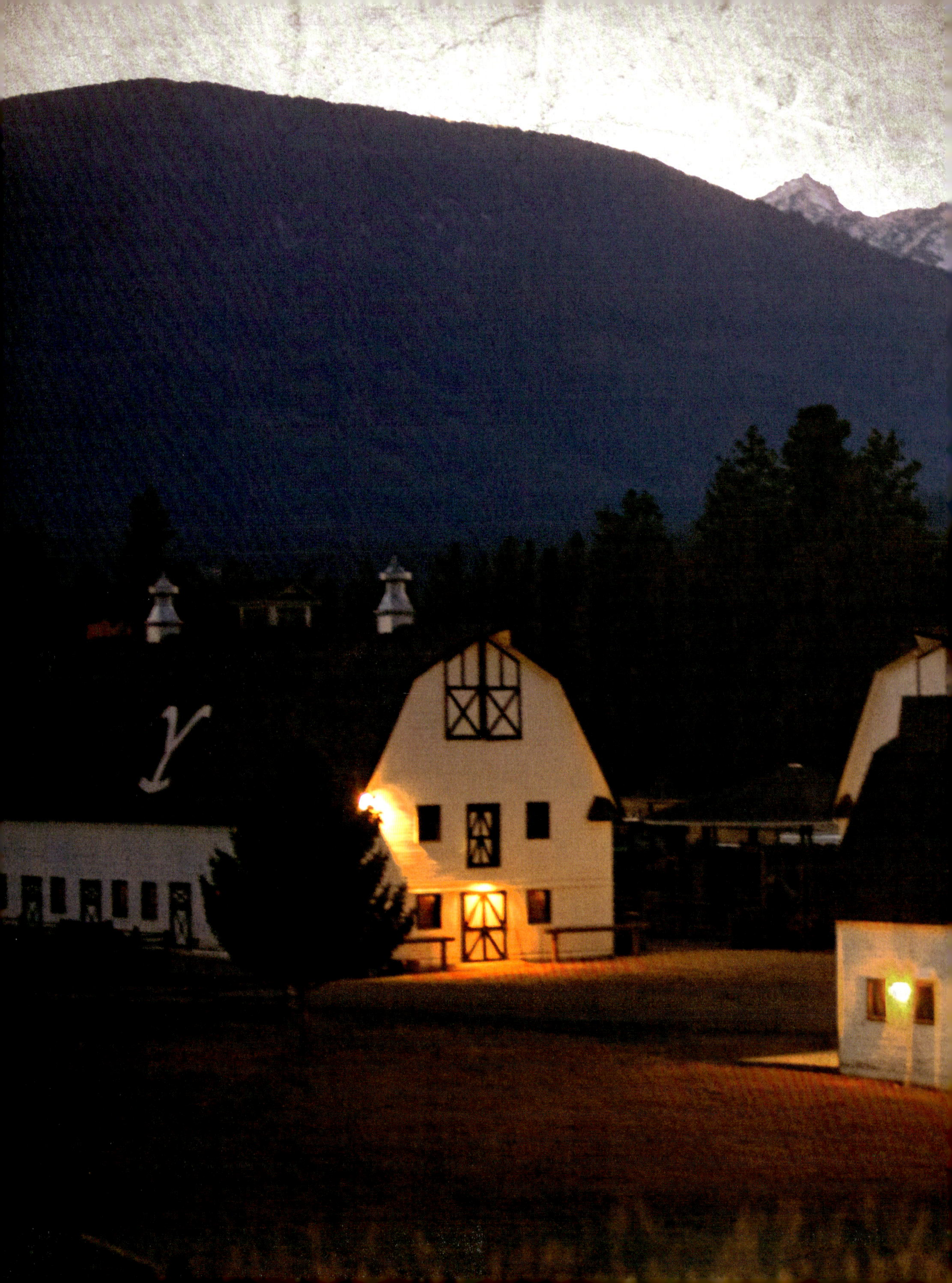

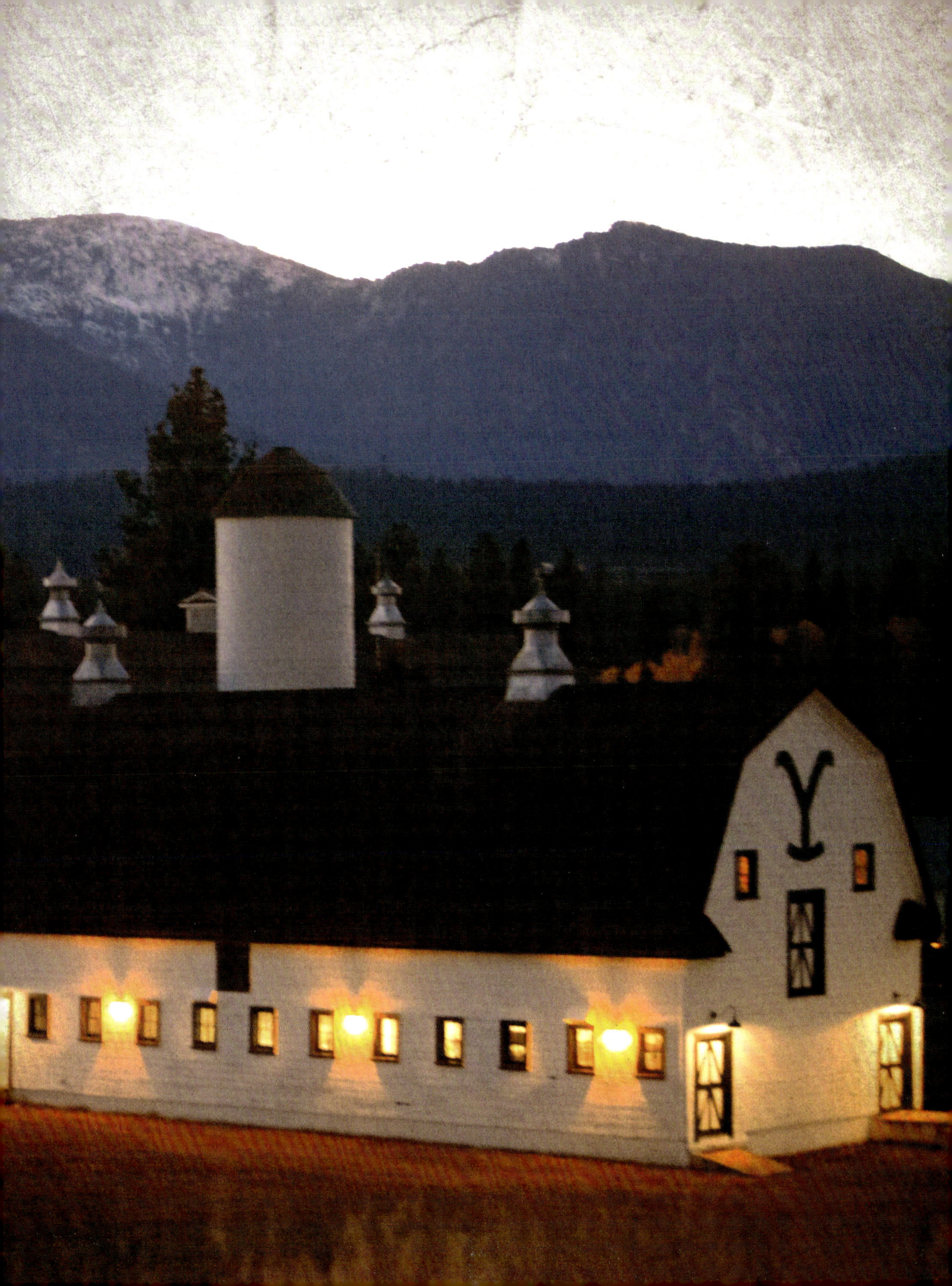

INDEX

A

almonds
  Crunchy Coleslaw, 119
  Summer's Wheatgrass Smoothie, 154
apples
  Beth and Rip's Bourbon Apple Cider Old-Fashioned, 158
  Chopped Salad with "Dutton Ranch" Dressing, 19
avocados
  Summer's Wheatgrass Smoothie, 154

B

bacon. *See also* pork
  BBQ Bison Burgers with Maple-Bourbon Bacon, 52
  Beth and Jamie's Twice-Baked Potatoes with Bacon and Cheese, 124
  Big Ranch Breakfast, 41
  Golden Squash Casserole, 106
  John, Kayce, and Tate's Glazed Venison Meatballs, 28–30
  Ranch Hand Baked Beans, 112
  Rip's Fry Bread with Scrambled Eggs and Bacon, 42
bananas
  Summer's Wheatgrass Smoothie, 154
beans
  Big Ranch Breakfast, 41
  Ranch Hand Baked Beans, 112
  Rodeo Cowboy Caviar, 116
  Smoked Turkey Legs with Red Beans and Rice, 87–88
beef
  Beth's Cheesy Hamburger Mac Casserole, 63
  Bunkhouse Beer-Braised Beef Stew with Root Vegetables, 49–50
  Gator's Cajun Dirty Rice, 59
  Helluva Grilled Flank Steak with Mustard-Mushroom Sauce, 55
  Jimmy's Cowboy Beef Chili, 45
  John's Perfect Ribeye Steak, 46
  Lee's Garlic Butter Steak Bites, 34
  Mama's Beef Pot Roast, 56
  Taylor's Beef Jerky, 33
bison
  BBQ Bison Burgers with Maple-Bourbon Bacon, 52
black-eyed peas: Rodeo Cowboy Caviar, 116
blueberries
  Beth and Rip's Sweet Blueberry Cobbler, 131
breads
  Bourbon Pineapple Bread Pudding, 142
  Cornbread Dressing, 107
  Gator's Louisiana Fried Shrimp Po'boys, 23
  Hush Puppies, 111
  Monica's Jalapeño-Cheddar Cornbread, 104
  Rancher's Chicken and Biscuit Dumplings, 82–85
  Rip's Fry Bread with Scrambled Eggs and Bacon, 42
  This Is How You Make a F*$%ing Biscuit, 103
  Yeasted Bunkhouse Beer Rolls, 108
broccoli
  Chopped Salad with "Dutton Ranch" Dressing, 19

C

cabbage
  Crunchy Coleslaw, 119
carrots
  Bunkhouse Beer-Braised Beef Stew with Root Vegetables, 49–50
  Chopped Salad with "Dutton Ranch" Dressing, 19
  Mama's Beef Pot Roast, 56
  Rancher's Chicken and Biscuit Dumplings, 82–85
cashews
  Chopped Salad with "Dutton Ranch" Dressing, 19
cheese
  BBQ Bison Burgers with Maple-Bourbon Bacon, 52
  Beth and Jamie's Twice-Baked Potatoes with Bacon and Cheese, 124
  Beth's Cheesy Hamburger Mac Casserole, 63
  Big Ranch Breakfast, 41
  Golden Squash Casserole, 106
  Grilled Portobello Mushroom Burgers, 60
  Jimmy's Cowboy Beef Chili, 45
  Monica's Jalapeño-Cheddar Cornbread, 104
cherries
  Beth and Rip's Sweet Blueberry Cobbler, 131
  Beth's "Two Scoops of Ice Cream, Three Shots of Vodka" Smoothie, 153
  John, Kayce, and Tate's Glazed Venison Meatballs, 28–30
chicken
  Gator's Cajun Chicken and Sausage Gumbo, 76
  Jamie's Smothered Chicken in Brown Mushroom Gravy, 73–74
  Kickin' Chicken Tenders with Pickled Jalapeño Sauce, 68–71
  Rancher's Chicken and Biscuit Dumplings, 82–85
  Western Butter Chicken with Rice, 79–80
chiles
  Corn Maque Choux, 115
  Gator's Cajun Chicken and Sausage Gumbo, 76
  Gator's Cajun Dirty Rice, 59
  Jimmy's Cowboy Beef Chili, 45
  Kickin' Chicken Tenders with Pickled Jalapeño Sauce, 68–71
  Monica's Jalapeño-Cheddar Cornbread, 104
  Rodeo Cowboy Caviar, 116
  Smoked Turkey Legs with Red Beans and Rice, 87–88
  Western Butter Chicken with Rice, 79–80
chocolate
  Big-Ass Chocolate Chip Cookies, 146
  Carter's Cast-Iron Coffee-Chocolate Cake, 135
  Maw Maw's Chocolate-Pecan Fudge, 145
coffee
  Beth's Coffee Vodka Martini, 162
  Carter's Cast-Iron Coffee-Chocolate Cake, 135
  Great Aunt Cara's Iced Irish Whiskey Coffee, 165
corn
  Corn Maque Choux, 115
  Monica's Jalapeño-Cheddar Cornbread, 104
  Potato Corn Chowder, 20
  Rodeo Cowboy Caviar, 116
cornbread
  Cornbread Dressing, 107
  Monica's Jalapeño-Cheddar Cornbread, 104
cornmeal
  Fried Okra, 31
  Hush Puppies, 111
  Jimmy's Cowboy Beef Chili, 45
  Monica's Jalapeño-Cheddar Cornbread, 104
cranberries
  John, Kayce, and Tate's Glazed Venison Meatballs, 28–30
crawfish
  Crawfish Cakes with Lime Cream, 24

D

dates
  Summer's Wheatgrass Smoothie, 154

F

fish
  John and Tate's Pan-Roasted Walleye, 90
  Lee, Jamie, and Kayce's Fire-Grilled Wild Trout with Chimichurri, 94–97

G

grapefruit
  Bunkhouse Bitter Beer–Bourbon Cocktail, 157

greens
  Chopped Salad with "Dutton Ranch" Dressing, 19

H

huckleberries
  John and Jamie's Huckleberry Whiskey Sour, 161

L

lemon
  Beth and Rip's Sweet Blueberry Cobbler, 131
  Beth's Coffee Vodka Martini, 162
  Bunkhouse Bitter Beer–Bourbon Cocktail, 157
  Chopped Salad with "Dutton Ranch" Dressing, 19
  Crawfish Cakes with Lime Cream, 24
  Grilled Octopus with Lemon and Roasted Potatoes, 93
  John and Jamie's Huckleberry Whiskey Sour, 161
  John and Tate's Pan-Roasted Walleye, 90
  Lee, Jamie, and Kayce's Fire-Grilled Wild Trout with Chimichurri, 94–97
  Western Butter Chicken with Rice, 79–80
lettuce
  Gator's Louisiana Fried Shrimp Po'boys, 23
  Grilled Octopus with Lemon and Roasted Potatoes, 93
  Grilled Portobello Mushroom Burgers, 60
lime
  Crawfish Cakes with Lime Cream, 24
  John and Tate's Pan-Roasted Tuna, 90
liver
  Gator's Cajun Dirty Rice, 59

M

macaroni
  Beth's Cheesy Hamburger Mac Casserole, 63
mushrooms
  Bunkhouse Beer-Braised Beef Stew with Root Vegetables, 49–50
  Grilled Portobello Mushroom Burgers, 60
  Helluva Grilled Flank Steak with Mustard-Mushroom Sauce, 55
  Jamie's Smothered Chicken in Brown Mushroom Gravy, 73–74
  Wild Rice Pilaf, 123

O

oats
  Evadelle's Lace Cookies, 141
octopus
  Grilled Octopus with Lemon and Roasted Potatoes, 93
okra
  Fried Okra, 31

orange
  Beth and Rip's Bourbon Apple Cider Old-Fashioned, 158
  Beth's "Two Scoops of Ice Cream, Three Shots of Vodka" Smoothie, 153
  John, Kayce, and Tate's Glazed Venison Meatballs, 28–30

P

parsnips
  Bunkhouse Beer-Braised Beef Stew with Root Vegetables, 49–50
pecans
  Classic Southern Pecan Pie, 132
  Evadelle's Lace Cookies, 141
  Maw Maw's Chocolate-Pecan Fudge, 145
pineapple
  Bourbon Pineapple Bread Pudding, 142
pork. See also bacon; sausage
  Gator's Cajun Dirty Rice, 59
  Maw Maw's Honey Bourbon Barbecued Ribs, 64
  Smoked Pulled Pork, 67
potatoes
  Beth and Jamie's Twice-Baked Potatoes with Bacon and Cheese, 124
  Big Ranch Breakfast, 41
  Bunkhouse Beer-Braised Beef Stew with Root Vegetables, 49–50
  Gator's Mustard Potato Salad, 120
  Grilled Octopus with Lemon and Roasted Potatoes, 93
  Jamie's Smothered Chicken in Brown Mushroom Gravy, 73–74
  Potato Corn Chowder, 20
  Rancher's Chicken and Biscuit Dumplings, 82–85
  Sweet Potato Bourbon Pie, 136–139

R

ramen
  Crunchy Coleslaw, 119
ribs
  Maw Maw's Honey Bourbon Barbecued Ribs, 64
rice
  Gator's Cajun Chicken and Sausage Gumbo, 76
  Gator's Cajun Dirty Rice, 59
  Jamie's Smothered Chicken in Brown Mushroom Gravy, 73–74
  Smoked Turkey Legs with Red Beans and Rice, 87–88
  Western Butter Chicken with Rice, 79–80
  Wild Rice Pilaf, 123

S

sausage. See also pork
  Big Ranch Breakfast, 41
  Gator's Cajun Chicken and Sausage Gumbo, 76

shallots
  John, Kayce, and Tate's Glazed Venison Meatballs, 28–30
shrimp
  Gator's Butter-Roasted Shrimp, 27
  Gator's Louisiana Fried Shrimp, 23
spinach
  Chopped Salad with "Dutton Ranch" Dressing, 19
  Summer's Wheatgrass Smoothie, 154
squash
  Golden Squash Casserole, 106
sweet potatoes
  Sweet Potato Bourbon Pie, 136–139

T

tomatoes
  Beth's Cheesy Hamburger Mac Casserole, 63
  Bunkhouse Beer-Braised Beef Stew with Root Vegetables, 49–50
  Corn Maque Choux, 115
  Gator's Louisiana Fried Shrimp Po'boys, 23
  Grilled Portobello Mushroom Burgers, 60
  Mama's Beef Pot Roast, 56
  Rodeo Cowboy Caviar, 116
  Western Butter Chicken with Rice, 79–80
turkey
  Smoked Turkey Legs with Red Beans and Rice, 87–88

V

venison
  John, Kayce, and Tate's Glazed Venison Meatballs, 28–30
vodka
  Beth's Coffee Vodka Martini, 162
  Beth's "Two Scoops of Ice Cream, Three Shots of Vodka" Smoothie, 153

W

wheatgrass
  Summer's Wheatgrass Smoothie, 154
whiskey
  Beth and Rip's Bourbon Apple Cider Old-Fashioned, 158
  Bunkhouse Bitter Beer–Bourbon Cocktail, 157
  Great Aunt Cara's Iced Irish Whiskey Coffee, 165
  John and Jamie's Huckleberry Whiskey Sour, 161

Y

yogurt
  Western Butter Chicken with Rice, 79–80

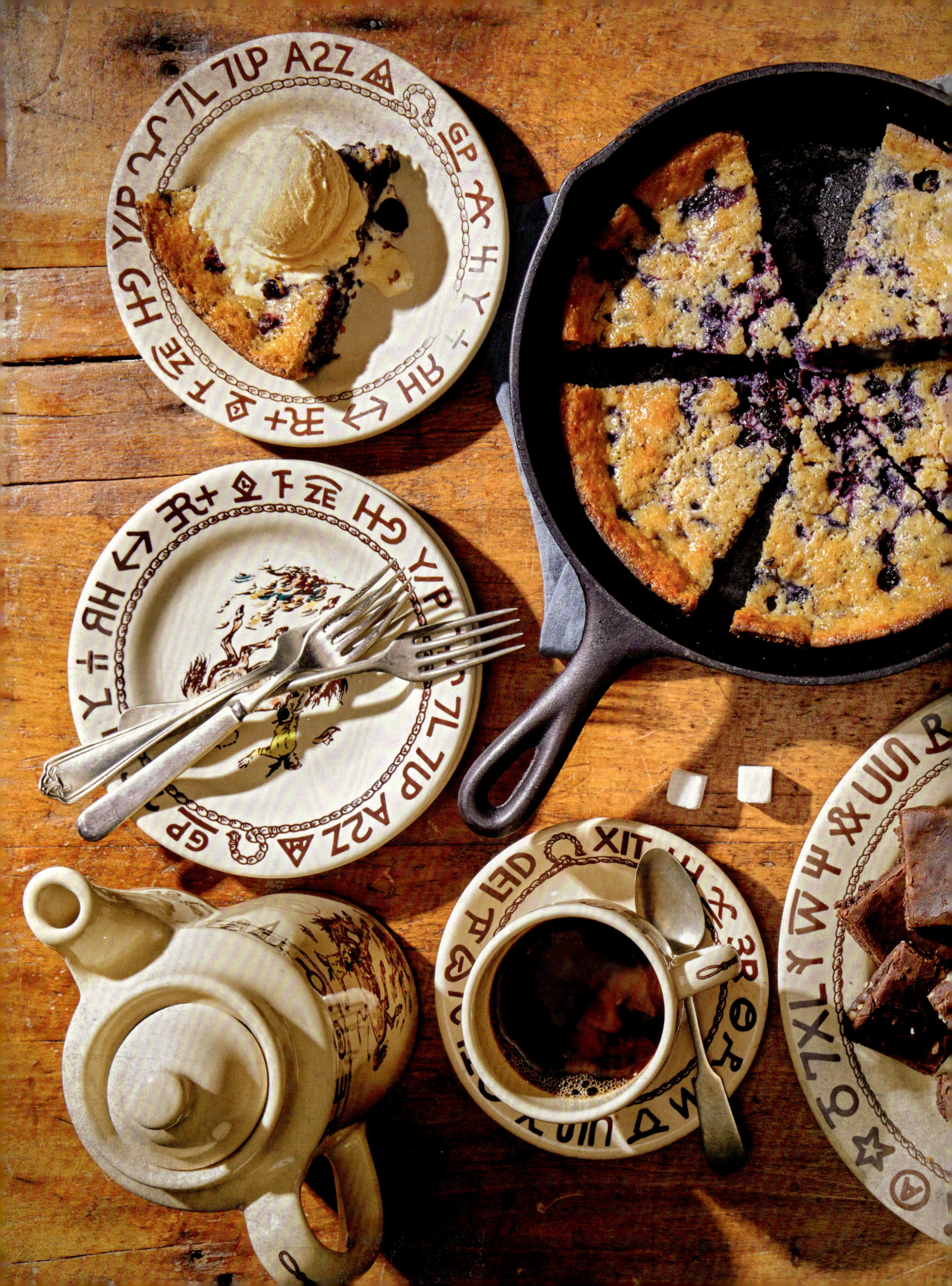

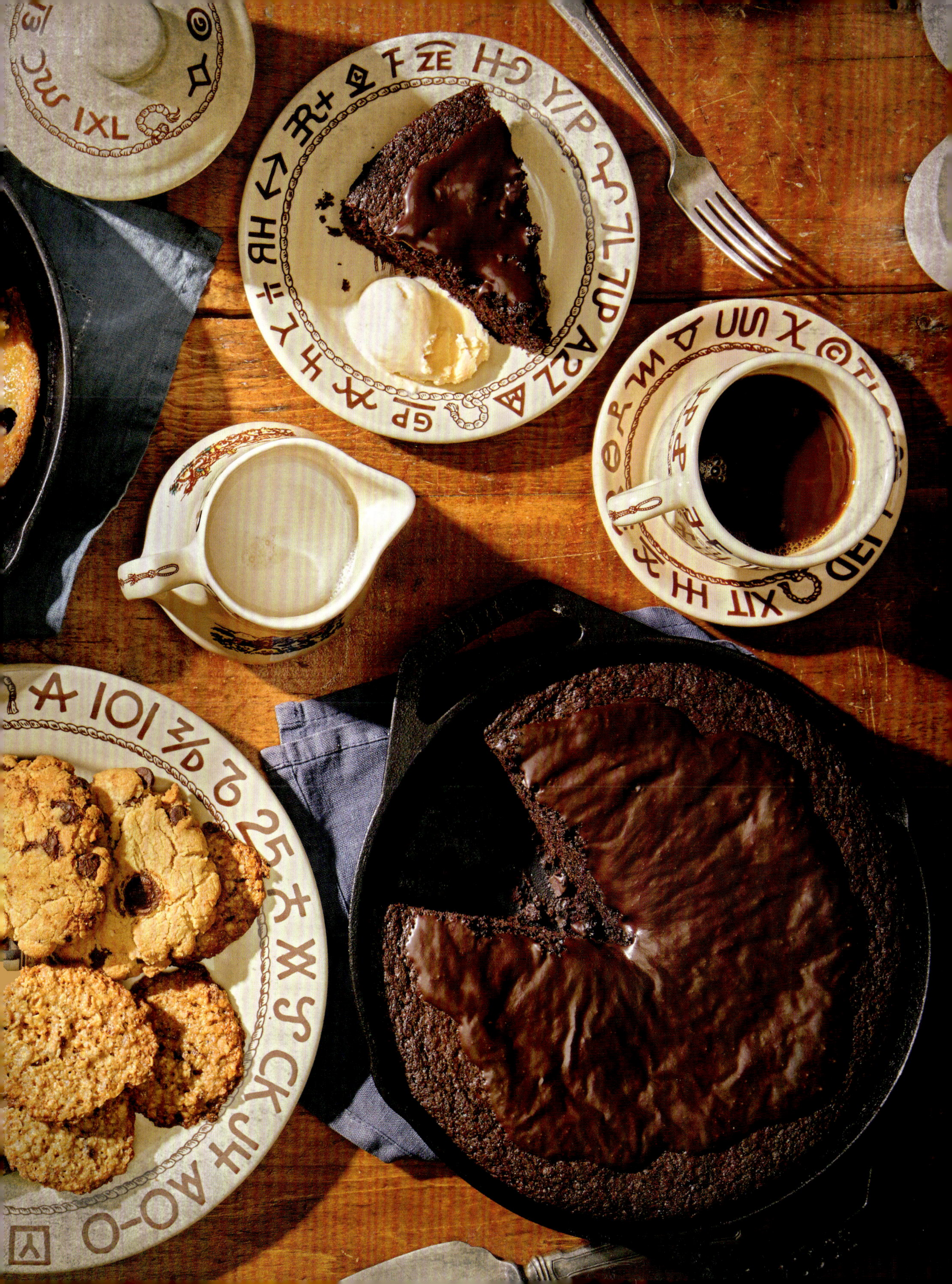

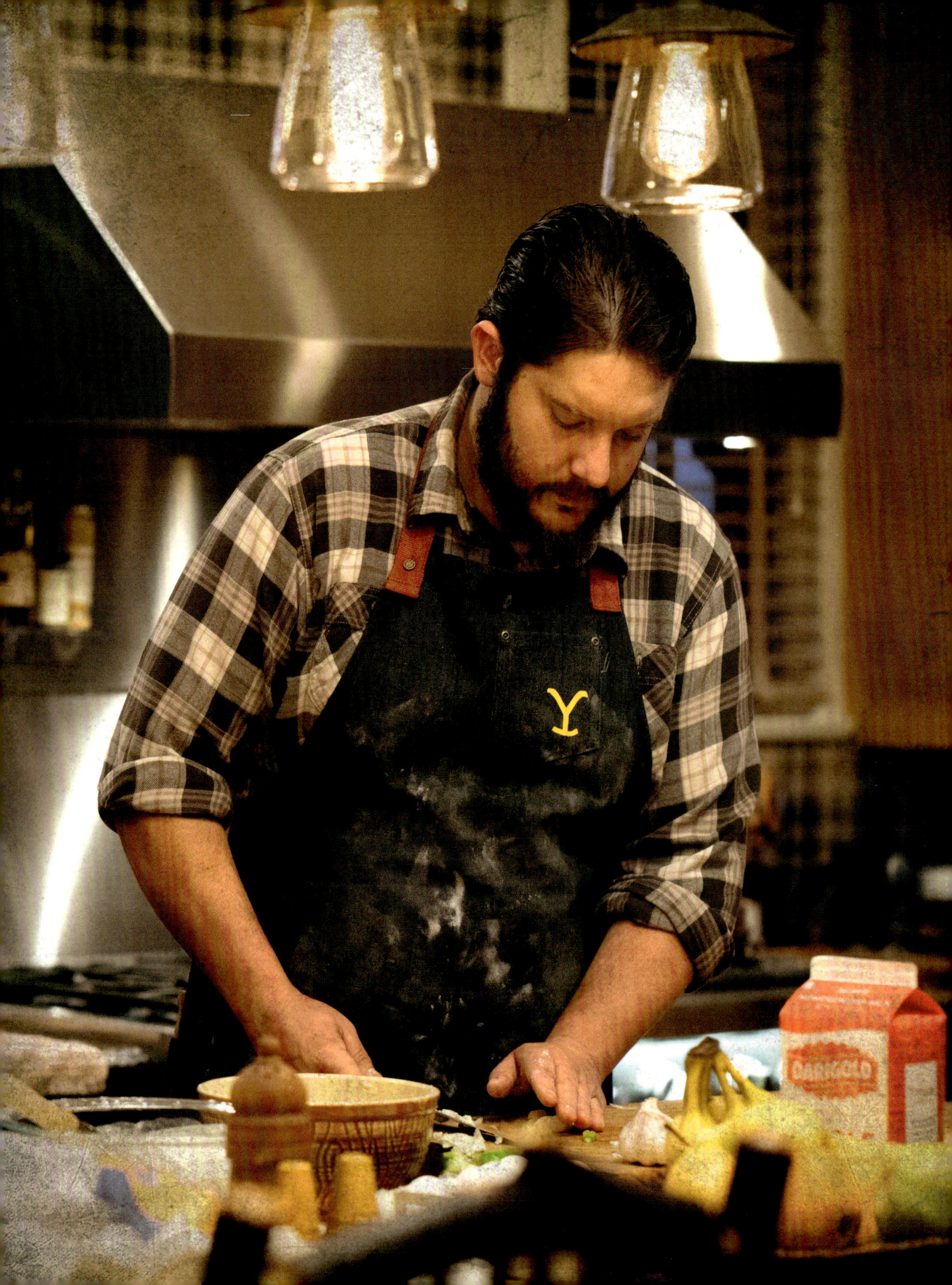
DARIGOLD

ACKNOWLEDGMENTS

First and foremost, I'm thankful for my family: my dad, Cajun, my mom, Donna Moss, and my grandmother, Evadelle Guilbeau. They taught me not only to love food, but also to love life. For that, I am eternally grateful.

None of this would have been possible without my good friend Taylor Sheridan. Without him and his vision, this cookbook, this *Yellowstone* world we all love, would not exist.

A very special thanks to my brothers, Snake and Tuna, who are always there in the best of times and the worst of times, and ready to smile with me as we made craft service dreams come true.

To everyone at Insight Editions and the Paramount family who helped enable this opportunity that I'm honored to be a part of, thank you for letting me share it with the fans.

Finally, to all those who have been a part of me getting here: Pete McGrew, Tex, all the PAs, teamsters, electricians, camera people, and every single grip that had whiskey and chicken with me through the years!

ABOUT THE AUTHOR

Gabriel "Gator" Guilbeau originally hails from North Hollywood, California, but formed both his culinary identity and Gator persona over many youthful summers spent in the heart of Cajun Country—Acadiana, to be exact. At least three generations of outstanding Cajun chefs comprise the South Louisianan portion of his family tree—most notably his grandmother, Evadelle Guilbeau, and his father, David "Cajun" Guilbeau, a renowned fixture in the culinary sector of the film industry himself. It was from these influences that he learned about not only his heritage but also the unique culinary tradition of Cajun Cooking. Blending both refined techniques and an improvisational cooking style, Gator combines imagination, emotion, and an emphasis on local ingredients to create perfect dishes for every occasion. With a focus on sights, sounds, smells, and flames, Gator and his creations are a show not to be missed.

Gator is best known by his fans for his role in the hit television series *Yellowstone*, where he plays the personal chef to the Dutton family. His character—like the professional chef—is lauded for his Cajun cooking and one-of-a-kind style. Although Gator's Cajun Chicken and Sausage Gumbo (page 76) and Cajun Dirty Rice (page 59) are among his signature dishes, he is most well-known his Kickin' Chicken Tenders with Pickled Jalapeño Sauce (page 68), a Southern-fried, spicy, jalapeño-glazed chicken dish. It's known to have been requested by more than one award winner. Never one to rest on his laurels, Gator's next project is his own branded line of Gator's Hot Sauce. After refining his flavor concepts with the cast and crews of *Yellowstone*, *1923*, and *1883*, Gator has opened his own food-processing company, Trapper Peak Foods LLC, to lab test, market, and distribute his hot sauce to friends and fans alike.

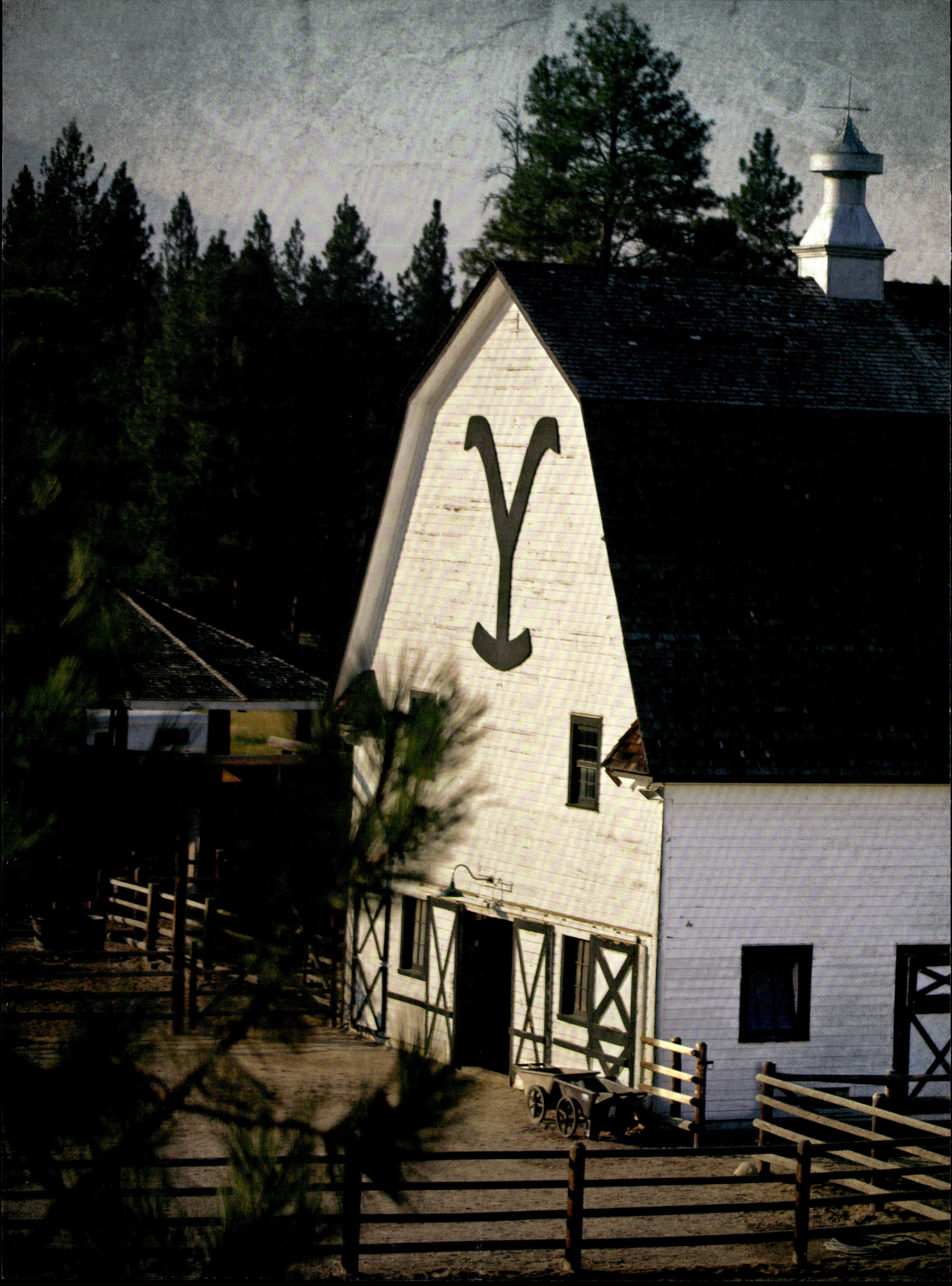

TITAN BOOKS

144 Southwark Street
London, SE1 0UP
www.titanbooks.com

f Find us on Facebook: www.facebook.com/TitanBooks

X Follow us on **X**: @titanbooks

Used Under Authorization. Published by Titan Books, London, in 2023.

© 2023 Spike Cable Networks Inc. All Rights Reserved. Yellowstone and all related titles, logos and characters are trademarks of Spike Cable Networks Inc.

No part of this publication may be reproduced, stored in a retrieval system, or transmitted, in any form or by any means without the prior written permission of the publisher, nor be otherwise circulated in any form of binding or cover other than that in which it is published and without a similar condition being imposed on the subsequent purchaser.

Published by arrangement with
Insight Editions, PO Box 3088, San Rafael, CA 94912. USA.
www.insighteditions.com

A CIP catalogue record for this title is available from the British Library.

ISBN: 978-1-80336-718-7

Publisher: Raoul Goff
VP, Publisher of Weldon Owen: Roger Shaw
VP of Licensing and Partnerships: Vanessa Lopez
VP, Creative: Chrissy Kwasnik
VP, Manufacturing: Alix Nicholaeff
Editorial Director: Katie Killebrew
Art Director & Designer: Allister Fein
Senior Editor: John Foster
Editorial Assistant: Kayla Belser
Senior Production Manager: Joshua Smith
Senior Production Manager, Subsidiary Rights: Lina s Palma-Temena

Unit still photography by Emerson Miller
Food photography by Waterbury Publications Inc.
Cover, interior, and endpaper texture courtesy of Shutterstock

ROOTS of PEACE   REPLANTED PAPER

Insight Editions, in association with Roots of Peace, will plant two trees for each tree used in the manufacturing of this book. Roots of Peace is an internationally renowned humanitarian organization dedicated to eradicating land mines worldwide and converting war-torn lands into productive farms and wildlife habitats. Roots of Peace will plant two million fruit and nut trees in Afghanistan and provide farmers there with the skills and support necessary for sustainable land use.

Manufactured in China by Insight Editions

10 9 8 7 6 5 4 3 2

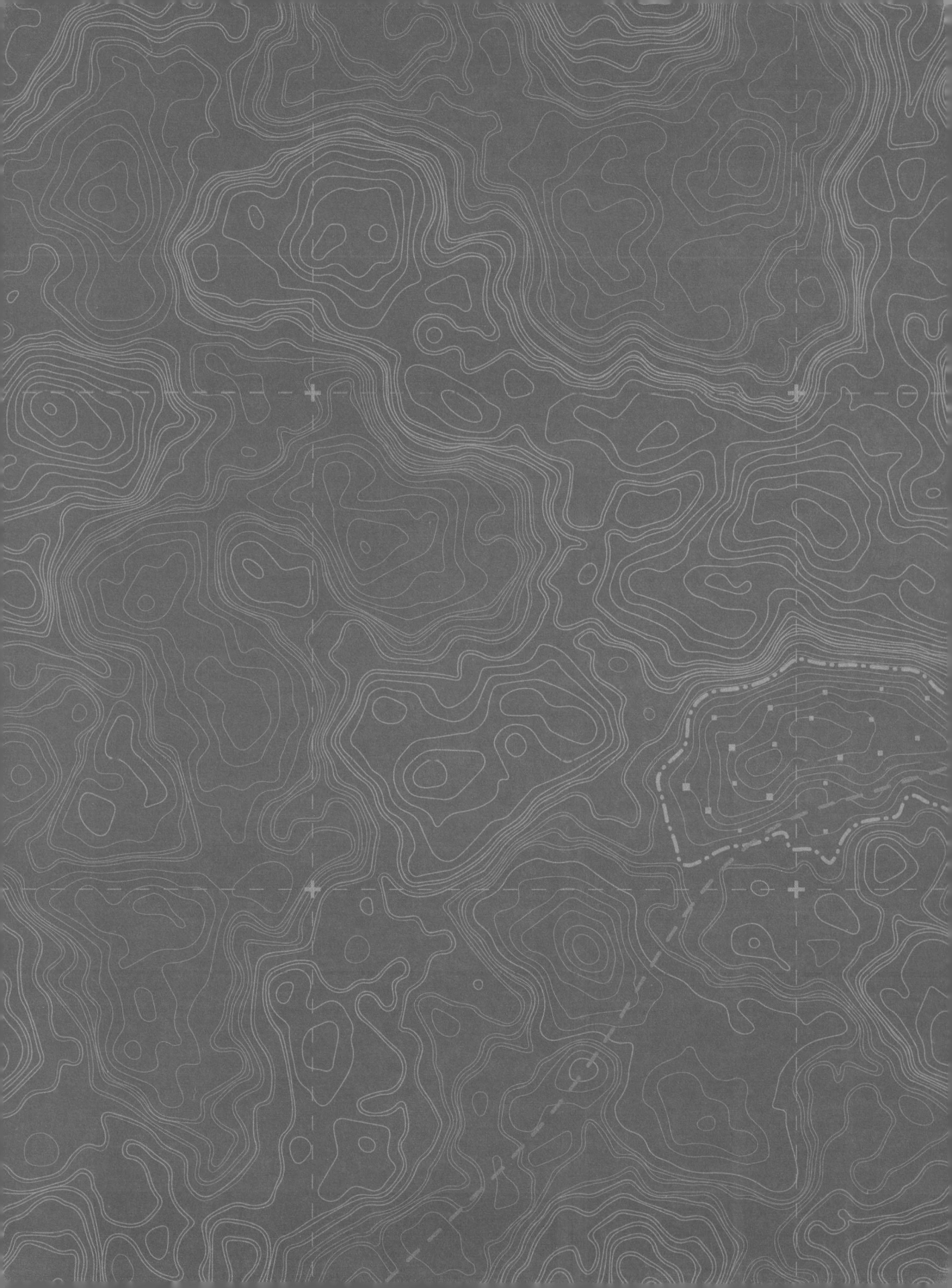